CHINA
CULTURAL AND POLITICAL PERSPECTIVES

CHINA
CULTURAL AND POLITICAL PERSPECTIVES

A Selection of Papers Presented at The
First New Zealand International Conference
on Chinese Studies, University of Waikato,
1972

Edited by D.Bing

LONGMAN PAUL

Longman Paul Limited
182–190 Wairau Road, Auckland 10, New Zealand

Longman Australia Pty Limited
Hawthorn Victoria Australia

Associated companies, branches and representatives throughout the world

First published 1975

ISBN 0 582 71739 6

The publication of this book has been assisted by
a grant from the Lee Foundation, Singapore.

Filmset in Hong Kong by Asco Trade Typesetting Limited
and printed in Hong Kong by Sheck Wah Tong Printing Press

Contents

v

Foreword

When the First New Zealand International Conference on Chinese Studies was held at the University of Waikato in May 1972 there was no contact at the official level between New Zealand and China. It is significant, I think, that a selection of Conference papers is now to be published under the title *China: Cultural and Political Perspectives* some months after diplomatic relations have been established between New Zealand and the People's Republic of China. It is clear that the desire to re-open communication with China was generally welcomed in New Zealand. The Government believed, and the view was widely shared, that for too long New Zealand had been unnecessarily cut off from the most populous nation in the world, one that has played and will continue to play a vital role in the Asian Pacific region. Generally speaking our objective in establishing relations was to build up a friendly and constructive relationship with China. Events since 22 December 1972 have fulfilled our expectations, and relations between New Zealand and China continue to improve.

Political communication is, however, only one method of making contact and increasing understanding of another country. Equally important is the study and careful scholarly discussion which this book represents. That is why I would like to commend the organizers of the First New Zealand International Conference on Chinese Studies and welcome the opportunity to contribute a foreword to this book. Studies of this kind complement the efforts made by the Government to improve international understanding.

There has long been a fascination about China in the Western world: the problem has always been to obtain sufficient factual and objective information and to interpret the material that is available. The Government's hope is that there will be a greatly increased flow of information and people between New Zealand and China. Our policy is in fact to encourage and foster a greater degree of contact between the two countries. Establishing diplomatic relations was only the initial step.

As we move to expand this contact, I believe that the publication of this book, *China: Cultural and Political Perspectives*, is most timely. I trust that it will, like the Conference, contribute to our understanding and appreciation of China.

Norman Kirk
Prime Minister

Preface

Had I been told six or seven years ago that I should be asked to write a preface to a collection of lectures delivered at an international conference on Chinese studies held in New Zealand in 1972, I should have been very surprised indeed since, although a few courses in Asian studies were offered in New Zealand universities before 1966, major developments have largely been since that year. Interest in and enthusiasm for Asian studies has been such over the past seven years that most New Zealand universities are now offering courses in the history and politics of the Asian region, and some: for example, Canterbury, Victoria, Massey, Waikato, and Auckland, have introduced language and literature courses, the majority of which have already been developed beyond the elementary stages.

Nor have these developments been limited to the universities. Asian languages are now taught in technical institutes in Auckland and Wellington, in privately organized classes and, at the time of writing, in more than twenty-five secondary schools throughout the country, both as part of the normal secondary schools curricula and of their adult education programmes held outside regular school hours. Interest in Japanese language studies has become so great that plans are afoot to have this subject made examinable at University Entrance examination level from 1974.

The holding of The First New Zealand International Conference on Chinese Studies in May 1972 was due in large measure to the enthusiasm and drive of Mr Dov Bing, a former student of the University of Auckland who is now Lecturer in Modern Chinese History and Politics at the University of Waikato. Aided and supported by the Vice-Chancellor of that university, Dr D.R. Llewellyn, and by a number of his colleagues, the Conference proved to be something of a landmark in the development of Asian studies in this country. A unique feature of the Conference was the decision to invite the public to participate. As Dr Llewellyn pointed out in his foreword to the Conference handbook,

> The gathering together of scholars and students with members of the public is something of a departure from traditional conference organization, but in the light of present world events there is clearly great value in providing for more extensive dissemination of knowledge about China. Since the Conference will deal with widely ranging aspects of Chinese society, both ancient and modern, it is particularly appropriate that it should bring together scholars, students and laymen . . . .

If there were doubts as to the wisdom of this decision prior to the Conference, they were quickly dispelled once it got under way. Approximately two hundred members of the public registered for the Conference, providing substantial audiences for the public seminars held each day as well as for the Public Lecture Series presented on the four evenings of the Conference. The participation of both interested laymen and scholars in the discussions which followed the reading of papers proved to be a stimulating and interesting experience for the lecturers.

As was to be expected in a conference of this nature, the majority of papers read and the dominant interest of the public were concerned with modern developments in China and with China's diplomacy in recent years. The scholarly papers presented and the 'workshops' held throughout the Conference centred largely on China's economy, education, and foreign relations. Other aspects of sinological studies were not neglected, however, and papers on Chinese art and literature, archaeology, religion, science, medicine, and agriculture all found a place. For sinologists working in New Zealand the highlight of the Conference was undoubtedly the opportunity it afforded to meet and listen to twelve scholars from overseas and to gain at first hand a knowledge of developments in their respective fields of research. This experience was especially valuable in view of the fact that scholars working in New Zealand lack the opportunity of those in the northern hemisphere to attend sinological conferences with any frequency.

The papers included in this volume, though only a selection of those read at the Conference, are a fair representation of the areas covered: they fall broadly under the headings of politics, arts and science, education, and economics.

Papers dealing with politics cover China's internal affairs as well as her relations with Japan and the West. The reader with little previous knowledge of the subject will find it helpful to begin by reading Mr Bing's historical survey of China's relations with the

West, and then to read Dr S.A.M. Adshead's paper on the Cultural Revolution. These should be followed by Mr W.A.C. Adie's examination of Chinese diplomacy in action, and then by the papers of Professor D.H. Mendel and Professor J.H. Jensen, which seek to relate Chinese political developments to Japan, the United States, and Rumania. Finally, in this section the reader is presented with suggestions by Professor W.T. Roy as to the lines along which relations between New Zealand and China may develop.

It is inevitable that those who seek to probe beneath the surface of Chinese propaganda will differ in their interpretations of the political scene. For one thing no 'China watcher' can detach himself completely from the intellectual and political climate of the society in which he lives and works, and this climate is bound to have some effect upon his evaluation of what is happening in China. Nevertheless we have in the papers presented here sufficient facts and a wide-enough range of judgments to allow the interested reader to pursue his study of modern Chinese history and politics with greater discernment than heretofore.

In the two papers on Chinese education by Mr R.C. Hunt and Mr R.I.D. Taylor one is forcibly reminded that even the cultural sphere in modern China is dominated by political considerations. In Mr Taylor's words, '... the Chinese leaders have regarded education as an instrument through which economic development may be furthered. To that extent emphasis has been placed upon collective interests rather than upon those of the individual. Academic freedom for the individual has been strictly subordinated to the demands of national sovereignty.' However, both Mr Taylor and Mr Hunt draw the reader's attention to the fact that there is a certain identity of purpose between the educators of China's old imperial society and those of today in that both have regarded ideology and politics as supreme.

Although only one paper on agriculture is included in this volume, those interested in China's agricultural development in recent years will find Dr John Wong's analyses and the comparisons he makes with the situation in New Zealand both informative and helpful.

The papers covering certain of the arts and sciences of China are a reminder that this nation has a long and distinguished history of cultural achievement. Although our knowledge of Chinese history, philosophy, religion, and literature has steadily increased since the arrival of the first Jesuit mission in China in the late sixteenth century, Chinese contributions to science were only imperfectly understood until comparatively recent times. Indeed it is only through the current researches of Professor Joseph Needham and his colleagues that anything like a complete picture of Chinese scientific achievements has been made available to the western reader. New Zealanders attending the Conference were therefore very fortunate to have one of Professor Needham's co-workers, Professor Ho Peng Yoke, speak to them on modern science in China.

As Professor Ho makes clear in his first sentence, what he means by modern science is 'the form of science that grew up in post-Renaissance Europe and that is now regarded as universally valid.' This does not prevent him, however, from describing certain features of traditional science in China before going on to show how modern science was gradually introduced and absorbed. Professor Ho does not dwell at any length on the fortunes of science in China since 1949, perhaps because of the difficulty in recent years of obtaining reliable information. Sir Douglas Robb's comments therefore on what he saw of medical science during his visit to China in 1966 are particularly valuable.

As translators like Arthur Waley and the spate of books on Chinese art have long made us aware, poetry, painting, and ceramics have flourished in China and achieved incomparable standards of perfection over several millenia. Dr Margaret South, in 'Let the People Sing', reminds the reader that no matter how exquisite a poem may be adjudged by purely aesthetic standards, it forms, in the Chinese tradition, a part of a literature whose value generally was believed to reside in its 'social utility' – a fact which provides a link between the literary tradition of imperial China and the China of today.

The two papers in this volume contributed by Dr Liu Wei-ping and Mr T.J. Bayliss offer the reader valuable information on Chinese landscape painting and ceramics. Dr Liu draws attention to the important part played by Buddhism and Neo-Confucianism in the development of landscape painting and to the connection between painting and poetry. Mr Bayliss examines the place of Chinese ceramics in both Eastern and Western civilizations, and traces the route along which the influence of Chinese pottery travelled before it finally 'set the stage for the present studio pottery scene in New Zealand.'

Even a casual observer of the New Zealand scene today is bound to notice a quickening of interest in the nations of East and Southeast Asia; but the Conference, and in particular the papers in this volume, show that, if this interest is ever to be more than superficial, a growing number of New Zealanders must begin the hard task of acquiring those skills which will allow them to investigate the region in depth.

Douglas Lancashire

Acknowledgements

We are grateful to Doubleday & Company, Inc. for permission to reprint selections from *Twentieth Century Chinese Poetry* by Kai-yu Hsu. Copyright © 1963 by Kai-yu Hsu.

Notes on the Contributors

Professor D. Lancashire is head of the Department of Asian Languages and Literature at the University of Auckland. He was educated at the University of London, and spent nine years in Hong Kong. During the early sixties he taught Chinese language at the University of Michigan and from 1962 to 1965 was at the University of Melbourne. He became the founding Professor of the Department of Asian Languages and Literatures at the University of Auckland in 1966. Professor Lancashire has published various articles in scholarly journals; his main research interest is modern Chinese Buddhism.

Mr D. Bing was born in Holland and graduated BA from the Hebrew University and MA from the University of Auckland. He is Lecturer in Politics (Modern Chinese History and Politics) in the School of Social Sciences at the University of Waikato, and is currently completing a doctoral thesis on the establishment of the Chinese communist party. He has been a guest lecturer at the major sinological institutes in the United States, Europe, and the Far East, and has participated in academic conferences in Sweden, the United States, Holland, and Australia. Mr Bing has published in many academic journals and much of his work has been translated into Chinese. His research interests are the history of the Chinese communist party, Sino-Soviet relations, and the industrial cooperatives in China.

Dr Margaret T.S. South is Senior Lecturer in Classical Chinese at the University of Auckland. She was educated at the Australian National University and has published various articles in scholarly journals. Dr South is New Zealand's leading scholar on Chinese poetry.

Dr Liu Wei-ping is Associate Professor in the Department of Oriental Studies at the University of Sydney. A gifted painter himself, he is one of the foremost authorities in his field. He has published widely on the subject of Chinese painting and has been a frequent guest lecturer at academic institutions.

Mr T.J. Bayliss is Curator of Applied Art and Assistant Director of the Auckland Institute and Museum. In 1965 he spent a year studying the Chinese collections in American and European museums, and is New Zealand's leading authority on Chinese ceramics.

Mr R.C. Hunt graduated BA (Hons) from the School of African and Oriental Studies at the University of London. He taught English at the Foreign Languages Institute in Peking for two years (1965–6) and revisited the People's Republic of China for a month in April 1971. He is now Lecturer in Chinese Studies at the Asian Studies Centre, Victoria University of Wellington. Mr Hunt's particular research interest is recent developments in Chinese education. He is the author of a recent series of NZBC broadcasts on modern China.

Mr R.I.D. Taylor was born in London and studied at the School of Oriental and African Studies at the University of London, where he obtained his degree in modern Chinese and political science. He is Lecturer in Asian Politics at the University of Auckland. His main research interest is educational policies in the People's Republic of China; he is also interested in China's foreign policy, especially her relations with Southeast Asia. He is a frequent contributor to the NZBC and has participated in academic conferences in Australia and New Zealand.

Dr S.A.M. Adshead is Reader in History at the University of Canterbury. He holds an MA from Harvard and Oxford universities and a PhD from Harvard University. He is the author of *The Modernization of the Chinese Salt Administration, 1900–1920* (Harvard University Press, 1970) and has published many articles in academic journals. He is currently working on vice-regal government in Szechwan, a study which will contribute to the debate on regionalism and modernization in the late Ch'ing period by analyzing the operations of the Szechwan government and the reasons for its overthrow.

Mr W.A.C. Adie is a Senior Research Fellow in the Department of International Relations at the Australian National University. He gained his MA from Oxford University and served with the British Foreign Service in the 1950s. He is co-author of several books on Chinese and Soviet foreign relations. At present he is completing a book on China's policy in Africa and is also engaged in writing other books, including a study to be entitled *The Cultural Revolution in Perspective*.

Professor D.H. Mendel is Professor of Political Science at the University of Wisconsin. He holds a PhD from the University of Michigan, and is one of the foremost specialists in the United States on Japanese-American and Sino-Japanese relations. He has published many articles in learned journals and two of his books were published in both English and Japanese. The third, *Politics of Formosan Nationalism* (1970), is a study of local Taiwanese attitudes.

Professor W.T. Roy was born in Lucknow, India, and was educated at La Martiniere Military College and the Indian Military Academy. He served in the 14th Army during the Burma Campaign (3/3 Gurkha Rifles) and later attended Lucknow and Auckland universities. He has been on the staff of both Auckland and Waikato universities and is at present Professor of Politics at the University of Waikato. His research interests are immigration law, policies, and problems, in particular those relating to ethnic minorities in New Zealand; the politics of multi-racial societies in the Southwest Pacific; bureaucratic structures (including the Chinese mandarinate); and international relations between states in the Asia/Pacific region.

Professor J.H. Jensen holds a PhD from the University of Pennsylvania and has taught at that university, Rutgers University, and Massey University. He is now Head of the History Department at the University of Waikato. He has published a number of articles and reviews on Eastern Europe and particularly on Rumanian history, and has also written and edited several secondary school textbooks. His particular research interests are Balkan international relations, transport and economic development in Rumania and Bulgaria, and peasant society in Rumania.

Dr John Wong was born in Canton and graduated from the University of Hong Kong. He obtained his PhD from the University of London in 1966. From 1966 to 1970 he lectured in economics at the University of Hong Kong, and in 1972 joined the Department of Economics at the University of Singapore. He has published papers in various professional journals on the economics of the People's Republic of China and Hong Kong, his particular interests being agriculture and trade in these countries. Dr Wong is currently completing a book on land reform in the People's Republic.

Professor Ho Peng Yoke was born in Perak, Malaysia. He obtained his DSc in physics from the University of Singapore and his PhD (also in physics) from the University of Malaya. Professor Ho is one of the world's leading authorities on modern science in China and is the author of a number of books, including *Science and Civilisation in China,* vol. 5 (in collaboration with Professor J. Needham); *Clerks and Craftsmen in China and the West* (Cambridge University Press, 1970); and *The Birth of Modern Science in China* (University of Malaya, 1967). He is Dean of the School of Asian Studies at Griffith University, Australia.

Sir Douglas Robb CMG MD FRCS Hon. LLD was formerly Chairman of the New Zealand Medical Council and Senior Surgeon (thoracic and cardiac) at Greenlane Hospital, Auckland. He was president of the British Medical Association from 1961 to 1962 and Chancellor of the University of Auckland from 1961 to 1967. Sir Douglas's many publications include an autobiography, *Medical Odyssey.* He had a lifelong interest in the Chinese people and in 1966 spent over a month in China as a guest of the Government of the People's Republic.

China and the West:
An Historical Perspective

D. BING

With a recorded history of almost four thousand years, Chinese civilization is one of the oldest and richest in the world. But, until the fifteenth century, this great civilization and the West were only intermittently in contact through the voyages of western traders and explorers. It was not until early in the seventeenth century that Chinese explorers reached the coasts of Africa, and Portuguese and Spanish envoys arrived in South China via the new sea routes, bringing in their wake missionaries, and traders in larger numbers. The Russians did not reach the Manchurian border until the middle of the seventeenth century.

During the centuries of closer contact that followed, the dialogue between China and the West was mainly one of mutual misunderstanding which in the end led to a disastrous collision. This paper attempts to analyze and explain some of the misconceptions about China that existed in the West for so long. It takes the view that these misconceptions were often due to the incompatibility of Western ideology and attitudes with the Chinese picture of themselves in relation to the world.

Throughout the ages the western nations have formed varied opinions of China, so varied that one asks oneself whether they can in fact have been describing the same civilization. One notion was of an incredibly rich and mighty China. It originated in the accounts of several overland travellers who reached the court of Ghengis Khan in the thirteenth century when the Mongol empire extended from the Ukraine to the borders of China. Of these travellers the most famous were the Italian Franciscan, Giovanni de Piano

Carpini; the Flemish Franciscan, William of Ruysbroeck; and of course the Venetian merchant, Marco Polo.

Piano Carpini was sent by Pope Innocent IV to the court of the Great Khan in 1245. In his brief account of his travels Piano Carpini describes China as a country of great material prosperity. 'Cereals, wine, gold, silver, silk and everything that human nature needs for its sustenance were to be found in great abundance', he wrote.[1] A few years later the Fleming, Ruysbroeck, set out for the capital of the Great Khan. His account says more of China's fabulous treasures: '... there is a city with walls of silver and ramparts of gold'.[2] However, Piano Carpini's and Ruysbroeck's reports had only a minor influence on their contemporaries and subsequent generations. Both men were overshadowed by that great traveller and magnificent observer, Marco Polo (1254–1324). This talented young Venetian became an important official in the service of the Great Khan and in that capacity he travelled widely throughout the Mongol empire, and criss-crossed China several times. In the year 1298 he dictated an account of his journeys to a friend. Its publication under the title *Description of the World* stunned provincial Europe.[3] For the first time the existence of another vast and highly-civilized world was revealed to the Christian West.

The dominant theme of Marco Polo's book is public administration in China. He describes the organization of the state, the monetary and fiscal system, and the excellent postal service. Unfortunately he barely mentions Chinese intellectual life. That he was a most accurate observer can, however, be seen by his famous description of Hangchow, the capital of the southern Sung dynasty. But no one in the West believed his reports of a highly civilized Eastern people. It was at variance with the accepted western view of the place of Christians in the world. Not surprisingly Marco Polo was nick-named *Il Milione* and asked on his deathbed to recant and expunge all exaggeration from his book. Though *Description of the World* was soon translated into many western languages, unfortunately most of the translators had bizarre imaginations and gave strange, and sometimes sinister, versions of Chinese customs. Thus Marco Polo's accurate description of a highly civilized China was distorted and replaced by a myth which has been believed in the West until the present day. Moreover, though Marco Polo's description of a wealthy China was accurate at the time, during the fifteenth and sixteenth centuries China's standard of living declined rapidly while Europe's rose with equal rapidity. But the western belief in a wealthy China persisted long after the West had surpassed her in material progress. Towards the end of the eighteenth century T.R. Malthus still believed that China was the richest country in the world.[4]

The second western notion I should like to discuss is that of 'a reasonable China governed by enlightened philosophers'. The Jesuits were mainly responsible for this belief. The most important person in the Jesuit mission was the Italian, Matteo Ricci (1552–1610). His writings introduced Confucius to Europe.

Ricci arrived in Macao in 1582, and after persistent requests was allowed to settle in Peking in 1601. There he won acceptance where many others had failed. He applied himself to an intensive study of Chinese and, after six years of reading Chinese classic writings, he was accepted by scholars and officials. In 'becoming as the Chinese' Ricci was following the orders of Alexandro Valignano, Visitor-General to the Indies, who in 1577 had ordered the Jesuits to adapt themselves to Chinese culture instead of trying to lead the Chinese towards Portuguese culture.[5] Matteo Ricci was the first and most successful exponent of this policy, and in this way he prepared for the entry of Christianity into the mainstream of Chinese life and thought. Living and thinking as a learned Chinese, advancing Christianity not by preaching but rather by discussion and conversation, he communicated with China through the medium of Chinese learning, and respected it just as the Chinese scholars came to respect him. He wrote in his journals:

> Whoever may think that ethics, physics and mathematics are not important in the work of the Church, is unacquainted with the taste of the Chinese, who are slow to take a salutary spiritual potion, unless it be seasoned with an intellectual flavouring. It was by means of a knowledge of European science, new to the Chinese, that Father Ricci amazed the entire philosophical world of China; proving the truth of its novelty by sound and logical reasoning. Once this new knowledge became known to a few, it was not long before it found its way into the academies of the learned. One can see how Europe's reputation was enhanced in this way and how they were slow to describe it as being barbarous, and ashamed at a later date to refer to it as such.[6]

Ricci's journals, which cover the years 1583–1610, probably had a greater effect on the literary, scientific, philosophical, and religious aspects of life in Europe than any other book published in the seventeenth century. Many of Ricci's successors in the Jesuit mission added to the stream of books, letters, and pamphlets pouring into Europe. The Jesuits described a reasonable China governed by philosopher-statesmen; a strong, united, and self-sufficient state, a China ruled by an emperor and his officials in accordance with the moral and political maxims of the Confucian classics. This new western knowledge of China raised many religious and philosophical questions, and the Jesuits' description of pure Confucianism attracted many of the best minds of Europe at that time. Voltaire thought that the theory of a universal religion of reason existed in reality in China. He wrote: 'One does not have to be an enthusiast for the achievements of the Chinese to recognise that the contribution of their Empire is the most excellent the world has ever seen, and the only one based on patriarchal authority.'[7]

Voltaire was of course just one of many Westerners whom the Jesuits misinformed or informed inadequately. For example they did not say that there were different schools of thought within Confucianism. They did not write about the evils of religious persecution and the corruption of some court officials. They were silent about peasant rebellions and the ill-treatment of minority peoples. They said no word of the influence of Buddhism or of the Ming-Manchu struggle of the seventeenth century.

The Jesuits did not like the materialistic agnosticism of contemporary Confucianism. For that very reason they had returned to what they regarded as the authentic religious tradition of ancient China. They believed that most of the ideas in the Confucian classics could be brought into accord with Christianity. They of course opposed Taoism and Buddhism as false beliefs which had corrupted pure Confucianism. In fact, by trying to adapt Catholicism to the Chinese way of looking at life, the Jesuits gave Europeans the impression that China was a country of high political morality. Although this picture of China faded soon after the decline of the Jesuit mission, the idea of a reasonable China governed by enlightened philosophers continued to have a very strong influence in the West.

The third misconception that I should like to discuss had become almost universal in Europe by the end of the nineteenth century. It was the view of China as a degenerate, sinister, corrupt nation which rejected the blessings of western liberalism. This was a complete reversal of the Jesuit view.

This nineteenth-century picture of the Chinese empire was of an old, rotten state which would disintegrate under the pressure of western economic progress and enterprise. Western opinion was unanimous: China was degenerate, calcified, unable to react in a 'normal' manner. To Westerners who believed that this picture was

4

true the Chinese indeed seemed blind. They believed that the Chinese simply ignored the prospects held out by commerce and industry. So it was from the western point of view. The Chinese saw the advanced western nations as barbarian states with a certain technical superiority. They resisted attempts to establish diplomatic relations until western military strength compelled them to give way. In Chinese perspective one can interpret China's reaction as a sign of strength, as proof of the life-strength of a great tradition, which in spite of disturbing and undermining influences continues to operate.

The West approached China as a sovereign nation. To the western mind, the relations between the West and China should rest on a basis of equality. The western powers expected the Chinese government to promote trade as a matter of 'national interest'. The Chinese had never done this, and were not in the frame of mind to do so. There was no place in the Chinese political system for two-way diplomatic relations.

What was the traditional Chinese system of government? The imperial government of China was very different from western government of the nineteenth century (e.g. constitutional monarchy). Compared to the western machinery of state, it appeared ineffective and incompetent. However, the basic reason for China's success in the act of government was that the community was held together by ethical beliefs and customs rather than by the power of law as it was understood in the West. To Chinese political thinkers, ethics and politics were one and the same; the state and the individual were regarded as one entity because they were under the influence of the same principle or code of ethics. Hence the Chinese maintained that good government depended not upon legal and institutional principles, but upon good administration. This attitude underlined the need for a morally cultivated ruling class. Imperial China was indebted to Confucius and his followers for an ethico-political system under which the emperor was expected to set a perfect moral example for his officials and his people so that all would be ruled by the power of his goodness and imbued with his virtue and moral influence. The most important duty of a sovereign, in Confucius' view, was to gain his people's confidence. Of the three essentials for good government Confucius believed that to have the people's confidence was the most important. (The other two essentials were to have sufficient food and arms.) Confucius said: 'From time immemorial, death has been the lot of all men; but a people that no longer trusts its ruler is lost indeed.'[8]

The key to the imperial government was the emperor. He held the kingdom both as the 'Son of Heaven' and as a kind of father to his people. He exercised his parental authority through a vast bureaucracy of 'superior men'. In theory the emperor was supreme over all the people in the empire and was the sole source of authority. He was the administrative director of the state, and officials derived their authority and titles from him. The power of legislation resided in him, and he was the supreme judge. Therefore the whole power of government – legislative, executive, and judicial – was vested in his person. In practice of course most of this imperial power had to be delegated.

The Chinese system of international relations was based on a system of tribute, which was the application to foreign affairs of those Confucian teachings by which the emperor gained ethical sanction for his exercise of political authority. Just as the good ruler, by his moral example, enjoyed prestige and influence among his people, so it was believed that he irresistibly attracted the barbarians who were beyond the pale of Chinese culture. To a Confucian scholar it was unthinkable that the rude barbarians of the West should not appreciate China's cultural superiority and therefore seek the benefits of Chinese civilization. As the emperor held the Mandate from Heaven to rule all mankind, he should be compassionate and generous to all barbarians. This imperial benevolence should be reciprocated, it was felt, by the foreigner's humble submission. Once the foreigner had recognized the unique position of the Son of Heaven he would inevitably humbly kowtow to him and bring him tribute. This was 'the mechanism by which barbarous non-Chinese regions were given their place in the all-embracing Chinese political, and therefore ethical, scheme of things'.[9] In theory the tribute system was ritualistic, based on the sacred lord-vassal relationship. In practice many so-called envoys, far from wanting to pay tribute, were traders who were eager to receive valuable presents – and some commercial privileges – from the Son of Heaven. About 1600 Matteo Ricci wrote about several of these swindlers, as he called them.[10] For the central government of China the tribute system had never been of economic importance; however, under the pressure of the western powers it became increasingly a vehicle for trade.

Western envoys did not understand the ideological role they were playing in Chinese eyes. They merely felt insulted by the endless ceremonials of the kowtow. First they returned home surprised, then disappointed, and finally very angry.[11] After the Opium War of 1839 the British thought they had defeated the tribute system. For the Chinese, however, the war had changed nothing in principle. Many incidents and disputes followed this war. Several powerful western nations insisted that the Chinese interior should be opened up for trade and missionary work. This policy seemed to be in line with Lord Palmerston's pronouncement that all semi-civilized nations like China needed a good beating every eight or ten years just to remain in form.[12]

And how did the Chinese statesmen react to western attitudes and western manners, to western intrusions and the use of force? As already mentioned, in western eyes their reaction seemed slight and then only according to their time-honoured central tradition of the Confucian state. It was precisely in this period (1860s) that progressive Chinese scholars began their famous 'Self-strengthening Movement'. These scholars believed that western technology and science should be adopted for practical reasons, and that their adoption would in no way spell the destruction of traditional Chinese institutions and way of life. Of course this proved a mistaken belief. But how could those Chinese orthodox leaders realize that it would be impossible to restrict technology and science to the building of schools and steamships? How could they realize that these influences would irrevocably change Chinese society? To them the old dogma of the central tradition was untouchable. To them technology and science were practical but not very important services. For centuries the Chinese Son of Heaven had had foreign technological advisers, both scientific and military, in his service: Indian monks, Moslems from Central Asia, and western priests. In the seventeenth century the Jesuits had not realized that they also were merely playing their part in this ancient Chinese tradition of making use of foreigners. Their religious status was merely a bizarre detail, tolerated but not accepted. This tradition of engaging foreign experts under strict governmental control continued until late in the nineteenth century. Among such experts, Sir Robert Hart, Inspector-General of the Chinese Maritime Customs, and Timothy Richard, adviser to the Emperor K'ang-hsi, spring to mind.

Japan defeated China in 1894–5 and annexed Formosa. At this stage several western nations joined in a mad scramble for concessions and China was divided into spheres of influence. It was well on the way to becoming fragmented colonial territory. The literati agreed that China needed desperately to protect herself. But they did not agree on the method of protection. Chang Chih-tung believed that to strengthen China was to uphold the dynasty and tradition. Liang Ch'i-ch'ao believed that radical modernization was in the true Chinese tradition. In 1895 a number of scholars led by K'ang Yu-wei (1858–1927) petitioned the throne to reject the treaty with Japan. K'ang Yu-wei urged broad changes for China's government based on the Japanese model of constitutional monarchy. K'ang's proposals were ignored until the Germans seized Shantung in 1897. In this desperate situation K'ang Yu-wei and other literati succeeded in their reform movement. They even gained the sponsorship of the Emperor Kang-hsi. Scores of decrees hastily were issued. They dealt with the importance of scientific studies, the adoption of western military drill, the improvement of agriculture and education, the abolition of the eight-legged essay in the official examinations, the dismissal of conservative officials, and so on. But three months later tradition showed its strength. Conservatives under the leadership of the Empress Dowager Tz'u-hsi staged a coup d'état. They revoked all the new decrees and declared the Emperor insane. Not long after this came the anti-western Boxer Rising (1900), the final bankruptcy of the old order, sealed by the abolition of the Confucian examinations in 1905. It was now clear that reform was needed. Moreover it had become evident with the abolition of the Confucian examinations that reaction in China was dead. Accordingly the thought of revolution was becoming clear in the young Chinese mind.

The fourth and final belief I should like to discuss is that of the foreign adviser and philanthropist in China. In fact the adviser has been mentioned several times already. He plays a very important role in the relationship between China and the West. For the last three centuries many western advisers have served the Chinese people in one capacity or another. These advisers were usually regarded as heroes, saints, and pioneers in the West. They began by bringing knowledge of the stars and of planetary motion. They ended by introducing the Chinese to aerial warfare and the mysteries of the atom. Most western advisers and philanthropists believed that they stood in a position of superiority to the Chinese. This superiority rested on two bases: the possession of advanced technical skills, and a belief in their moral rightness. Chinese refusal to accept western goals and Chinese rejection of western advice were met with bewilderment or anger. Today all western aid and advice is rather simplistically brushed off by Chinese patriots as 'imperialism'. For example, missionary hospitals are classed as 'cultural imperialism'. Professor King Fairbank has wisely remarked that this blanket use of the word 'imperialism' to malign even the noblest motives of western philanthropy may well remind us of one basic fact: the West expanded into China, not China into the West. The foreigners even in their best moments were in this sense aggressive; they were agents of change and thus destructive of the old order.

Not so long ago a new breed of western advisers appeared in China: selfless, dedicated people like the famous Canadian doctor, Norman Bethune, and the English educator, George Hogg. In his introduction to Hogg's *I See a New China,* the New Zealander Rewi Alley wrote the following words about his dear friend: 'He is one of those Westerners who have brought to China a real contribution, and made some amends for the sins of those who have come to this country to take away livelihood – not bring it. Through his being and working, many blades of grass will grow in places where none grew before.'

These words apply equally to Rewi Alley himself. When Alley arrived in Shanghai in April 1927 he took a job with the Shanghai Municipal Council Fire Brigade as a factory inspector and during his periods of leave he helped with famine and flood relief, particularly in Suiyan and Hankow. In 1938 he organized the Chinese Industrial Cooperatives – known to the western world as 'Indusco' or 'Gung Ho' ('work together'). These small-scale industries produced the goods required by the community during the Japanese invasion. The industrial cooperatives, which numbered approximately 2 000, flourished, and Rewi extended his activities to building training schools for their apprentices and organizers – notably the schools of Shuangshihpu in Shansi and Sandan in Kansu. The 'Sandan experiment' founded by Rewi Alley was the prototype for the present self-sufficient village commune in China. Of all the western experiences in China since Marco Polo, the New Zealander Rewi Alley has had the most influential and also the most intimate. If a new and better relationship has been established between China and the West, it is to no small degree due to people like Bethune, Hogg, and Alley.

Notes

1 F. Risch, *Johann de Piano Carpini. Geschichte der Mongolen und Reisebericht 1245– 1247*, Leipzig, 1930, p. 120.

2 F. Risch, *Wilhelm von Rubruk. Reise zu den Mongolen 1253–1255*, Leipzig, 1934, p. 169.
3 Yule-Cordier, *The Book of Ser Marco Polo*, 2 vols, London, 1903. Benedetto, *Marco Polo, il milione*, Florence, 1928. Moule-Pelliot, *Marco Polo, The Description of the World*, 2 vols, London, 1938.
4 T.R. Malthus, *First Essay on Population*, London, 1926.
5 G. Dunne, *Generation of Giants*, Notre Dame, Ind., 1962, p. 19.
6 L.J. Gallagher (trans.), *China in the Sixteenth Century: The Journals of Matthew Ricci, 1583–1610*, New York, 1953, p. 326.
7 *Oeuvres complètes*, Gotha 1785, xxxviii, p. 492; quoted from A. Reichwein, *China and Europe*, New York, 1925.
8 *Analects*, xii, 7.
9 J. King Fairbank and Ssu-yü Teng, 'On the Ch'ing Tributary System', *Harvard Journal of Asiatic Studies*, vol. vi, no. 2, June 1941, p. 129.
10 *Ibid.*, p. 172.
11 The English tribute mission of Lord Macartney refused to kowtow in 1793. See Ssu-yü Teng and J. King Fairbank, *China's Response to the West, a Documentary Survey 1839–1923*, Harvard University Press, Cambridge, Mass., 1954, p. 19.
12 J. King Fairbank, *Trade and Diplomacy on the China Coast*, Harvard University Press, Cambridge, Mass., 1953, p. 380.

Let the People Sing –
Three Thousand Years of Protest

MARGARET T.S. SOUTH

Almost three thousand years ago, according to tradition, the early rulers of the kingdom of Chou sent officials into the countryside to collect the songs of the common people. From these they were to learn of the people's hopes and fears, of their needs and requirements, and whether content or discontent prevailed within the various feudal principalities of China. Some three hundred of these poems and songs were later selected, polished, and formed into the collection now known as the *Shih-ching* (variously translated as the *Book of Songs*, the *Book of Odes*, or the *Classic of Poetry*). The compilation of this work is commonly attributed to Confucius although this view has never been substantiated. He is known, however, to have given it the seal of his approval and the collection has long formed part of the Confucian canon.

Less than twenty years ago, in 1958, the government of the People's Republic of China sent officials, teachers, writers, and students into the countryside to record the songs of the peasants and manual workers. Nation-wide poetry contests were organized, from which another vast number of poems and folk songs were collected and published. Some three hundred of these were later selected by the distinguished writer Kuo Mo-jo and formed into a collection known as the *Hung ch'i ko yao* (*Songs of the Red Flag*). Ostensibly these latter-day poetry officials were not looking for criticisms as had their predecessors – for once the socialist revolution was complete what serious grounds for complaint could remain? Primarily they were taking part in a great cultural revolution from which it was hoped a new socialist literature would emerge. Their aim was not merely to observe and record but, by personally sharing in the labours of the people, to come to appreciate more nearly and hence to convey more truthfully their thoughts and

11

feelings. Whether this ideal has yet been fully realized and whether this new collection of three hundred poems and songs will survive to be as profoundly influential in the cultural life of the Chinese people as the *Book of Odes* has been is a matter for a future literary historian. What is of immediate interest, however, is the long-standing tradition of which both collections form a part – a chunk as it were of that 'Chinese bedrock' remarked upon by Hu Shih[1] which underlies the changes wrought by social revolution. In this context the common or continuing factor linking the policies of Mao Tse-tung to those of the early kings of Chou is the centuries-held belief in the social utility of literature.

This concept has played an important role in the development of the Chinese poetic tradition and predominated throughout the first five hundred years of its recorded history. Though other theories of the nature and function of poetry were later to emerge and be observed, the essentially pragmatic and didactic view has always had strong adherents among those belonging to the Confucian school. Moreover, while these other theories have usually taken precedence, and didactic and satirical poems have been fewer in number and often less highly regarded as poetry, the view that literature should have a social and moral purpose has always been considered legitimate and respectable in China. Today it has been restored to its former pinnacle. At the Yenan forum on art and literature held in 1942 its principles were unequivocally restated by Mao Tse-tung and in China today the poet is continually re-minded that his first duty is to employ his art in the service of the revolution and the people.

Many people who have come to know Chinese poetry only in translation may not be aware of the strength of this tradition. Didactic or satirical poems often require much annotation and for that reason tend to be omitted from anthologies prepared for the general reader. In this paper I propose therefore to examine some poems of this kind and hope in so doing to modify in some degree an impression still fairly prevalent in the West; namely, that Chinese poetry is almost exclusively concerned with bamboo groves, lotus ponds, and autumn chrysanthemums, or inevitably permeated by that gentle melancholy induced by the drinking of wine, the playing of the lute, or moonbeams shining through the bed-curtains. These images are deservedly admired by jaded Westerners seeking tranquillity from an Eastern muse, but to judge all Chinese verse by such images alone is to fail to appreciate the important social role poetry has always played in China and to underestimate its function as a vehicle for the communication not only of feeling and emotion but of comment, opinion, and criticism on a wide variety of topics.

As indicated above, the *Book of Odes* was compiled from a collection of songs believed originally to have been gathered together for a social purpose. They are for the most part 'songs of the people', representing the whole range of popular activity: work songs, love songs, songs about feasting, about war, about hunting, about agriculture. Some were happy, some sad. Some depicted the simple life of the countryside, others the sophisticated pleasures of the court. In the main they purport to be the songs of those personally involved, of whatever class: peasant or conscript, soldier or bureaucrat.

A pleasant example of a simple work ditty is no. 8, the 'Plantain Song'. It is sung by women gathering plantain, a plant believed to ensure easy childbirth:

> Gathering the plantain
> Now we gather it
> Gathering the plantain
> Now we grasp it
>
> Gathering the plantain
> Now we pick it
> Gathering the plantain
> Now we pluck it
>
> Gathering the plantain
> In aprons held out
> Gathering the plantain
> In aprons tucked in*

*Except where otherwise indicated, all translations are by the writer. However, those from the *Shih-ching* (Book of Odes) are based on translations by B. Karlgren and Arthur Waley, and that of 'The Cloth-seller's Song' on a translation by Winnie Une-shing Tsang.

Ode 188, 'I travel through the countryside', reveals a lady in less happy circumstances, although not, it would seem, unduly cast down:

> I travel through the countryside
> Luxuriant are the Ailanthus trees
> Because we were to wed
> I went to your house
> As you do not care for me
> You have sent me home to my own land
>
> I travel through the countryside
> I pluck a dock leaf
> Because we were to wed
> I went to dwell with you
> As you do not care for me
> I am going back home again
>
> I travel through the countryside
> I pluck the *fu* plant
> Not thinking of your old wife
> You went looking for a new one
> It can't have been for the money
> It can only have been for a change

In more serious vein is ode no. 40, 'Northern Gate', the complaint of an overworked and ill-used official:

> I leave by the northern gate
> My heart is sore distressed
> In want indeed and poor
> No one knows my troubles
> Well it's finished now
> Truly Heaven caused it
> Why then talk about it
>
> The King's business was assigned to me
> Government business increasingly was given to me
> Whenever I came in from outside
> The people of the house would all reprove me
> Well it's finished now
> Truly Heaven caused it
> Why then talk about it

> The King's business was heaped upon me
> Government business increasingly was left to me
> Whenever I came in from outside
> The people of the house would all repress me
> Well it's finished now
> Truly heaven caused it
> Why then talk about it

What practical conclusions were drawn from such songs by those who originally commissioned their collection is not known. However, by the time Confucius was commending it to his disciples, the *Book of Odes* appears to have become something more than a mere anthology of popular songs. Possibly through its having been subjected to the refining attentions of the court poets and musicians, the collection was now felt to be imbued with some kind of moral power. In some way it had been transformed into an instrument of that civilizing process which, in the Confucian view, is the proper function of good government. 'By studying the *Odes*,' said Confucius, 'one can be stimulated, one can observe, one can be sociable, one can learn the art of resentment.'[2] The *Odes*, he believed, assisted men to act correctly, to do their duty towards parents and prince, to converse intelligently – in other words, to inculcate correct social attitudes. For him, as a moralist and an educationist, the intrinsic literary merit of the collection was of less significance than its effectiveness as a moral and transforming influence.

His successors, the scholars of the Confucian school, wholeheartedly adopted this view. Moreover, for them the *Book of Odes* became not only a work to be read for its general moral tone but one to be used as a source for particular moral lessons. Some of the *Odes* were intended from the beginning to convey a message or a complaint, to be satires or allegories. A great many however were merely love songs or work ditties with no political significance. It nevertheless became the practice to treat them all as allegories. In songs of courtship or marriage, for example, the relationship between husband and wife was seen as an allegory for the relationship between a prince and his minister. A rejected suitor was clearly a symbol for an official denied office, a discarded wife for a minister out of favour with his prince. During the Han dynasty (206 B.C.–A.D. 220), a time when Confucian orthodoxy came to be pre-eminent, prefaces were added to these odes, providing each one with a moral or political interpretation. It was difficult to read very much of that nature into such ditties as the 'Plantain Song'. Nevertheless the attempt was made and its preface reads: 'The "Plantain Song" is about the Queen's goodness. There was harmony and peace and so the women delighted in bearing children.'

The preface to ode 188 simply states: '[The ode] "I travel through the countryside" criticises King Hsuan.' In this ode the husband to whom the lady addresses herself represents King Hsuan. The lady herself, the discarded wife, represents a minister originally engaged by the king from a neighbouring state but now dismissed for some trivial reason in order that he may employ someone else.

The traditional interpretation of the ode 'Northern Gate' is that it was specifically directed against oppressive conditions in the kingdom of Wei. Its preface reads: 'In the kingdom of Wei everyone was fearfully oppressed. The families of the common people could not keep together. So, helping each other to pack up, they all moved away.'

Such specific ascriptions often appear unwarranted by the words of the text. Nevertheless they cannot be discounted. Accepted for many hundreds of years (they were not seriously disputed until the eleventh century), these interpretations are almost as important as the text itself, especially if one wishes to understand the significance of allusions to the odes in later poetry.

It may thus be seen that by the time of the Han dynasty an important literary precedent had been established. From believing that the simple songs of the *Book of Odes* contained subtle political allegories and bitter satirical protest it was but a short step to assuming that subtle political allegories and bitter satirical protest were best embodied in the form of simple songs. Furthermore, because the *Book of Odes* had immense prestige as the sole work of poetry in the Confucian canon, it was natural for the Chinese writer to regard poetry as a proper vehicle for social criticism. Until the third century A.D., after which time Chinese poetry, to its great enrichment, gradually came to be recognized as an art in itself, this purely utilitarian view of its function predominated. However, while poetic content continued to be governed by the principles educed from the *Book of Odes*, poetic form was not so restricted.

The four-word line of the *Book of Odes* in time became stereotyped and poets came to prefer more contemporary metres. Those of the second great anthology of early Chinese poetry, the *Ch'u-tz'u* (*Elegies of Ch'u*), from the third century B.C., are entirely different,

16

being based on a couplet of two six-word lines linked by a meaning-less syllable, *hsi*. During the Han dynasty another new form, the *yueh-fu* ballad, emerged and became very popular among poets who had a social message to express. One of the duties of the *yueh-fu* or Music Bureau, from which the new form took its name, was the collection of popular songs for use at court feasts and other enter-tainments. At the same time, following the Chou tradition, poetry officials were sent out among the people to gather songs by which the authorities might gauge public opinion of the effectiveness of the administration in general and the efficiency of individual officials in particular. J.P. Dieny suggests that these two activities were quite unrelated.[3] Albeit, the songs thus collected all came to be known as *yueh-fu* and, as might be expected, had many features in common. *Yueh-fu* metres, for the most part based on irregular or on five-word lines, were more attractive to the ear than the more formal four-word lines of the *Book of Odes*. Moreover, in their simplicity of expression and concrete imagery, *yueh-fu* had universal appeal. Hence the *yueh-fu* form and style were frequently adopted by those who wished to express their grievances effectively.

The following song, 'To the East of P'ing-ling', illustrates the genre at its best:

> To the East of P'ing-ling
> Pines, cedars, and *wu-t'ungs*
> Someone, we know not whom, has abducted our master
>
> Has abducted our master
> 'Down by the high hall
> Hand over two million cash and two riding horses.'
>
> And two riding horses
> 'Tis indeed truly difficult
> One glance at the Investigator and our hearts are sick
>
> Our hearts are sick
> Our blood drains away
> We go home and tell them to sell the yellow calf

Even in translation the language is simple and concise, the lines of irregular length, the rhythm natural. The use of direct speech and of reiteration – the repetition of the last words of one line at the beginning of the next – are also characteristic features of the genre. The treatment is realistic; the complaint, thinly veiled, is implicit in the situation described and not overtly stated. Ostensibly the poem concerns a person abducted by bandits and held for ransom, with little hope of rescue by the authorities who are investigating the affair. At the same time, however, one receives a distinct impression that the authorities themselves are responsible. If this is so the poem may well be a complaint against unscrupulous officials who have arrested a householder for non-payment of dues, possibly illegally imposed.[4] The hardships incurred by the people from rigorously imposed taxes are a constantly recurring theme in *yueh-fu*.

Another recurring theme, that of the displaced wife, is illustrated in the next song, 'She went up the hill to gather herbs':

> She went up the hill to gather herbs
> She came down the hill and met her former husband
> Bowing low she asked her former husband
> 'Your new wife, what kind of girl is she?'
>
> 'My new wife, though I will say she is good,
> Is not to be compared with the old one.
> In looks there's little to choose between the two
> But the new one is not so clever with her hands.'
> 'Yet the new wife through the front door entered in
> While the old wife through the side door went away!'
>
> 'The new wife is good at the weaving of raw silk
> The old wife is good at the weaving of white silk
> The one, of raw silk weaves a roll a day
> The other of white silk fifty feet and more.
> But when you compare the raw silk with the white
> The new wife is not as skilful as the old.'

This is an example of a *yueh-fu* in the regular five-word-line metre. Both these poems are short and to the point. However, not all *yueh-fu* were as brief. 'The Orphan', a very famous and well-loved poem in which the sufferings of an orphaned lad at the hands of his brother and sister-in-law are described, has over fifty lines.[5] The 'Chiao Chung-ching', a long narrative poem relating the misfortunes of a young bride unable to please her mother-in-law, has over three hundred.[6] The language of these longer *yueh-fu* is, however, as vivid and alive as that of the shorter poems, the narrative equally simple and expressive, the message as direct.

After the end of the Han dynasty significant changes took place not only in poetic form but also in poetic content. Along with the development of the five-word-line *shih* poem as the major lyric form, poetry came to be recognized as a vehicle for the expression not merely of ideas of social and moral value but of all kinds of personal feeling. It gradually became acceptable for poets to record in verse the pleasures they experienced at feasts or excursions or at meetings with friends; their enjoyment of the beauties of the landscape; their personal anxieties and their philosophical ideas. Poetry no longer had to be directed towards a 'useful end' but was recognized as an end in itself. This new freedom naturally led to some abuse. Released from the Confucian obligation to include material of moral worth, some writers found expression of greater interest than content and there were cases of over-elaboration and over-complexity of style, especially in the fifth and sixth centuries. Such extravagances were later censured by those who held a more moral view of the function of poetry.

Poets such as Ch'en Tzu-ang in the early years of the T'ang dynasty (618–905) reacted strongly against this kind of writing, the so-called 'decadent and florid style' of the Ch'i-Liang period, and called for a return to the principles of the *Book of Odes*. Initially few poets responded to this call. The great poets of the High T'ang can scarcely be accused of displaying a 'decadent and florid' style but the social content of their work is minimal. Even Tu Fu, who was to write some very bitter lines about the poverty and distress he encountered in his own life and in his travels throughout the country, does not appear to have set out deliberately to write poems of social criticism. Nevertheless his work was not without its influence in this regard, and later reformers quoted such poems as his 'Recruiting Officer at Hsin-an', 'Recruiting Officer at Shih-hao', and 'Frontier Officer at T'ung Kuan' with approval and as models to be followed.[7]

In the early part of the ninth century a group of younger writers, under the influence of a Confucian revival in literature headed by the great prose writer Han Yu, reaffirmed the view that literature should have social and moral content, and consciously devoted their talents to writing poems of protest. Included among them were such poets as Po Chu-i, Chang Chi, Wang Chien, Li Shen, Yuan Chen and, somewhat surprisingly, the precocious young genius Li Ho. Li Ho's writing is not generally characterized by either simplicity or straightforwardness. Nevertheless, the poem which follows, no.2 of a series entitled *Moved to Satirize*, uses the *yueh-fu* form to great advantage.

In Ho-p'u there are no bright pearls
In Lung-chou there are no oranges
So it seems that even God himself
Is powerless to meet the Governors' demands
The woman of Yueh has not yet started weaving
The silkworms of Wu have only just begun to wriggle
When the District Officer rides up on his horse
With fierce mien and curly purple whiskers
In his pocket a single square of paper
On the paper several lines of writing
'If you were not the cause of the Governor's anger
Why should I have come to your house?'
The woman of Yueh bows to the District Officer
'The mulberry shoots at present are still small
You'll have to wait until the end of spring
Then only will the silk-reeling begin'
While the woman of Yueh has been explaining
Her sister-in-law has been preparing millet gruel
Barely has the District Officer gulped it down and gone
Than the Records clerk is in the hall again

Ho-p'u was in Han times a district famous for its pearls. Under a corrupt governor the pearl beds were depleted. A neighbouring state acquired all the pearls, trade declined, and many Ho-p'u people died of starvation. At the time this poem was written China was suffering a similar depletion of its silk through an unequal trade treaty with the Uighur tribes to the north. The women of the silk-weaving households were greatly oppressed by the impossible demands made upon them. Some even resorted to such devices as coarse weaving and incorporating spiders' webs and lotus-root fibres to make up the required amounts. The situation in Ho-p'u was resolved by the appointment of a competent governor who quickly restored prosperity to the state. Li Ho thus infers that the restoration of an efficient and incorrupt administration would do the same for the T'ang.

Li Ho's poem is very simple and direct and conforms in almost every respect to the *yueh-fu* tradition. He was himself of course one step removed from the situation and, as a literary man writing about a social abuse, he used the literary man's device of a somewhat obscure allusion in the first lines. Nevertheless this is a realist poem of a very high order.

In his *yueh-fu* poems Li Ho was in general surpassed by other members of the group. Chang Chi, for example, was especially praised by his contemporaries for his devotion to the principles of the *Book of Odes* and for the writing of *yueh-fu* ballads. His ballad 'The Old Countryman' is typical of his work. In it he describes the plight of a peasant farmer who labours a whole year to produce the tax grain and is then left with nothing with which to supply the needs of his own family:

> The old farmer is poor and lives in the mountains
> He ploughs and sows a mountain field of half an acre or so
> The plants are sparse, the taxes many, so he doesn't get the food
> That goes to the state granary where it moulders into dust.
> The year at an end, his hoe and plough by the side of his empty house
> He calls to his sons and climbs the mountain in order to gather acorns
> The trader on the West River has pearls by the bushelful
> The dogs reared on his boat are always fed on meat

In this poem Chang Chi speaks for the farmer and does not allow him to speak for himself. The poem therefore lacks the immediacy and personal involvement typical of the other examples quoted so far. Yet it is not without impact. This is achieved through an ironic contrast drawn between the lot of the poor peasant farmer in the mountains and that of the rich pearl trader on the West River, a contrast all the more striking when one recalls that of the four traditional classes in Chinese society – scholar, farmer, artisan, and merchant – the merchant, being non-productive, was the least highly regarded.

A great admirer of Chang Chi's poetry was the poet Po Chu-i. The most prominent among the ninth-century group of reformist poets, he was destined to become one of the greatest names in Chinese poetry. Early in his official career he wrote and circulated a series of more than a hundred poems drawing attention to various abuses in the society of his day. These, as he had intended, came to the attention of the Emperor, Hsien-tsung, who was greatly impressed by them and subsequently ordered Po Chu-i's promotion. Thus encouraged, Po Chu-i wrote more poems of social criticism, using the *yueh-fu* form, and made a special collection of fifty poems which he called *Hsin yueh-fu* (*New Ballads*) and for which he wrote a preface very much after the style of the preface to the *Book of Odes*. Though in many respects these new *yueh-fu* employ the techniques of the old *yueh-fu* and retain much of their simplicity, they are primarily literary works and use literary devices such as allusion

21

and allegory to a far greater extent than their Han counterparts had done. The poems which follow all belong to this series of fifty *Hsin yueh-fu* and were written during the fourth year of Hsien-tsung's reign, the year 809 of our calendar. In the first, 'A man of Tu-ling', he writes, as did Chang Chi in 'The Old Countryman', of the plight of a poor farmer. Unlike Chang Chi, however, he allows the farmer to speak some lines on his own behalf:

> A man of Tu-ling
> He dwells in Tu-ling
> Each year tilling his fifteen-acre tract of barren land
> In the third month no rain fell, drought winds arose,
> On the wheat shoots no ears formed, many yellowed
>   and died.
> In the ninth month frosts descended, and autumn early
>   turned cold
> Ere the ears of grain were ripe, all had blackened and dried
> The chief clerks, though well aware, did not report the
>   disaster
> But zealously exacted extortionate levies with an eye to
>   their merit assessment.
> 'If I mortgage the mulberry trees and sell my land to pay
>   the official taxes
> For next year's food and clothing whatever shall I do?
> You strip the cloth from my body
> You snatch the grain from my mouth
> In oppressing men and harming living creatures you are
>   like wolves
> But why must you use hooklike claws and sawlike teeth
>   to eat our flesh.'
> I do not know who it was informed our august Emperor
> But the Emperor's heart was touched when he learned of
>   the people's plight
> On white hemp paper he wrote out an act of grace
> The capital territory was completely absolved of this
>   year's taxes!
> Just yesterday the village clerk arrived at the gates
> In his hand a dispatch which he posted up in the village
> But out of ten families, nine had already paid the taxes
> And vainly received our ruler's kindness in remitting
>   them.

This poem was occasioned by the severe drought in the spring of the year 809, which had caused widespread distress. Po Chu-i and his colleague Li Chiang had already sent up a memorial requesting the emperor to extend relief to those most affected by remitting their annual tax. Po Chu-i subsequently submitted a further memorial requesting additional relief. This poem was intended to reinforce his arguments.

In their memorial Po and Li had also pointed out to the emperor that the number of women then being retained in the palace was excessive and that economies might be effected in such a time of natural disaster by dispensing with their services. The emperor acted upon this advice and, in addition to carrying out the other measures proposed, sent more than three thousand of these women back to their homes. Shortly afterwards rain fell and the drought was broken. The following poem, 'The Lady of Shang-yang', was written to support the submission concerning the palace women. Po Chu-i appears to have had a very special sympathy for the misfortunes of women. 'Do not be born a woman,' he wrote in his poem 'The T'ai-hang Road', 'dependent on others for every joy and sadness.' In 'The Lady of Shang-yang' he reveals the plight of the imperial concubines. Many thousands of these women were recruited at a very early age and taken into the Inner Palace for the emperor's pleasure, but few were ever seen by him. The greater number endured for the rest of their lives a barren and lonely existence. Some who were especially beautiful, having incurred the jealousy of already established favourites, were sent away to distant palaces, such as that of Shang-yang, where the chance of being brought to the emperor's notice was equally remote.

> The Lady of Shang-yang
> The Lady of Shang-yang
> Her rouged face sallow with age, her white hairs newly
>   come
> Where the green-clad supervisors guard the palace gates
> Once shut up in Shang-yang how many springs have
>   passed
> It was during Hsuan-tsung's last years that she was first
>   chosen for entry
> On entry she was sixteen, now she is sixty
> Those chosen at the same time numbered over a hundred
> Now wasted away and full of years only she remains
> She recalls the past when, swallowing her grief, she parted
>   from her family
> As they helped her into the carriage, they told her not to
>   cry
> Everyone said that on entering the palace she would gain
>   the imperial favour

23

For her face was like a lotus flower, her breasts white as
   jade
But before his Highness was allowed to catch a glimpse
   of her
Yang-fei out of the corner of her eye had seen her from
   afar
And, jealous, ordered her banishment to the Palace of
   Shang-yang
Thus her whole life is spent sleeping in an empty room
Sleeping in an empty room, the autumn nights are long
The nights are long and sleepless and dawn never comes
Flickering, the expiring lamp casts shadows behind her on
   the wall
Sough, sough the night rain sounds as it beats against the
   window
The spring days linger
The days linger as she sits alone, dusk never falls
The palace orioles with their hundred cries in her grief she
   tires of hearing
Of the swallows nesting on the beams, growing old she has
   stopped being jealous
The orioles return, the swallows depart but always she is
   sad
Spring goes, autumn comes, she no longer counts the
   years
Alone in the depths of the palace she looks up at the
   bright moon
Which, from east to west, has gone round four to five
   hundred times
Today within the Palace, she is the oldest one
And the Emperor from afar has given her the title
   'Mistress in charge'
Putting on her pointed shoes and gown with narrow
   sleeves
In sombre hues she paints her eyebrows, her eyebrows
   fine and long
People on the outside cannot see, but to see would make
   them laugh
At her make-up in the style of the last years of T'ien-pao
The lady of Shang-yang
When young she suffered
Now old she suffers
Her suffering young, her suffering old, what can be done
   about it?
Have you not seen in a former time Lu Hsiang's *Fu* poem
   'The Beautiful Lady'
And do you not see today the song of 'The Shang-yang
   Palace Lady's White Hairs'

In sending home the palace ladies Hsien-tsung may perhaps have been influenced more by expediency than compassion, but he could hardly fail to have been moved by this very touching picture of the Lady of Shang-yang. In this poem Po Chu-i uses the *yueh-fu* technique of reiteration most effectively to create an atmosphere of interminable loneliness. Especially poignant is the little stir caused by the lady's being granted a new title, when, womanlike, she hastens to change her dress and repair her make-up still in the style of her youth sixty years before. This poem reveals Po Chu-i as not only a keen observer but also a poet of deep compassion. So too does the following poem, 'A mother parted from her sons', in which, with great understanding, he relates the plea of yet another supplanted wife.

A mother parted from her sons
Sons parted from their mother
The bright sun does not shine, the sound of weeping is
   bitter
The Kuang-hsi Grand Cavalry General just recently
For defeating the Caitiff tribes last year has had his name
   recorded
By Imperial Order he was given a two million cash reward
And in Lo-yang he has wedded a lady lovely as a flower
Since the new wife came, the old wife's been set aside
On the palms of the one lotus flowers, in the eyes of the
   other thorns
His taking a new wife and setting aside the old one is not
   worth my grief
I grieve because my husband's family is keeping my two
   sons
One has just begun to walk with help, one for the first
   time is sitting up
The sitting one howls, the walking one weeps as he
   clutches at my skirt
To permit you husband and wife to have fresh pleasures
You condemn us mother and sons to life-long
   separation
Even the crows and magpies in the forest are better off
The mother does not lose her chicks, the cock
   companions the hen
Like the peach and plum trees in the garden is how it
   ought to be
The flowers fall in the wind but the fruit remain on the
   branches
New wife, new wife, hearken to my words
In Lo-yang there are countless 'red-tower' ladies

My one wish is that the General establish his merit again
And bring home with him another new wife, one far
   better than you

Investigation has failed to reveal the identity of the Kuang-hsi
Grand Cavalry General. However, as the poem appears to be an
indictment of a general social evil rather than of one particular man,
this is perhaps of little moment. In it Po Chu-i shows his ability
not only to enter into the feelings of those whose grievances he is
describing but also to re-create them in his readers. It is for such
perception and understanding that he became known as 'the
humane genius'.

The poets of the *Hsin yueh-fu* (New *yueh-fu*) movement wrote
many poems critical of the society in which they lived, though in
general none surpassed Po Chu-i in expression or feeling. Nevertheless the literary principles they promoted, the essentially Confucian
principles of morality and didacticism in poetry, were not widely
adopted even among their contemporaries. Nor indeed was their
own work exclusively governed by these principles. The great
bulk of Po Chu-i's critical *yueh-fu*, for example, was produced
during his early years in office when his youthful idealism was still
untempered by any real necessity to avoid giving offence. The first
years of Hsien-tsung's reign were clearly favourable to this kind of
writing; but the political climate was soon to change and poets
were no longer encouraged to express their criticisms in verse.
It is probably true to say that such propitious times were not to
recur for many hundreds of years.

One should not think however that the writing of protest poetry
ceased. During the interval between the ninth and twentieth centuries individual poets, as occasion arose, continued to express both
personal and social grievances in verse, not only in *yueh-fu* form
but also in the other forms available to them—in the regulated
five- or seven-word *shih* poem, in *ku-shih* (old-style) verse, and even
in the *tz'u* lyric. Poetry officials, as Po Chu-i had complained in
'The Poem Collectors', were no longer sent to collect the people's
songs, but the people still sang and poets continued to resort
to folk songs from time to time for fresh inspiration. New metres
for formal poetry, such as the *tz'u* lyric, an irregular song form with
lines of unequal length and prescribed tonal patterns, which was
popular during the Sung dynasty, and the later *san-ch'u* or dramatic

lyric, a shorter and less restricted form associated particularly with Yuan drama, both evolved out of popular tunes.

After the revolution of 1911 literary reformers again sought new models. After a great struggle the classical or literary language was discarded and the vernacular or *pai-hua* adopted as the vehicle for a new national literature. Western literatures were explored for inspiration, and the writings of English, French, and Russian authors appeared in translation. Poems in the new *pai-hua* forms influenced by western traditions began to appear and experimental literary groups with widely divergent views were formed. At the same time, however, the traditional source for the revival of poetry was not neglected. Having won the battle over the introduction of the vernacular, literary men such as Hu Shih turned once again to the songs of the people in search of literary renaissance. Societies such as the Folk Song Collection Bureau and the Folk Song Research Society were founded in Peking, and in 1922 a journal, the *Folk Song Weekly*, began publication. The aim of its editors was to bring to light songs expressive of the feelings of the people and thereby to promote the development of a new, truly national poetry. The collection of songs was also seen as a means of acquiring knowledge of social conditions and bringing to light social abuses, both prerequisite to social reform. By 1925 over 13 000 songs had been collected and over 2 000 published in the *Folk Song Weekly*.[8] It is not surprising that poems by some of the early reformers appear to owe less to new western literary theories than to an indigenous tradition going right back to the Han *yueh-fu* and to the *Book of Odes*. 'The Cloth-seller's Song' by Liu Ta-pei illustrates not only the poet's awareness of contemporary problems but also his debt to an earlier literary convention:

> Sister-in-law weaves cloth
> Elder brother sells cloth
> He sells the cloth to buy rice
> There is rice for them to eat
>
> Sister-in-law weaves cloth
> Elder brother sells cloth
> Who comes and buys the cloth
> The rich man from the next village

> Local cloth is coarse
> Foreign cloth is fine
> Foreign cloth is cheap
> The rich man likes it
> Nobody wants local cloth
> Sister-in-law and elder brother starve

The period between the founding of the first republic in 1911 and the People's Republic in 1949 was one of great social upheaval and intellectual ferment. Western economic pressures, Japanese military aggression, and civil war were added to the disruption attendant upon the break-up of the Ch'ing dynasty and the fall of the Manchus. Thousands of young writers were uprooted and forced into situations where the distressed condition of the common people – peasant farmers, artisans, conscript soldiers – was inescapably presented to them. Many turned to communism for a solution to the grievous social ills besetting their country. The poets among them, filled with compassion for the oppressed and bitterness against the oppressors, and with their traditional assumptions about the social function of literature reinforced by the literary precepts of Marx and Lenin, responded with poems of social realism.

Some very bitter poems in this genre were written during the thirties and forties. Among them Yuan Shui-p'ai's 'Old Mother Blinds Her Own Son', and Liu Chia's 'Yen Hsi-shan's Tax Agent' stand out. The first, according to the author, was occasioned by a report published in the *Wen-hui Daily* of Shanghai in January 1947 of a mother who had blinded her son to ensure his rejection for military service.

> It's snowing hard
> The river froze
> We finished the nation's war, but now we fight our own
>   people
> Conscription could not reach the rich men
> It only reached my son, over twenty years old
>
> I entreated heaven, heaven did not respond;
> I pleaded with the earth, the earth had no power
> I begged other people, but no one sympathized
> I cried my eyes dry, dreading the arrival of dawn
> For at dawn my son was to report to the army camp

While my son was asleep
And the neighbourhood lay in total silence
'Ah my son
Don't blame your mother for being too cruel
Don't blame your mother for being too cruel.'

I took needles
Two steel needles
And plunged them into my son's eyes
He screamed and blood spurted out
'Ah, my son, they don't take a blind man in the army.'[9]

(trans. Kai-yu Hsu)

The unhappy lot of the conscript is a constantly recurring theme in protest songs. This one recalls Po Chu-i's *yueh-fu* 'Old man with the Broken Arm', which tells the tale of a young man who smashed his own arm with a rock in order to avoid being sent to Yunnan, from which few conscripts ever returned. Liu Chia's poem, from which I quote only a few lines, recalls the rapacious tax collectors in Po Chu-i's 'A man of Tu-ling', but is infinitely more shocking:

From down the road came a woman running
She rushed forward, her hair flying
Pushing the crowd aside
She threw down a sack:
'This is the tax grain, ah!
To be handed in to Governor Yen. If not enough...
Take me to the Governor.'

The village chief was stunned.
Opening the sack he poured out the contents
Everyone fell back, horrified – Good Heavens!
There were two children's heads, still dripping blood[10]

(trans. Kai-yu Hsu)

Under the new régime such extreme abuses were to end and the people – of the proletariat at least – were to have fewer and fewer grounds for complaint. This did not mean that their literary champions were at liberty to return to the luxury of writing 'for writing's sake'. Military conquest was only the first phase of the revolution which, Mao Tse-tung had made it plain at Yenan, it was the function of literature to serve. The people had been liberated but had yet to be educated. They were now free but, never having experienced freedom, needed to be told how free people behaved and thought. This was to be the task of the writers and artists of the new People's Republic.

To this end extensive literacy campaigns were instituted throughout the country. The people were encouraged to express themselves. Their songs and poems were collected and suitable selections published. Like the poem collectors of old, of whom Po Chu-i wrote in his *yueh-fu* of that name,[11] the literary cadres 'collected poems, listened to songs and induced the people to speak!' Unlike those poem collectors, however, they did not 'seek for satires', and little criticism is to be found in the anthologies so far published. Theoretically writers still had a duty to expose the blemishes in the new society, but their immediate task was not so much to portray 'life as it really is' but to depict 'life as it ought to be'. In other words, in their writing they were to be governed by the principles of socialist realism.

The *Songs of the Red Flag*, the collection of popular songs to which reference has been made at the beginning of this paper, exemplifies these principles. The songs are bright, cheerful, rhythmic, and colourful. Their general tone is bracing, their effect stimulating. They extol the achievements of the Great Leap Forward (1958–9) and encourage their readers to fresh endeavour. Unlike the *Book of Odes* they contain no criticism and express little resentment. Like the *Odes* they perform a social function and are valued not so much for their intrinsic literary merit as for their transforming influence.

The two poems that follow are taken from part two of the collection, entitled 'Songs of the Great Leap Forward in Agriculture'. The first poem, 'Longridge Slope', praises the achievement of the Cooperative in improving the lot of the hill farmers, of whose harsh existence Chang Chi had written a thousand years before. The land from which individual farmers had been unable to wrest a living is now fully productive through cooperative labour.

Longridge Slope, Longridge Slope,
four things in plenty once it had:
plenty of stones, plenty of thorns,
plenty of wild beasts, plenty of weeds;
no flying bird dared settle there,
it earned the name of 'devil slope'.

Longridge Slope, Longridge Slope,
spring breezes blow the peach into flower;
an advanced co-op has been formed in the valley,
the members go up the hill together.
The stones make way, the tigers flee,
a silver river's been lodged round the hill.

The silver ribbon wanders free,
the bottom slopes are gold with grain.
The hill-top trees bend low with fruit,
a scented breeze invades the heart.
We sing as one of Chairman Mao,
for life is good for hill-folk now.[12]

(trans. A.C. Barnes)

The second poem, 'The Young Bride's Gone Home to Visit her Mother', brings to a happy conclusion the succession of 'young wife' poems quoted in this paper. Of course even in Chou times not every bride was unhappy in her marriage but, as Po Chu-i remarked, her happiness was always dependent upon the whim of others. The bride in this song has a new air of confidence, and it is the groom who is anxious. In the new China this wife need never fear her husband's rejection for is she not a model worker eager to support the Cooperative and anxious not to miss her evening classes?

The peach is in flower
like a mass of sunset clouds,
the young bride's gone home to visit her mother.
What was she wearing?
Pale blue trousers and a patterned quilted jacket.
And on her head?
White pear blossom twined in her hair.
Who saw her off?
My brother saw her off.
Who saw her go?
I saw her go.
I also heard what passed between the pair.
He asked her:
'When will you be back home again?'
Sister-in-law
dropped her head
and she blushed like the peach-blossom:
'There's no need for you to worry,
I'll be back home tomorrow.
For I don't want to hold up the co-op's work,
and I don't want to miss my evening class.'[13]

(trans. A.C. Barnes)

Notes

1 Hu Shih, *The Chinese Renaissance*, University of Chicago Press, Chicago, 1934.
2 *Analects* Book 17/9.
3 J.P. Dieny, *Aux origines de la poesie classique en Chine*, Brill, Leiden, 1968.
4 In a later work, Chang Chi's *yueh-fu* 'The Fierce Tigers', the yellow calf is a symbol for unauthorized taxes imposed by local authorities over and above the ordinary dues.
5 For a translation see A.R. Davis (ed.), *Penguin Book of Chinese Verse*, introduction pp. iii and iv, Penguin Books, 1972.
6 For a translation see *Chinese Literature*, no. 4, 1959, pp. 3–14.
7 For translations of these poems see W. Hung, *Tu Fu, China's Greatest Poet*, Harvard U.P., Cambridge, Mass., 1952.
8 W. Eberhard, *Folk Tales of China*, University of Chicago Press, Cambridge, Mass., 1968; foreword by R.M. Dawson, pp. vii–x.
9 Kai-yu Hsu, *Twentieth Century Chinese Verse*, Anchor Books, Doubleday, New York, 1964, pp. 410–11. I have been unable to see the original Chinese text of this and the three following poems quoted.
10 *Ibid.*, p. 435.
11 'Ts'ai shih kuan' ('The Poem Collectors') in *Po Hsiang-shan chi*, Wan-yu wen-k'u edn, Taiwan, 1964, chap. 4.
12 Kuo Mo-jo and Chou-yang (comp.), *Songs of the Red Flag*, Foreign Languages Press, Peking, 1961, p. 52.
13 *Ibid.*, p. 90.

The Art of Chinese Landscape Painting

LIU WEI-PING

Western visitors to a Chinese art gallery are usually confronted with and puzzled by the overwhelming display of landscape paintings. Why do Chinese painters think so much of landscape? How significant is landscape painting to the study of Chinese art? These may be the questions a western admirer would like to ask.

Ching Hao, the great painter and art critic of the tenth century, said: 'There are thirteen categories in painting, and landscape is the first.' Another artist, Kuo Hsi, of the eleventh century, added:

> Why is it that a scholar is so fond of landscape? The reason is that he often lives a retired life in his garden, he enjoys his excursions by the springs and rocks, he makes friends with fishermen, wood-cutters and recluses and he loves to watch the monkeys and cranes. It is only human nature to resent the restless life of the common world and dream about, though not always achieve, the care-free life of immortals.... Now, all these have been skilfully produced by excellent artists. Without leaving one's house, one can fully enjoy the beauty of streams and mountains. To be able to hear the sounds of the birds and monkeys and see the reflection of mountains and the colour of the water, isn't this the most satisfying pleasure in one's life? This is the reason why people value landscape paintings.*

These remarks indicate that the Chinese are great lovers of natural scenery, but they give only a superficial reason for the popularity of Chinese landscape painting. The real cause is the overwhelming respect Chinese tradition pays to scholars, particularly to those who

---

*All translations in this paper are by the writer.

live in solitude and disengage themselves from worldly affairs, such as business and government service. The esteem in which Chinese scholars have held landscape painting can be attributed to the following two causes: first, the influence of Ch'an Buddhism, and second, the close relationship between painting and literature, particularly poetry.

Although we know very little about the beginnings of Chinese painting, we may assume that its earliest form was the drawing of human and animal figures. Among the oracle bones (tortoise shells and ox scapulae on which an ancient form of writing was carved) dating from the Shang dynasty (1766–1122 B.C.), there is one tortoise shell on which, besides notations of cyclical dates relating to divination, there is a drawing of an elephant with a smaller elephant in its stomach – evidently symbolizing pregnancy. This could be the earliest example extant of Chinese drawing. It is now in the possession of the National Palace Museum in Taiwan.

Many accounts of commemorative portrait painting have also been recorded in Chinese written sources. The emperors of various early dynasties engaged artists to paint their ancestors, meritorious officials, and historical figures. Later they also entrusted artists with the decoration of their palaces. None of these early paintings has survived and we can now judge them only from fragments of stone carvings which are believed to be reproductions of original paintings.

We may assume, however, that because of the enormous space an artist was given for mural painting, he had to seek additional elements to fill out the composition. This is thought to be the origin of landscape painting, which gradually became an independent form and enjoyed a more fruitful development than any other type of painting in the field of Chinese art.

From the third century A.D. for several hundred years, as a result of internal disorder and external invasion, China suffered from political instability. The nation was divided between north and south, and the north was under barbarian occupation. This political chaos, coinciding with the spread of Buddhism, stimulated the most rapid and diverse development in art in Chinese history. Painting, calligraphy, sculpture, and poetry all flourished and enjoyed great popularity, as scholars and artists devoted their best creative energies to their chosen fields.

One of the main principles of Ch'an Buddhism is that enlightenment can be achieved by meditation practised in a state of *ch'u-shih* (出世) or 'being out of the world'. Buddhists believe that worldly affairs are all vulgar and commonplace and they therefore attempt to remain physically distant from the world of the laity. For this reason most well-known Chinese Buddhist temples (unlike churches in western countries which are usually situated close to the city for the convenience of the congregation) are located amid picturesque scenery. There is a saying which goes: 'Most of the famous mountains in the country are occupied by monks.' Buddhists also believe that people who love natural scenery are likely to have outstanding character and a refined understanding. Wang Wei (701–61) of the T'ang dynasty once wrote to his friend describing his life in the mountains in these words:

> I would often go to the mountain, and rest in the Temple of Mercy and then leave after having a meal with the monks. I would travel north to the Yüan Embankment where the moon is bright and clear. In the evening, I would ascend the Hua-tzu Hill. The water of the Mang River rippled under the reflection of the moon. In the distance, from the cold mountains, lights flickered among the forest. In the long lanes, shivering dogs barked like wolves. From the villages, the sound of grain-pounding in the night mingled with the occasional bells from afar. I would sit there alone meditating, while my servant retired and all was quiet. Then I often recalled the days when we went out together composing poems. Now I should wait until the spring comes when the grass and plants will be luxuriant and then I shall be able to watch the distant spring mountains. Fish will appear above the water and white sea-gulls will soar high on their strong wings. Dew will wet the green ground and there will be early pheasants flying over the wheat field. All these won't be long now. Will you be able to make the trip with me? It is just that you are a person with high enlightenment; otherwise, I should not bother you with this.

It was with this innate fondness for natural scenery, in addition to his devotion to Buddhism, that Wang Wei practised the art of poetry, music, calligraphy, and painting. He was renowned as 'an artist who has poetry in his painting and painting in his poetry'. He is also believed to be the first person to have discarded the use of colour in landscape painting and to have applied only simple black ink, a technique known as *hsüan-tan* (渲淡) or colouring with light washes. Hence he is regarded as the leader of the Southern School in the history of Chinese painting.

While an artist can achieve enlightenment through his fondness for natural scenery, a Buddhist can also achieve it by practising meditation in beautiful surroundings. In their philosophical dialogues Buddhists often use the description of landscape as a metaphor. For instance, the following is a dialogue between the eighth-century monk, Ch'ung-hui (崇慧) of the T'ien-chu (天柱) sect, and his disciple:

The disciple asked: 'What is the principle of the T'ien-chu sect?'
The Master replied (in the form of a couplet):
'Occasionally there are white clouds coming to fill the doorway; no longer do the wind and moon float around the hills in the four directions.'
The disciple asked: 'Where does the spirit of a deceased monk go?'
The Master replied: 'On top of the lofty Ch'ien Mountain, the greenery always accumulates; the moonbeams above the Shu River are brilliant.'
The disciple asked: 'What is the benefit the monks offer to the public?'
The Master replied: 'One fall of rain benefits the whole world; and adds elegant blue colour to thousands of mountains.'
The disciple asked: 'How do the members of the T'ien-chu sect go along?'
The Master replied: 'Strolling alone on the tops of thousand hills; wandering among the nine-curved streams.'

In this type of dialogue Buddhist masters use description of natural scenery to illustrate their religious principles. At the same time each line of the couplets could well be used as the theme of a landscape painting.

The classification of Chinese painting into Northern and Southern Schools was in complete imitation of the divisions in Ch'an Buddhism. The first person to suggest this analogy was Mo Shih-lung (莫是龍, second half of the sixteenth century) who was obviously a devout Buddhist. His classification was based less on the historical background of painting than on his personal interest in Ch'an Buddhism which had already divided into Northern and Southern sects. Mo Shih-lung said: 'In Ch'an Buddhism there is a division into Northern and Southern sects which started in the T'ang Dynasty; it was also about the same time that painting became similarly divided.'

36

Tung Ch'i-ch'ang (董其昌, 1555–1636), the great painter of the Ming dynasty, named Li Ssu-hsün (李思訓, 651–716) and his son as the founders of the Northern School and Wang Wei as the founder of the Southern School. This classification was supposed to be based upon their different techniques. The painters of the Northern School were usually colourists. They endeavoured to preserve the identity of subjects and the purity of colour. Most of them specialized in painting palaces and buildings with 'fine brushwork', and their style was known as 'gold and green landscape'. When painting mountains and rocks they applied clear-cut lines, a technique known as 'axe-chopping'. The members of the Southern School, however, preferred 'colouring with light washes'.

There has long been controversy over whether this classification and definition are justified or even necessary. In general it is believed that the Southern School is the origin of the 'scholars' painting' in Chinese art. Most scholar-painters, though they may not have been devout Buddhists, showed great interest in the principles of Ch'an Buddhism. The practice of bringing a philosophical flavour into painting, particularly landscape painting, later became a main element in the works of the Southern School.

Although Ming artists trace the classification into Northern and Southern Schools back to T'ang, the division did not become really obvious until later dynasties, and it was not until the Sung dynasty that the technique of *hsüan-tan* became prevalent. Even in the Imperial Hanlin Academy of Painting, the members of which were mainly 'fine brush-work' painters, there were many artists who showed a fondness for painting landscape in the Southern School style.

During the Northern and Southern Sung periods the hopelessness of the political situation and the constant threat of foreign invasion drove most artists first into a psychological seclusion and then to an escape into Ch'an Buddhism. In both poetry and painting they showed an eagerness to evade the desperate reality of the times and a desire to seek peace and tranquility 'out of the world'. This seemed possible only through devotion to unworldly religious beliefs. As a Ming art critic pointed out, they first learnt from the ancients, then from nature, and finally from their own minds. This learning from their own minds corresponded to the 'enlightenment' of Ch'an Buddhism.

The abstract and metaphysical theories of the Neo-Confucians of the Sung and Ming dynasties had great influence on the development

of landscape painting. These Neo-Confucians believed that knowledge gained by study was insufficient without an accompanying
achievement of enlightenment. Without enlightenment, poetry
would become mere pedantry and painting mere artisans' work.

A second characteristic of Chinese landscape painting is its close
affinity with poetry.

One of the main principles honoured in both painting and poetry
is *ch'i-yün* (氣韻) which can be translated as 'spiritual expression'.
Hsieh Ho (謝赫), an art critic of the early sixth century, made *ch'i-
yün sheng-tung* (氣韻生動), 'spiritual expression and liveliness', the
first and most important of his six principles in painting. Chinese
critics have also been very fond of using natural scenery to illustrate
poetry. In his well-known book, *Shih-p'in* (詩品), Ssu-k'ung T'u
(司空圖, 837–908) of the T'ang dynasty adopted an entirely new approach to poetic criticism. He classified poetry into twenty-four
'modes': for example, Imposing and Perfect, Quiet and Insipid, and
Refined and Elegant. To define each of these modes, he composed
a twelve-line, four-character poem, explaining the style and the
'world' of poetry of each mode according to his own observation
and opinion. Thus he presented, through his description, a picture
of the circumstances in which each particular type of poetry should
be composed and its characteristic mood. For instance, under the
section on the Refined and Elegant Mode, he wrote:

> Welcoming spring with a jade wine-pot,
> I enjoy the rain in a thatched hut.
> In the company there are worthy scholars;
> There are tall bamboo to left and right.
> There are white clouds in the sky just after rain,
> Birds in seclusion follow each other.
> I lay the lute down in the green shade,
> With a flying waterfall overhead.
> The falling petals are soundless,
> I am as quiet as the chrysanthemums. . . .

Every poem in fact stands by itself as a picture of natural scenery.
In addition Ssu-k'ung T'u emphasized the importance of *yün-wei*
(韻味, rhythm and taste), which is extremely close to the criterion
ch'i-yün in painting. In his opinion, a poem of high standard should
have the qualities of *yün-wai-yün* (韻外韻, rhythm beyond rhythm)
and *wei-wai-wei* (味外味, taste beyond taste): that is to say, a quality
of suggestion which carries the reader beyond the actual expression
of the words.

Wang Shih-chen (王士禎, 1634–1711), the great poet of the early Ch'ing dynasty, compared one literary work with the paintings of Kuo Chung-shu (郭忠恕), a well-known painter of the Sung dynasty, which 'have only a few mountain peaks against the distant sky, added with a few touches of the brush. . . .' Wang said: 'However, what attracts the viewers' admiration lies beyond the brush and ink.' A view which 'lies beyond the brush and ink' in painting is the same as 'an idea which exists beyond the words' in poetry, and both are usually regarded as the highest achievement of poets and painters.

In principle, a scholar's painting should concern itself more with the expression of an idea than with a simple representation of a scene or an object. It must be able to evoke an intellectual response, not just visual pleasure. Theoretically there should not be any unpainted space left in a picture, especially a landscape painting. Even the blue sky should be positively treated by the artist. But a landscape painter, particularly a scholar-painter, seldom fills every inch of his paper. In order to achieve a sense of mystery and infinity he purposely leaves open spaces. This is what is expressed in the principles of 'having a few touches of the brush' and 'lying beyond the brush and ink'.

One of the principles of the scholars' painting is that one should not simply strive for likeness. This is why portrait painting has been the least developed genre in Chinese art. In portrait painting, it seemed to the Chinese, one has very limited freedom to demonstrate one's philosophical principles. Tung Ch'i-ch'ang admitted that he could never paint a portrait. In fact very few scholar-painters could. Even if they undertook portraits they would only be portraits executed with a few quick strokes, seeking to grasp the expression and spirit of the subject, not fine and detailed work.

Another important element in both poetry and painting is the practice of *chi-t'o* (寄託, the conveying of a second idea). In painting, Chinese scholars believe that landscape and 'the four gentlemen' paintings, i.e. paintings of plum blossom, orchid, bamboo, and chrysanthemum, are the best vehicles for the expression of *chi-t'o*.

For instance, Tu Fu (杜甫, 712–70), in his poem 'The Lovely Lady', wrote: 'In the mountains, the spring water is clear; when it leaves the mountains, it becomes muddy.' These lines have been used as a metaphor indicating that a scholar living in retirement has a pure, lofty, and virtuous character; but once he is involved in 'worldly affairs', as, for example, if he takes up a government position, he will become vulgar, common and, consequently, 'muddy'. A painter once presented to his friend who was a scholar-official a picture of a waterfall among mountains, with these lines added: 'Flowing into the world, it benefits the people with irrigation, but the clearness and purity which it possessed in the mountains is, after all, lost.' The 'second idea' conveyed is that, although a scholar may turn out to be an honest official who serves his people and country, he will no longer possess the same outstanding character and lofty virtue as a scholar who lives in retirement.

This example typically reveals the close relation between poetry and landscape painting in Chinese art. With this support from Buddhism and poetry, Chinese painters certainly enjoy more freedom than western painters in the demonstration of their ability to express and to create through painting.

Chinese Ceramics,
Their Place and Their Influence
on Western and Eastern Civilizations

T.J. BAYLISS

Pottery, made either by hand-building or by throwing on a wheel – as distinct from mass production by machinery – is closer to man and reveals his way of life and his characteristics more than any other craft. The wet plastic clay receives the potter's intentions directly from his hands, without the medium of a tool, and this tends to make the finished article reflect the potter's emotions as well as his craft skills. A potter in an excited state will throw a pot completely different to one made when he is bored and listless; similarly, a people with a sensitive approach to form, colour, and texture will produce a completely different version of an object to one produced by potters in a grossly materialistic society. Studio potters of today recognize in a fellow potter's wares many of the characteristics of the maker.

If we look at a pot from a past era we can make a fairly accurate estimate of the values held by that society. A seventeenth-century Hispano Moresque dish, with its emphasis on heraldic designs, quarterings, and so on, tells us that the people who used these wares were concerned with status and the worship of power and position, and not overly concerned with subtleties of form and tone. If we examine a stoneware teapot from Onda in Japan, glazed in a soft glowing turquoise, we realize that this pot was made for a sensitive people, knowledgeable about form, with a liking for understatement, and with priorities vastly different from those of the Spanish grandee.

At the same time few crafts are as dependent as pottery-making upon the technological level of the society of which they form a part. Earthenware which is fired at temperatures of around 800 degrees centigrade can be produced in any open fire and requires only the lowest level of technology. The production of stoneware, in which the clay is vitrified and thus impervious to water, requires a kiln – basically a chimney with a bulge in the middle for holding the pottery – to enable heat to be trapped and built up to temperatures around 1 300 degrees centigrade. Porcelain requires further advances in clay refinement and in the chemistry of glazes. So that examination of a pot may also reveal the technological level of the society in which it was made.

When pottery is made for a closed society such as Japan was in the fifteenth century, it reflects only the general taste of that society, but in a country like China, for over two thousand years the centre of a worldwide market ranging from Indonesia through Central Asia to the Atlantic seaboard, pottery shows the influence not only of the local society but of the market. It is obvious that flooding a market with foreign wares will alter the buyers' way of life; but, if the market is large enough, the makers of the wares will also produce objects to the buyers' taste and thus modify their own products. From well before the Christian era until the present day China has exported to most parts of the known world, and during the seventeenth and eighteenth centuries she produced porcelain to the taste of England and all the other countries of Europe, Japan, Southeast Asia, Persia, and North America.

The Stone Age pottery of China, made without the use of a wheel, was unglazed and decorated in manganese and iron with swirling designs much akin to those seen throughout Polynesia (Plate 1). Some of these pots are very large, up to 60 centimetres in height. During the Han dynasty (206 B.C.–A.D. 220) the first stonewares appeared and lead glazing became common. The glazes used were lead-based and were stained green with copper, and brown, red, and yellow with iron.

The potters during this Han period were shackled to the glories of the bronze workers of the Shang and Chou dynasties and managed to make their clay objects look like cast bronze (Plate 2). Society is always reluctant to accept changes in an article reproduced in a new material, and there is usually a time lag during which the styles of the previous medium are copied. For example, throughout the nineteenth century cast-iron furniture was made in the style of heavy carved wood; and the first motor cars were made in the style of horse-drawn vehicles. Consequently during the Han dynasty it was a century or so before the users were prepared to give up bronze forms.

Under the T'ang dynasty (618–906) pottery underwent considerable development. This dynasty, powerful and aggressive, maintained its contacts with the West. Our most vivid picture of the period comes from tomb figures, representations of all the life surrounding the T'ang well-to-do – camels, dogs, chickens, hares, and oxen, and those marvellous battle chargers, modelled from the horses obtained at the cost of persistent visits by ambassadors and later by armies to the land of Kokand to obtain breeding stock to replace the smaller Chinese horses seen in earlier paintings and sculptures. Also represented in T'ang pottery were the women – plump and satisfied (Plate 3), dancing girls, priests, soldiers, and swarthy hooknosed traders from thousands of kilometres along the Silk Trail. These figurines filled the tombs of the wealthy, no doubt to provide solace during the long dark hours ahead. Lead glazes typical of the period were coloured bright green, red, and yellow. The potter allowed his glazes to run down the surfaces of the pots, thus providing a general liveliness.

If we look at Persian pottery of the T'ang period we find replicas of T'ang pots, differing only in the poor quality of the clay compared with the superb clays found all over China. This indicates of course the pressure of Chinese exports upon the Persian market and the potters' need to copy or starve. The Greeks and Romans were too conscious of their own abilities to ape Chinese pottery or be influenced by it. There was no room in that world for the Chinese art form, but the Chinese were quick to adapt Roman, Greek, and Persian forms. The long-necked vase illustrated (Plate 4) is a Chinese potter's version of the small pot often held in the left hand of early Maitreya-Buddhist figures. The form of this small pot travelled from Greece with the armies of Alexander the Great (356–323 B.C.) to Northwest India, and thence, with the spread of Buddhism, through Tibet to China.

By the end of the T'ang dynasty in 906 ceramics were well developed; stoneware was common and feldspathic glazes were used, one of which was celadon. This glaze, in varying shades of jade green, is produced by firing a glaze containing around 1 to 2 per cent of iron oxide, under reducing conditions. These conditions are obtained in the kiln by using an excess of fuel which burns up all the free oxygen, thus preventing oxidization of the iron.

With all these advances, however, the potter had still not realized his full potential – he was still not exploiting to the full the plastic nature of his clay. This development was to come during the Sung dynasty (960–1279), the classic era of the arts in China. All the arts flourished: music, poetry, painting, and sculpture, and none more than pottery. What then are the qualities of these pots, so admired ever since throughout the East, and more tardily in the twentieth-century western world? First, the potter has taken full notice of the plastic nature of clay and used it to its limit; forms are full-blown, curves are lively, and changes of direction occur at satisfying places. By the use of a crisply-carved foot the pot thrusts strongly from the base. Decoration is always subservient to the pot form: it amplifies the statement of shape but does not compete with it.

This decoration consists usually of natural designs incised in the clay body and bold brushwork as in Tz'u Chou pots, usually in manganese black (Plate 5), or in the manipulation of glaze varia-tions: for example, the breaking of black glazes into reddish-brown on rims and shoulders, the pooling of celadons, the flow and conse-quent dripping bulges of Chün, that exquisite, optical-blue glaze (Plate 6). Above all the Sung potter was a master in the art of understatement, in texture, colour, and line. Unlike brash, catchy melodies appealing at first hearing and a bore at the sixth, Sung pots gradually take hold of the senses of sight and touch so that they become as much a part of their constant beholder as a favourite tree, hill, or flower.

If we look again at Persian pottery of the same period we shall see the facsimile; once again the potter must copy or starve. Two countries to the south of China, the Philippines and Indonesia, are today rich sources of Sung export pottery.

The Sung period saw the peak of stoneware and porcelain, the crisp Ting ware and the fabulous sky-blue celadon, Ch'ing pai. Our present-day studio pottery is derived from this period. The Japanese folk potter has always held Sung pottery in highest regard and, when Bernard Leach, the English artist, became involved with the folk-craft revival in Japan, he became himself a potter in that Sung tradition and set up a pottery in England. New Zealanders worked with Leach in the 1940s and set the stage for the present studio pottery scene in New Zealand.

Two neighbouring countries, Korea and Thailand, were strongly influenced by Sung pottery. The Korean Koryo-period wares are outstanding in their own right but their debt to the Sung potter is obvious. The short life of Thai potting is a kind of tribute to Sung, a charming but much less technically efficient and more naïve version.

The Ming dynasty (1368–1644) was one of rapidly increasing contact with the West, and the development of transport by sea between East and West enabled enormous quantities of porcelain to be sent to Europe. This was truly the period of porcelain: now came the development of the crisp white porcelain body, and the use of cobalt oxide as an underglaze blue decoration. The first Ming blue and white retains many of the virtues of the earlier dynasties – the matt glazes, subtle forms, and the use of decoration as a complement to the pot, not a competitor (Plate 7). The early blue decoration is line drawing, not painting. Compare it with the blue and white of the Ch'ing dynasty (1642–1912) and we can see how the later decorators have used painting techniques of tone on tone.

As well as continuing the production of celadons the Ming potters developed a range of monochromes, among them lustrous pure yellow, aubergine, and pure white porcelains.

One of the great technical advances was in the enamelling technique. In temperatures of above 1 100 degrees centigrade most of the brighter colours, such as yellow, orange, and green, volatilize, and it was found necessary first to fire the glazed wares to the high temperature, then to apply low-temperature glaze decoration and refire at a low temperature. This enamelling technique is used on porcelain throughout the world today but the resemblance between a modern enamelled porcelain tea-set and a Ch'eng Hua stem cup of the fifteenth century is faint indeed. The Ch'eng Hua wares are of a warm, thick, lustrous porcelain, with a design in vibrant enamels – glowing reds, yellows, and greens, with occasionally a soft underglaze blue.

During this period the city of Ching te Chen produced increasing amounts of pottery and, with the growing obsession of the Imperial Palace for more or less novel effects, a change in the character of the pottery became evident throughout the later part of the period. When we look at a group of later Ming export porcelain we can also clearly see the effect of the market upon the wares. The designs upon wares for the Portuguese and Dutch markets bear little resemblance to those made for internal use. On the other hand it is interesting to look at the so-called Swatow wares, made in south China towards the end of the period for export to Southeast Asia (Plat 8). These are beautiful freely-designed bowls, fully in the tradition of early Ming and Sung pottery, because taste in this market resembled the potters' own.

With the Ch'ing dynasty came ever-increasing exports. The chimneys of Ching te Chen smoked day and night and the East

India Companies carried enormous quantities of porcelain to Europe. In 1721 the Port of London alone landed two million pieces of blue and white porcelain (Plate 9).

The first effect of these imports was, as usual, on the buyer. European potters, with a technology capable only of producing brown pottery, were faced with this deluge of, to them, gem-like porcelain. Yet again it was copy or starve! The copy was achieved by mixing tin oxide with their clear lead glazes, and so making a white surface that obscured the brown clay. On top of this, designs in blue were painted, thus producing a ware with at least a superficial likeness to Chinese porcelain. In Holland and England this ware was known as delft, in France as faience, and in Italy as majolica.

Of course in the early eighteenth century Europe was desperately trying to find out from China the 'recipe' for porcelain, but it was independently discovered in 1709 by the Meissen chemists under Böttger. The rest of Europe had to wait three-quarters of a century for it and, as delft was not of comparable quality to Chinese porcelain, a further substitute, known as soft-paste porcelain, was made in scores of European potteries by adding powdered glass to white earthenware clay. Among these potteries were those in Chelsea, Worcester, Bow, Sèvres, and Capodimonte.

In the eighteenth century Chinese pottery penetrated every world market: blue and white went to Persia, celadons to India, and wares of every kind to Europe. In Canton a guild of manufacturers known as the Hong was established beside the harbour, and ships arriving from Europe and America brought orders with them. The Hong decorated with the required design blanks of table wares and decorative wares previously brought down from Ch'ing te Chen, and the wealthy families of Europe ate from services emblazoned with their crest or arms, all made in China (Plate 10).

By this time industrial England had set the wheels of Staffordshire in motion and the struggle began for dominance in what had by now degenerated into the 'crockery trade'. All that was innately good in Chinese ceramics was sacrificed to the effort to satisfy the customer, and Chinese potters increasingly devoted their energies to copying European-style wares and underselling them (Plate 11). By 1830 it is probable that Staffordshire had won the sales battle, but both Staffordshire and China had lost the battle for that quality in pottery which the Chinese had established during the Sung dynasty.

Plate 1 Hand-built earthenware pot, second millennium B.C., height 35·5 cm (Auckland Museum)

Plate 2 Bronze-form pot, Han dynasty, height 32 cm

Plate 3 Court lady, T'ang dynasty, height 33 cm (Auckland Museum)

Plate 4 Stoneware vase of Graeco-Roman form, T'ang dynasty, height 22 cm (Auckland Museum)

Plate 6 Stoneware bottle with Temmoku glaze, Sung dynasty, height 26·5 cm (Auckland Museum)

Plate 5 Tz'u Chou pot, Sung dynasty, height 11 cm (Auckland Museum)

Plate 7 Blue and white porcelain, early Ming dynasty, height 7·2 cm (Auckland Museum)

Plate 8 Large 'Swatow' dish, late Ming dynasty, diameter 36 cm (Auckland Museum)

Plate 9 Ch'ing dynasty porcelain, reign of K'ang Hsi, height 23·5 cm (Auckland Museum)

Plate 10 'Armorial' ware, *c.* 1800, diameter 21·2 cm (Auckland Museum)

Plate 11 Chinese porcelain copy of English soft-paste porcelain teapot, *c.* 1800, height 12·5 cm (Auckland Museum)

Some Aspects of Educational Reform Arising from the Great Proletarian Cultural Revolution

R.C. HUNT

'Some men work with their minds, and some work with
their hands. Those who work with their minds govern others;
those who work with their hands are governed by others....'[1]

Mencius

The traditional educational system in feudal China was geared to
the imperial examinations, a demanding and competitive process
designed to select the best men available to staff the civil service
bureaucracy necessary to administer China for the emperor. The
examination content was limited mainly to classical texts and to
eight-legged essays. Both texts and essays stressed the underlying
themes of loyalty, filial piety, and respect for the virtues: in· effect
the social morality as codified by Confucius.

By this means the emperor could exercise some control over the
scholar-official class that he needed to govern the country and reinforce his political power. In return for socio-economic status and
privileges the literati had a vested interest in maintaining a stable
society and the status quo. The literati also had the special function
of keepers of the Ethical Way; they were the repository of the Confucian ethic, and consequently they occupied a special position in
Chinese society.

In actual fact the examinations were open to the peasant masses
and it was possible for poor boys to lift themselves out of their rural
class into an official position of power and wealth. This was usually
achieved only at the economic expense of the boy's family and clan.
His success amply repaid their sacrifice, and the accruing honour
and status bestowed by the traditional Chinese value system was
reflected on all the clan. He often secured employment for his rela-

tives through his social position: the system in fact tended to be corrupting and encouraged nepotism. The Chinese have a saying: 'One man rises to officialdom, then all his dogs and chickens will be promoted.' Within this sociological background one can well understand the traditional respect of the Chinese peasants for learning and education, and their passivity and subordination towards the educated scholar-official class.

Since the abolition of the imperial examinations in 1905, the emerging structure of education has been based on a tertiary form of primary, middle, and higher education, patterned on American and Japanese lines. There have been later adaptations of Russian thought and practice, particularly in the 1950s; but recent developments show a more distinct Chinese style in the educational design. Before the Cultural Revolution (1966–9), primary school was for six years, from the age of 7 to 12, and middle school also for six years, from the age of 13 to 18. Thus there was the possibility of twelve years' schooling before entering higher education.

The New Socialist Man

When considering education in China today, one must have regard for the political background of socialist thought. It is not possible to review educational developments in isolation, detached from the mainstream of social philosophy and practice. There is great stress in the People's Republic of China on creating a new social morality, a new-style man to help achieve a socialist culture.

From Marxist concepts of human nature and the essence of man the Chinese have pursued the notion of the changeability of man's nature. They would seem to favour the argument that man's social being is mainly conditioned by his environment rather than dependent on innate abilities or characteristics. Mao Tse-tung has summarized the idea of different social classes having different natures and outlooks:

> Is there such a thing as human nature? Of course there is. But there is only human nature in the concrete, there is no human nature in the abstract. In a class society there is only human nature that bears the stamp of a class; human nature that transcends classes does not exist.[2]

Following from this the Chinese are very concerned with the philosophical thinking underpinning the educational structure, and with the keystone importance of education in the cultural infrastructure of society. The cultural matrix of society overlying the economic base is what the Chinese are referring to in their Cultural Revolution: that is, the way in which the society is organized and controlled and the resulting inter-relationships affecting individuals and groups within that social unit.

In contemporary China education, in the widest sense of the word, takes place in and out of the classroom, and as in traditional China the distinction between academic study on the one hand and moral-political education on the other is not clearly drawn. They are inextricably linked together, and one of the current slogans in education, 'Be Red and Expert', clearly illustrates this point: the younger generation should develop a socialist outlook as well as academic expertise. To help them build this proletarian outlook young people should spend some time with the peasants in the countryside, doing manual work, *laodong*. It is necessary for urban-based students to experience the peasants' life and gain some understanding of how four-fifths of the Chinese population live. This is an essential political education; and it will help to break down the traditional superiority of the educated class towards the rural masses. Carrying a shoulder pole and two baskets of manure should have some sociological effect on these students. Any revolutionary youth should be able to integrate with the peasants and work with them. The following essay was written in January 1966 by a nineteen-year-old student at the Peking Foreign Languages Institute after he had done four weeks' manual work on the Miyun-Peking canal project, just before the Cultural Revolution:

> We worked in the countryside for less than a month. It was a good chance to live with the poor and lower middle peasants. We learned a lot from them. They were not only hard working, but also had the happiness of the people at heart. They often said that they must produce more grain for the revolution. They also took good care of us. They let us live in the best houses, but they themselves lived in the worst ones. Once a comrade got ill, they nursed him back to health. There our main work was to dig the Peking-Miyun irrigation canal. All of us worked in real earnest. We were the first to bear hardships, the last to enjoy comforts. When we were tired we would think of the truth, 'After all, you are not a real revolutionary youth, if you are afraid of difficulties.' On thinking of this, we would screw up our courage at once. No matter how great the difficulties were, we could overcome them all. So everyday we finished the work ahead of time. After work

49

we always had a good time. Some studied Chairman Mao's works. Some read newspapers. Some sang songs. Some put things in rhymes. During physical labour, our life was full of happiness, because we created wealth with our own hands.[3]

Thus it is in the realm of education that the Chinese practice in support of their theory of the new socialist man can most clearly be seen. By their definition, a necessary attribute for this new man is a socialist or proletarian world outlook. In essence this is the antithesis of the bourgeois mentality, which is strongly individualistic, acquisitive, and 'self'-oriented. In comparison the proletarian world outlook should be unselfish and group-oriented, with a complete dedication towards one's fellow men. This concept of 'Serve the People' is exemplified by the three constantly read articles by Chairman Mao: 'In Memory of Norman Bethune' (1939); 'Serve the People' (1944); 'The Foolish Old Man Who Removed the Mountains' (1945). These give simple illustrations of some of the essential revolutionary qualities needed by the younger generation: unselfish service to the masses, the subordination of self to the needs of the community; persistence and patience in the face of all difficulties; the willingness to learn from others and flexibility of approach at all times.

The Cultural Revolution

At the start of the Cultural Revolution in Peking, in May 1966, criticisms were aimed at the fundamental ideology of the educational process with its traditional and gradualistic principles. Mao's directive of 7 May 1966 summed it up:

While the students' main task is to study, they should in addition participate in industrial and agricultural work and military affairs. They should also criticise the bourgeoisie. The period of schooling should be shortened, education should be revolutionised and the domination of our schools by bourgeois intellectuals should not be allowed to continue.[4]

This line of attack on the educational corpus had occurred before as one prong of the Great Leap Forward movement of 1958–9. The aim was the same – to transform the educational ethos from one of middle-class privilege to that of egalitarian socialism, with particular emphasis on such significant points as: selection into higher education; student participation in productive work; the coordination of practical experience with academic theory, teaching materials, and teacher attitudes; and the need for the students to go to the countryside to do some *laodong*.

During this Great Leap period the president of Ts'ingHua Univeristy, Peking, had expressed the new policy thus:

> The educational institution becomes not just a school, but at the same time a research institute, factory, designing institute and building concern. An end is put to the traditional concept of a school as a consumer unit, an ivory tower far removed from the surrounding life of society. Our policy bridges the gap between educational and production units.[5]

Yet the president of Peking University, Lu Ping, had reacted differently: 'So many factory workshops have been established in the school. Shall I be the director of a university or a factory?'[6] And soon he was asking for moderation, no doubt representing a considerable body of conservative opinion in China:

> The University must avoid and overcome the impetuous greediness for quantity and size, and impatience for success, as well as unwillingness to bear hardships, to act realistically and to do concrete work. Lofty revolutionary ambitions and long term targets of struggle must rest on a practical base of current work. Otherwise they would simply be illusions. We must combine these ambitions with the good academic tradition of learning with realism and perseverance.[7]

This approach was antithetical to the Maoist line. By 1960 it had diluted many of the aims of the Great Leap Forward reform programme, and had realigned students' sights on academic excellence, with minimal regard for productive work and political education. The swing was from 'red' to 'expert'. Six years later the general changes in education suggested by students during the Cultural Revolution were in essence the same reform programme that had been partly frustrated in the aftermath of the Great Leap Forward.

Mao's views of what education is about, and what lines it should develop along, were clearly summarized in Article 10 of the sixteen-point programme for the Cultural Revolution, laid down at the Eleventh Plenary Session of the Chinese communist party meeting from 1–12 August 1966:

In the Great Proletarian Cultural Revolution a most important task is to transform the old educational system and the old principles and methods of teaching. In this great Cultural Revolution, the phenomenon of our schools being dominated by bourgeois intellectuals must be completely changed. In every kind of school we must apply thoroughly the policy advanced by Mao Tse-tung, of education serving proletarian politics and education being combined with productive labour, so as to enable those receiving an education to develop morally, intellectually and physically and to become workers with socialist consciousness and culture.... The period of schooling should be shortened. Courses should be fewer and better. The teaching material should be thoroughly transformed, in some cases beginning with the simplification of complicated material. While their main task is to study, students should also learn other things. That is to say, in addition to their studies they should also learn industrial work, farming and military affairs, and take part in the struggles of the Cultural Revolution to criticise the bourgeoisie, as these struggles occur.

During 1968–9 there was continuous public debate on how to transform primary and middle school education. One important document, which was published in the *People's Daily* on 12 May 1969, was the 'Draft programme for primary and middle school education in rural areas' worked out by the revolutionary committee of Li Hsu County, Kirin Province. This programme incorporated many of the general points outlined in Article 10, and in retrospect it seems to have been adopted as the basis for subsequent experimentation and developments.

Length and Content of Courses
In primary and middle education in China today there is emphasis on a gradual reduction of the length of courses from six years to five years. According to observations made during a visit in April 1971, this is being carried out in a very cautious manner and is not being implemented in an arbitrary way. There were regional variations in the stages of development of this aim, and there seemed to be some local independence of action, indicating that a certain degree of decentralization had occurred. Chinese officials constantly stressed the experimental nature of the changes, and the need for pragmatic adjustment according to the demands of the situation. The final effect of this reduction in course length will be that Chinese children entering primary school at seven years of age will have the

possibility of ten years of education, up to the age of sixteen to seventeen years, instead of twelve years as before.

It is always necessary to differentiate between urban and rural schooling when considering the general educational system. With four-fifths of the population living in the countryside there is an imbalance in favour of the urban areas, not least of all in educational facilities and opportunities. The Chinese are working hard to reduce the disparity of what they call the 'Three Great Differences': that is, between town and country, between agriculture and industry, and between mental and manual work. One result of the Cultural Revolution has been the acceleration of the programme for improving health, educational, and cultural levels in the rural areas. Primary and middle schools in the countryside are concentrating on a syllabus that is more relevant to their daily life, with a blending of academic learning and practical subjects. For primary levels, the fundamentals are Chinese language, arithmetic, revolutionary art and literature, politics, agricultural knowledge, physical education, and production experience. At middle school level, agricultural knowledge includes elementary science and economic geography, and arithmetic is expanded to mathematics. In middle schools Mao Tse-tung's philosophy is studied also, and this encompasses Chinese and world history. In some cases a foreign language (usually English) is taught at a very simple level. Under this system pupils acquire some scientific understanding of the land, insecticides, fertilizers, and the processes of agricultural production, and also gain some technical knowledge that can be applied to small-scale countryside projects, such as building reservoirs, canals, and pump irrigation, and in simple engineering and machinery repairs.

In urban areas the school syllabus is substantially the same, except that the sciences are usually studied under the subject of common knowledge, as are history and geography. An important change since the Cultural Revolution has been the introduction of production workshops into the school environment, in both primary and middle schools. In middle schools there has also been the innovation of health science, which deals with human biology, anatomy, personal hygiene, sex instruction, simple acupuncture, some medical knowledge of common illnesses and their treatment, and instruction in first aid. *Laodong* was included in the middle school time-table before the Cultural Revolution, but more time is now being given to it: usually one to two weeks per year at senior primary school level and up to four weeks per year at middle school level.

In all schools there is continuous reappraisal of teaching materials and content: this aspect of education is still in the transformation stage, with various ideas, alternatives, and modifications being tried and discussed by all the people involved – administrators, parents, teachers, and pupils. As at April 1971 no teaching books or material had been finalized, although there was a wide variety of experimental material in use.

Teacher-pupil Relationships

> Gentlemen! We are students. Our lives are extremely bitter; the professors who teach us treat us like criminals, humiliate us like slaves.... They are interested only in making us read a lot of books, but we don't understand any of it, we merely exercise our memories to no good purpose.... Why are we so lethargic, so lacking in vivacity? Oh! It is all because the professors force us to refrain from moving or speaking out.... Our teachers are such obstinate pedants. They are constantly mouthing expressions such as 'We read in the *Book of Odes*' or 'The Master (Confucius) says'.... They are not aware that this is already the twentieth century, and they still compel us to observe the 'old rites' and to follow the 'old regulations'....[8]
>
> Mao Tse-tung, *Hsiang River Review*, July 1919

The imperial examination system, because of its specific function in the social order, tended to stultify and inhibit creative and original thinking, whilst encouraging rote learning and formalistic philosophical analysis. The products of this education, members of the scholar-official class, became an integral part of the fabric of the emperor's autocratic rule, and had a privileged élitist role. But they rarely attained the pure Confucian ideal of establishing harmony between a benevolent imperial power and contented peasant masses. Their political role did not allow for impartial detachment; rather it cultivated the attitude of 'severe to the people, compliant to the Emperor'. In the educational struggle to attain these privileges and socio-economic security only a small percentage of candidates finally succeeded in passing all the five-tier examinations. Many of the unsuccessful ones turned to teaching to support themselves during these years of study.

Teacher-pupil relationships developed within this social framework, and viewing Mao's comments of fifty years ago one can see the defects on both sides: an authoritarian approach from the teacher, reflecting the traditional superiority of the intellectuals towards the ordinary people; and an unquestioning obedience from the pupils, reflecting the political passivity of the masses under feudal autocratic rule.

The Cultural Revolution has focused attention on these attitudes and there are signs of positive change, although it would seem to be a long-drawn-out process, especially for the more conservative teachers. Teachers are making greater efforts to enliven their teaching techniques with an egalitarian approach of suggestion, discussion, and greater pupil participation. More efforts are being made to improve teaching materials and visual aids. As in the West, the change from an authoritarian role to one of group 'leadership' will make greater demands on the effort and creativity of teachers which, with high pupil-teacher ratios, will place more pressure on them, and on primary school teachers in particular. In higher education the aim is to cultivate a more positive and analytical response from students by using seminar discussion situations. Instead of the students sitting silently absorbing information like tape recorders, they must make contributions and ask questions. In return the teachers and lecturers should be able to accept the students' questioning of their arguments and theories without loss of face.

A further development is in the approach to formal examinations. At Ts'ingHua University the question of examinations was laughingly dismissed as 'setting ambushes for the students'; however, the students admitted that in some subjects written and practical tests were necessary, and they tried as far as possible to use continual assessment, including in some cases group assessments. This is yet another aspect of education that is being thoroughly investigated and discussed.

Admission into Higher Education

The beginning of the Cultural Revolution saw general criticism of the admissions policy for higher education from pupils in middle schools:

> The old system of examinations in the secondary schools is in contradiction with the educational line of Chairman Mao. It is a tool in the hands of the representatives of the bourgeoisie, who are using it for the purposes of class struggle

against the proletariat and for exercising a dictatorship over the sons and daughters of the workers and peasants. This system encourages students to indulge in cramming and learning dogmas by rote, and it impels them to take the path of specialists seeking personal glory and benefit. We propose the abolition of the examination system and suggest that all secondary school graduates join the ranks of the workers, peasants and soldiers, before entering higher education. If this is postponed until the completion of higher education learning, the young men and women might have already formed an individual world outlook by then, which would be hard to change. Students entering higher education should be selected directly by the Party.

Peking No. 1, Girls Middle School (June 1966)

This proposal for middle school students to do full-time productive work before entering higher education seems to have been adopted in an experimental form, and the old senior middle schools for sixteen to eighteen-year-olds, which were formerly the springboards to tertiary education, no longer function as such. Now all teenagers graduating from middle school must either work on the land, in a factory, or in an office, or join the armed forces. After two or three years' productive work they can apply for entry into higher education. This application must have the support of the workers in the applicant's work group, and also be recommended by the local communist party branch. Only then will the higher education unit consider the candidate and make its decision, based not on the results of written examinations as previously required, but on an assessment of the person's general outlook and socialist understanding. This system represents a swing towards ideology: the thinking and social philosophy of the individual is emphasized rather than mere academic expertise.

In this way preference will be given to the person who relates to his social group and participates in a positive manner: as the Chinese say, one who actively applies Chairman Mao's thinking in a living way. This policy would seem to net only highly motivated students. The 1970–1 intakes of students (which were the first groups selected in this manner) in fact allowed for a small percentage of students from bourgeois backgrounds, whilst the majority (about 90 per cent) came from the worker-peasant-soldier middle school graduates.[9]

56

The qualifications for entry into higher education as laid down by current educational policy are good health, correct political consciousness, two or three years' productive work experience, a junior middle school cultural level, and a maximum age limit of twenty-four to twenty-five years. This age limitation was not rigidly enforced: both Peking and Ts'ingHua Universities had accepted in their 1970–1 intake a 1 to 2 per cent group of veteran workers – people who were all over this stated limit.

Productive Work

The introduction of production workshops into schools and universities is an attempt to make the educated youth more resourceful with their hands and less concerned just with book knowledge: to be all-round in their skills and less specialized. The traditional Chinese scholar, superior and aloof in his long gown, has little social status in the value system of the new China, although the associated mentality of 'becoming an official' lingers on. As explained by the Chinese, the educational system before the Cultural Revolution still produced too many 'Sanmen' (three-door) officials:[10] that is, people with a very narrow work experience, who are insulated from life by their sheltered existence.

The need for technical education and expertise had long been apparent in nineteenth-century China. Sun Yat-sen, the first president of the Republic of China and leader of the Kuomintang, had suggested that one factor inhibiting China's development was the old, ingrained idea of 'Action is difficult but knowledge is easy'. If only this mental barrier could be overcome, then China would modernize at a much faster rate. But this was antithetical to the scholarly Confucian custom, and conservative opinion was strongly opposed to it.

Production experience in schools today is one way of diluting this traditional outlook. Workshops are 'not for profit, not for production, but for education'.[11] The pupils are involved in the work process and can see the finished product, which gives them some understanding and appreciation of technical tools and skill.

In practical terms, what is actually being done? At the Ch'eng-Hsian Road Primary School in Nanking in April 1971 there were woodwork and metalwork rooms as well as a small workshop for making oil filters for cars and metal fitments for buses. A nearby factory had helped to set up this workshop and the factory workers kept in close touch with the running of it.

No. 31 Middle School in Peking had four workshops where the standard of workmanship was quite impressive. The workshops were for car circuits, brake spares, and printed circuits for electronics and triodes (used in transistor radios). At first considerable help had been received from local factories, but later the school workshops were integrated into the factories' production lines and were able to maintain regular production without too many problems. The four shops occupied about one hundred pupils altogether, and each pupil spent two to three weeks a year on this work.

Higher Education: Linking Theory with Practice

The new experimental courses at university level are generally two to three years long. This excludes specialized fields which will still need longer periods of study. One obvious result of these shorter courses will be a greater number of graduates coming from universities and presumably some falling-off in academic standards compared with previous levels of attainment. But this is understood by the Chinese, and is a reflection of their re-assessment of priorities. Students and teachers alike follow a three-part time-table of study/teaching, productive work, and *laodong*. They must not be allowed to suffer the 'Three Divorces' – from the people, from production, and from politics.

Mao Tse-tung has always believed in the educative value of combining practical experience with the understanding of theory, and this is now being translated into a tangible form. There has been careful application of this concept in the realm of higher education, and the practical achievements are impressive. All colleges and universities have been called upon to set up their own factories and workshops: the linking of theory and practice is the cornerstone of what the Chinese call the 'three-in-one' combination of learning, research, and production. This should be carried out by teachers, students, and staff workers together in the various departments.

At the Canton Teachers Training College four workshops have been set up – for chemistry, biology, radio-electronics, and teaching aids. The biology group has done a full-scale project on plant research, in particular on the crossing and development of rice strains. In the radio-electronics workshop the students themselves build transistor radio audio-amplifier sets; the finished products have a useful value, since they can be used in the countryside and also in educational units.

At Peking University the biochemistry and organic chemistry departments have joined forces to build a pharmaceutical factory, and they produce a variety of medicines such as insulin, antibiotics, anti-asthmatic drugs, anaesthetics, anti-parasite tablets, and cytochrome C injections.[12] All these medical products are handled by the state organization and distributed through the Peking area.

Ts'ingHua University, which has always had a good reputation as an engineering university, has achieved a high technical level in its workshops. There is a motor vehicle factory producing about fifty lorries per year, as well as a machine-tool shop and an electronics laboratory. These last two units have combined together to make a simple computer, and they have also built milling machines that are automatically controlled by computer.

The usual method of acquiring practical experience on the work site has been followed wherever possible. For example, the hydraulics and water conservancy faculty at Ts'ingHua University – lecturers, workers, and students – all moved to the San Men dam project on the Yellow River for the 1970–1 academic year. But there is also a desire to involve arts faculty students as well, and not to limit extra-mural experience just to the sciences and engineering. Arts students can go to nearby factories and communes and help in preparing information boards and display materials; they can give language classes and cultural performances and assist in many such ways. Some students of Chinese language and literature went to a Peking rolling-stock plant that was involved in a campaign against waste and extravagance.[13] They were able to help the workers to prepare articles, to summarize their experiences, and to write comments and criticisms. They also publicized the investigations taking place and kept everyone informed of the latest developments. By living close to the workers and participating in factory life these students were establishing communication between the university and society, and thus putting the 'open-door' policy into practice. Whether this was a meaningful experience for the students remains to be seen. If in later life, when members of this generation reach positions of power, the individual has a deeper and more mature social understanding, then surely the experience will seem to have been a positive one.

During the Cultural Revolution many universities and institutions of higher education did not function as formal learning units for several years. At the present stage of development, with an agriculturally based population and an economy that is slowly industrializing, the Chinese want an educational system that blends with their society. This is a reappraisal period, involving re-evaluation of the relationship between centres of learning and society, as shown in the question posed at Ts'ingHua University: 'What is the function of a socialist university?' And there is an attempt also to realign the educational system into a form more appropriate to the socio-economic needs. China requires vast numbers of trained graduates and personnel to implement her national reconstruction programme; perhaps the changing educational system will be better able to satisfy these needs.

TABLE 1

Some Statistics for the 1970–1 Academic Year[a]

PEKING UNIVERSITY	TS'INGHUA UNIVERSITY
REVOLUTIONARY COMMITTEE	**REVOLUTIONARY COMMITTEE**
49 members	31 members

FACULTIES

Arts Chinese literature
Eastern languages
Economics
History
International politics
Law
Library science
Philosophy
Political science
Russian
Western languages

Science Biology
Chemistry
Geology-geography
Mathematics-mechanics
Physics
Radio-electronics

FACULTIES

Arts Foreign languages

Science Automatic control
instruments
Building
Civil engineering
Electronics
Electronics
Engineering physics
Hydraulic and water
conservancy
Industrial chemistry
Mechanics
Precision instruments
Radio

INTAKE

2 667 students (29% women)

10%	'bourgeois' class
1–2%	veteran workers
90%	(approx.) middle school graduates with 2–3 years' productive experience

INTAKE

2 800 students (20·5% women)

7–8%	'bourgeois' class
1–2%	veteran workers
90%	(approx.) middle school graduates with 2–3 years' productive experience

[a]According to information supplied during a visit to Ts'ingHua University, 22 April 1971, and Peking University, 19 April 1971.

Notes

1 *The Works of Mencius*, Book III, in James Legge (ed.), *The Chinese Classics*, vol. ii, Clarendon Press, Oxford, 1861–72.

2 Mao Tse-tung, '*On Literature and Art*' Foreign Languages Press, Peking, 1960.

3 A copy of the original essay, entitled 'My Experience during Laodong', is in the possession of the author.

4 The 7 May Instruction to Lin Piao: 'Long Live Mao Tse-tung's Thought'; quoted in Jerome Ch'en, *Mao Papers*, Oxford University Press, 1970.

5 *China Reconstructs*, February 1959.

6 Morris Wills, unpublished manuscript, Harvard University, 1965; quoted in Victor Nee and Don Layman, 'The Cultural Revolution at Peking University', *Monthly Review*, vol. 21, no. 3.

7 *Ibid.*

8 Stuart Schram (trans.), 'The Great Union of the Popular Masses', *China Quarterly*, no. 49, January/ March 1972.

9 According to information supplied in April 1971 during a visit to Ts'ingHua and Peking universities.

10 The 'three doors': the first was from home to school, the second from school to university, and the third from university to an 'official' bureaucratic niche (according to a responsible member of the Revolutionary Committee, Canton Teachers Normal College, 6 April 1971).

11 Responsible member of the Revolutionary Committee, No. 31, Middle School, Peking, 24 April 1971.

12 Visit to Peking University, 19 April 1971.

13 Committee of Concerned Asian Scholars, *China – Inside the People's Republic*, Bantam Books, March 1972.

Chinese Education
as a Strategy of Development

R.I.D. TAYLOR

When the Chinese communists acceded to power in 1949 they were faced with the overriding problem of national reconstruction. As the first rulers of China since 1911 to have achieved political unity, they have been concerned from the outset of their régime with the goal of national strength in order to guarantee the security of the state. Since the Chinese communists immediately embarked upon policies of rapid modernization, education has been given high priority and a heavy premium placed on certain types of specialist skill. In this context education can be seen as an integral part of development strategy. In common with the leaders of other developing countries in Asia and Africa, the Chinese leaders have regarded education as an instrument through which economic development may be furthered. To that extent emphasis has been placed upon collective interests rather than upon those of the individual. Academic freedom for the individual has been strictly subordinated to the demands of national sovereignty.

Seen in terms of development strategy, the educational policies of the Chinese communists are instructive. In contrast with many other developing countries, China has to a large extent avoided the phenomenon of large numbers of unemployable arts graduates who continue to form a large reservoir of social discontent. For example, the practices of sending cadres and intellectuals down to work in the countryside and the creation of part-time education have done much to bridge the élite-mass gap between urban and rural areas, which has been so much a feature of economic development in the new states. Modernization requires a delicate balance in education between élitism and popularization: between the need to concentrate resources on a few key sectors on the one hand and the demand for a literate and technically skilled population on the other. The conflict between these two requirements has been a consistent theme in Chinese communist educational policy since 1949.

As Chinese education is in itself a vast field of research, this paper focuses on higher education as a case study and, more specifically, examines enrolment policies. The Chinese communists have themselves described enrolment as the main battlefield between the two educational lines. This conflict came to the surface in the Cultural Revolution. Ultimately these two lines came to represent two different strategies of development. This struggle was latent from the very beginning of the régime, although signs of it were not apparent until 1958.

An understanding of this debate about educational policy cannot be complete without a brief examination of the traditional Chinese relationship between education and society. The Confucian ethic, which underpinned the authority of the imperial goverment, emphasized harmony rather than change. Man should not attempt to mould the physical environment but should harmonize with it. The summit of man's achievement was to be expressed not in terms of technological change but in the correct ordering of human relationships. Furthermore, since the merchant was also despised, there were no competing centres of economic power. In this sense all authority derived from the imperial government, and from its representatives, the scholar-officials. This bureaucracy of scholar-officials thus represented the only channel of social mobility.

Entry to the ranks of officialdom was generally only possible through success in the imperial examinations, which were based upon the acquisition of prescribed knowledge through study of the Confucian classics. These texts instructed candidates in the precedents of good government. Paradoxically, however, although the knowledge gained as a result of study was a kind of expertise, it was also an ethic or amateur ideal which the scholar-officials were to apply in their relations with the population as a whole. In short, the imperial bureaucracy was a meritocracy with a difference: the specialist knowledge which the scholar-officials possessed was only of worth in so far as it could be applied to concrete situations in everyday life. Neither the intellect nor this specialist knowledge were valued very highly for themselves. In this sense the Confucian ethic was humanist, and was honoured because of its capacity to achieve harmony in society and the correct ordering of human relationships. Furthermore the Confucian tradition postulated a unique relationship between rulers and ruled. Confucian teachings explained that man's nature was inherently good: 'the divine spark' was found in all men, but it could only be developed to the full through the correct training and by moral example. Since all men were naturally good, and only came to differ from one another through education, it followed that every individual had the capacity to discern the correct ordering of human relationships.[1]

This Confucian theory of knowledge led to two main conclusions. The first was an optimistic assessment of the miracles which could be worked in the social and physical environment, not by technology, but rather through moral training in social harmony. The second suggested that through the divine spark every person was capable both of being educated and of being the educator. Society itself was thus a vast educational process; and while all could reach the summit of human endeavour by right conduct, even the greatest paragons of virtue could fall from their pedestals through negative behaviour. To this extent society was a vast laboratory in which both rulers and ruled were being continually re-tested. Good character had to be constantly demonstrated in practice. The unconscious legacy of the Confucian theory of knowledge could not fail to affect the educational policies of the Chinese communists. In imperial society politics stood supreme because all relationships were political. Since the communist accession the party leaders too have placed 'politics in command'.

The impact of western might on China in the middle years of the nineteenth century forced people to adjust to modern technology. This process of adjustment is still continuing: the policies which the Chinese communists have pursued, for example in the educational field, can be seen as but the latest Chinese response to the demands of modernization. One of the first Chinese attitudes to the need for change was that of the T'ung-chih reformers in the 1860s, who put forward a programme of moderate reform to be carried out within the traditional framework of Confucian political values. Western technology was to be harnessed to the needs of the Confucian state; modern educational institutions were to be established while the political heritage of Confucianism was preserved.[2] But what the T'ung-chih reformers failed to realize was that foreign institutions would eventually affect native values; their moderate reforms were not practicable as a long-term solution.

In 1905 the abolition of the imperial examination system 'disenfranchized' the intellectual pool from which the scholar-officials were drawn. The nationalist fervour of the May the Fourth Movement of 1919 demonstrated the intellectuals' quest for a new ideology within which the modernization of China could be achieved.[3] The political disunity of this period allowed many schools of thought to contend. Yet there was a contradiction in the position of the intellectual leaders of the movement. On the one hand they played the role of critics of government; on the other the traditional political values by which they were unconsciously influenced led them to seek an authoritarian political creed to which they could render service. From the intellectual currents of the May the Fourth Movement came many of the future Kuomintang and communist party leaders.

During the 1930s the Kuomintang tried to construct an ideology on the basis of an amalgam of native and western political thought; sporadic efforts were made to assert party control over the universities, and certain academic subjects, for instance technology, were emphasized at the expense of other fields of study. Even in the Nationalist period education was to be directed not merely for the cultivation of individual excellence but for the service it could render to the strength of the nation. In the event, however, internal disunity and foreign invasion prevented the Kuomintang from moulding education in the image it desired. Chinese communist educational policy thus represented the later adaptation of western scientific and technological achievement to China's economic development. The weapons of the West could neither be accepted nor rejected in their entirety, but had to be adjusted to the unconscious legacy of traditional political thought, in order to resist foreign encroachment and to reassert national sovereignty.

The Chinese communists' rise to power was due to their ability to adapt Marxism-Leninism to Chinese conditions. But in 1949 the Chinese leaders leaned to one side, and the Soviet Union became their mentor in education, as in other fields. The Chinese communists abandoned the educational practices which they had developed at Yenan during the Sino-Japanese war years; Soviet curricula were translated and the institutional structure of higher education was reorganized. For the purposes of these reforms Soviet specialist personnel were employed, Chinese instructors were assisted by Russian experts, and new courses were introduced.[4] But if the Soviet example was followed in the fields of academic organization and curricula, it was supplemented by methods of control which owed far more to traditional political values than to Marxism-Leninism. Chinese intellectuals had sought a new ideology during the decades of disunity; now the communist party had replaced the ideology of Confucianism with that of Marxism, but in doing so it had merely replaced the medium through which political control was expressed.

In the early 1950s Soviet organizational structure and native political controls existed side by side in uneasy coexistence. Yet even when emulating the Soviet example in certain fields of educational work, the Chinese communists never completely lost sight of the kind of society which they intended to create. Politics still stood supreme, even above economics. Human relationships were more important than technological change. Imported institutions should not override native political values. The latent conflict between the two systems was not articulated until the early 1960s, but it existed nevertheless and was the channel through which the conflict between Mao Tse-tung and Liu Shao-chi over educational policy was eventually to come to the surface.

It is in the field of teaching methods that native political controls and the Chinese communist theory of knowledge have been most in evidence. Like its imperial predecessor Chinese communist society is a vast educational process. Where the Confucian ethic emphasized harmony, Chinese communist ideology has stressed struggle; but both have regarded education as the servant of society and have placed the individual in strict subordination to collective interests. According to the Chinese communist theory of knowledge, ability comes not from natural endowment but from the struggle of practice.[5] Knowledge has been directed towards changing the physical environment, and thus towards the promotion of national construction. Furthermore, precisely because ability is not endowed by heaven, the Chinese communists have formulated their own unique conception of the relationship between student and teacher: both may contribute to learning, since the teacher has no monopoly of knowledge.

Two cardinal principles epitomize the Chinese communist conception of higher education: the combination of theory and practice,[6] and collective study.[7] These two methods were designed to further two interrelated objectives: the dissemination of specialist knowledge and the establishment of the correct relationship between faculty and students. The aim of higher education was not merely to produce highly-qualified personnel, but to ensure that such specialists were motivated towards service to the people. Theory was to be united with practice: scientific theoretical knowledge was of no value unless it was continually tested and re-tested in practice.

Practice was the Chinese revolution and China's construction. The touchstone of a scientist's or technologist's work lay not in his scholastic achievement *per se* but in his contribution to national construction. Many bourgeois intellectuals, inherited from the pre-liberation period, were attacked for failing to realize that education was a weapon of class and production struggle and that it should serve politics.

In the same way the teaching method called 'collective study' meant a reassessment of the traditional position held by the university teacher. From now on both teaching and research were to be closely related to national construction. Individual achievement in research was only valued to the extent that it served the collective interest. In teaching, the old standard method by which the teacher taught and the students listened was abandoned. In collective study both teacher and students were linked in a common endeavour: education was a two-way – or rather three-way – process between the teacher and individual students. All could make contributions to knowledge, and collective understanding was eminently superior to individual excellence. Needless to say collective study would have individual study as its basis; but collective study, like the principle of theory and practice, was envisaged as the best method of motivation to satisfy the needs of national construction. It was through the correct ordering of human relationships that miracles could be worked.

Meanwhile the seeds of conflict between Soviet organizational structure and native educational theory were being sown. In terms of curricula and academic structure the Soviet model had been imitated; but teaching methods were permeated with an ideological intensity never witnessed in the Soviet Union. Chinese communist educational theory was based upon the manipulation of human relationships rather than upon the forces of organization. Yet in time the humanist ethic came to be overtaken by events and institutions began to influence values. The humanist ethic had been eminently suited to an imperial society which was agrarian and functionally diffuse. All relationships were political, since there were no competing centres of economic power. In the developing economy of communist China, however, the 'amateur ideal' could become a barrier to the development of national construction. An industrial base was now emerging, certain types of expertise were at a greater premium than others, and society was becoming functionally specific. New centres of power were being created; a technocratic élite was in the making. In higher education the party had to make concessions to personal incentives, even if teaching methods like collective study were designed to counteract an individual's selfish ambition. Soviet organization, on the other hand, tended to promote individual excellence. A hiatus began to appear between organization and ideology. This was essentially a product of the educational system itself, rather than a direct clash between individual party leaders. It was from this growing need for diverse types of expertise that the later conflict between the two educational lines was eventually to emerge.

In the early 1950s there was still outward unanimity among the party leaders on educational policy. The so-called capitalist roaders were to this extent products of the educational system, rather than the creators of an independent line deliberately formulated in opposition to that of Mao Tse-tung. The humanist ethic was in fact proving inadequate to contain the many non-political roles which a developing economy was demanding. The difference between the two educational lines lay in the extent to which the two protagonists were able to come to terms with the changes which the dynamic of modernization was bringing. While Liu Shao-chi was prepared to make certain adjustments, Mao Tse-tung showed much less willingness to do so.

Since the Maoist section of the Chinese leadership has stated that enrolment is the main battlefield, let us now examine the evolution of conflict between the two lines within the context of university admission policies. Analyzing twenty years of enrolment, a writer in the theoretical journal *Hung-ch'i* wrote in the Autumn of 1970: 'In the educational battlefield, conflict between the two classes and the two lines appears first of all in a concentrated form in enrolment.'[8] From the beginning, admission policies had two basic aims: the training of specialists for national construction and the creation of worker-peasant intellectuals. The latter was designed to produce urgently-needed technical manpower and to break the monopoly of bourgeois experts. But it was not immediately practicable to admit large numbers of worker-peasant elements to higher education. Home background and financial circumstances placed them at a considerable disadvantage in comparison with other candidates for higher education.

To remedy the academic deficiencies of workers and peasants, special rapid middle schools[9] were established by universities to prepare them for entry. Much publicity was given to these schools in the press. But despite the praise often lavished upon them, it was eventually shown that many university authorities were reluctant to expend time and effort on training worker and peasant students of only indifferent calibre, and in certain cases the attitude of faculty members towards them seems to have been one of open hostility.[10] Nevertheless there is evidence that worker and peasant students were succeeding in gaining admittance to universities through study in the rapid schools. For example, in 1954 it was claimed that worker-peasant candidates from rapid middle schools had excelled in an enrolment examination for Ts'ingHua University, one of the country's most prestigious institutions.[11]

This apparent conflict between the standard reached by students from the rapid schools and the attitude of faculty members towards such students can, however, be reconciled. It is true both that rapid middle school graduates did enter the universities and that faculty members were deeply concerned with the maintenance of academic standards. In this situation university teachers did not contradict the party's policy on the creation of worker-peasant intellectuals; what they did was to interpret it in the light of their own academic experience. While prepared to encourage the very able among workers and peasants, they were unwilling to compromise on levels of scholarship. In these circumstances the worker-peasant rapid middle schools became channels of limited social mobility for those of outstanding merit. But the ultimate implications of such a system would negate the very reason for creating worker-peasant intellectuals. The domination of the universities by those who were more 'expert' than 'red' would be perpetuated; there was always the danger that worker and peasant students would become divorced from their social origins. They would merely join the ranks of those students from the academic higher middle schools. The base of the academic élite would thereby be widened, but its composition would not be significantly altered.

There is every reason to believe that unanimity existed within both the party leadership and academic circles about the fostering of talent among workers and peasants; the differences between the associates of Mao Tse-tung and those of Liu Shao-chi lay in their interpretations of the function which worker and peasant rapid middle schools should perform. To Mao the creation of worker-peasant intellectuals was an article of faith, a value in itself; to Liu this policy was instrumental, directed towards the end of training specialist personnel from all available sources. Enrolment statistics provide substantial evidence in favour of the argument that academic authorities did not pursue a policy of excluding students of worker and peasant origin at all costs; instead they aimed to select the best potential students from both rapid middle schools and other sources outside the educational system.[12] In December 1962 an article in the *Peking Review* declared: 'half of China's total university enrolment is of worker or peasant origin.'[13] There is little doubt that worker-peasant elements were gaining admission to higher education, whether via the rapid schools or through preferential treatment in the enrolment process. The enrolment regulations for the summer of 1950 expressed the party's thinking on sources of applicants for admission to higher education. These statutes remained substantially unchanged into the middle 1960s.

Until 1956 the enrolment targets for higher education exceeded the number of available middle school graduates; consequently the remaining students had to be sought elsewhere. Since there was an acute shortage of qualified manpower, talent had to be tapped wherever it could be found. In addition therefore to higher middle school graduates and those of an 'equivalent level of scholarship',[14] certain other categories of applicants were given preferential treatment under what was known as the 'broad-range entry system'. Under this system certain categories of applicants could gain admission even if their performance in entrance examinations was unsatisfactory. According to the 1950 regulations those eligible under the broad-range rubric included in the main production workers and members of revolutionary cadres who had worked or served for three years or more. However, although these candidates eligible under the broad-range entry system were given preferential treatment in entry to higher education, they were far less free than students from higher middle schools to select their academic studies. All available evidence suggests that the majority of cadre members were allocated[15] to subjects closely associated with their former employment. That they were usually directed to certain fields is illustrated by the party's criticism that at least some of them were disregarding the national interest by insisting upon being admitted to subjects of their own choice.

The party's special treatment of cadres and workers under the broad-range entry system took account of three major considerations: the ideological need to create a corps of worker-peasant intellectuals dedicated to the revolution, the economic demand for technical personnel at various levels of production trained in the most advanced skills, and the practical requirement that these entrants be placed in academic fields to which their production experience suited them. These competing claims had somehow to be reconciled, so that workers and cadres were directed to fields of study where they acquired new expertise rather than intellectual breadth. The cadre members in particular were already in positions of leadership and had attained limited social advancement. Certainly after returning to production their status might well be enhanced, but their chances of achieving upward mobility were nevertheless considerably fewer than those of university graduates who had originally come from higher middle schools.

Élitist tendencies were also built into the institutional structure of higher education. Courses in universities consisted of two types: the basic courses (*pen k'e*) and the special training courses (*chuan hsiu k'e*). Great pains were taken to point out that both types were equal in academic quality; the special training courses differed only in their shorter study period and more concentrated curricula. But an *Enrolment Handbook*, published in 1955, casts doubt upon these claims; special training courses were practically designed to train technical cadres for immediate production needs. Furthermore they were confined to a relatively small number of technical fields and unpopular academic options like agriculture, forestry, and teacher training. Clearly the less able higher middle school graduates were placed in the special training courses, as were many of the students admitted under the broad-range entry rubric. In short, although revolutionary cadres received preference in enrolment through the broad-range entry system and the establishment of rapid middle schools, they were not necessarily admitted to prestigious institutions and departments. The party leaders had to reconcile their ideological and economic objectives: a new corps of worker-peasant intellectuals had to be created, but equally the country could not afford to neglect the training of technical cadres to fill key posts at various levels of production.

If the institutional structure of higher education had élitist implications, the results of the enrolment process were decidedly meritocratic. Leaving aside the special provisions provided for certain categories of workers and peasants, the entrance examinations through which the majority of candidates passed were intensely competitive. Under the system of unified enrolment and planned distribution, candidates were sent to institutions and departments on the basis of their examination performance.[16] This task was undertaken by the enrolment committees which took account of three considerations: the needs of national construction, the preferences of the students, and current academic standards. In applying for admission, candidates had to fill in preferences for departments and institutions. Since examination performance was the yardstick in allocating those with the same preference, there was strong competition for certain university places. The better departments and colleges attracted the best applicants; less desirable fields like agriculture and teacher training, where national needs were greatest, very often received the least able. Thus, in spite of the party's call to candidates to consider national needs first and their own interests second, the preferences of prospective students were very often concentrated in certain medical, scientific, and technical subjects, where rewards of future employment seemed to be the most promising.

Vast inequalities of opportunity existed in the enrolment process not only between the broad-range and rapid middle school candidates on the one hand and the remainder on the other, but also within the ranks of the privileged few – the academic students from higher middle schools. In the years from 1949 to 1958 an élite-mass structure was evolving in higher education. The arrangements made in the enrolment process to further the entry of worker-peasant elements confirmed rather than mitigated these tendencies towards élitism. Far from creating a corps of worker-peasant intellectuals, the structure of higher education was already producing an academic meritocracy, which itself had dire implications for the ultimate objective of an egalitarian society. It was in any case becoming clear by 1958 that revolutionary cadres, production workers, and worker-peasant children were finding it difficult to adjust to the rigours of college life. Home environment and limited financial support placed such students at a considerable disadvantage. A university education placed heavy burdens on poor rural families and factory workers' families.

As a means of producing worker-peasant intellectuals, the institutional measures of broad-range entry and rapid middle schools had failed. This drastic situation called for a drastic solution. An attempt to solve these problems came in a joint directive of the Central Committee of the Chinese communist party and the State Council, issued on 19 September 1958.[17] In the early years of the régime Soviet organizational structure had tended to override native educational philosophy; now the order was reversed. The new mea-

sures emphasized that education was to serve the interests of proletarian politics and to be integrated with productive labour. These
policies were given their strongest expression in the part-work part-
study schools which were established first at the middle school level
and later, more importantly, in higher education. There is every
reason to assume that unanimity existed within the party leadership
over the establishment of these schools, although Cultural Revolution sources have associated their creation with the name of Liu
Shao-chi. In fact Mao Tse-tung himself had already praised the
system in a visit to Tientsin University earlier in 1958. [18]

The part-work part-study institutions had both economic and
political objectives. In economic and practical terms these schools
and colleges were set up locally, could pay their own way without
public expenditure, and provided education, particularly at the
middle level, to students in the rural areas where it had formerly
been lacking. In addition the combination of education and production provided new sources of manpower with much-needed, even if
limited, expertise. In political terms the part-time institutions were
intended to eliminate the differences between mental and manual
labour, and thus to break the monopoly of bourgeois intellectuals.

Industrial enterprises in the cities set up middle technical schools[19]
which enrolled graduates from full-time junior middle schools.
These students were to be trained as technicians for the enterprise in
question. Similarly, on the rural front, agricultural middle schools
were established[20] and admitted graduates from full-time senior
primary schools. However, there were fewer part-time-study universities than middle schools. At the level of higher education part-
time study took two forms: the establishment of workers' universities in 1958, and the gradual transformation of full-time universities
into the part-time pattern. Of the first type the Kiangoi Communist
Labour University was a good example: it paid attention to local
needs, combined mental and manual labour, and offered courses in
agronomy, stock breeding, forestry, fishery, and sericulture. [21] An
instance of the second type was Ts'ingHua where students received
instruction in the classroom and the factory; 'all-round worker-
intellectuals' were to be created in this new-style university. [22]

But while there might have been agreement about the establishment of part-time institutions, disagreement existed over the function they should perform. The conflict between the two education
lines began to come to the surface. The part-time schools had

officially been justified in both economic and political terms; but in time these two justifications polarized into rival interpretations of the role of part-work part-study. While Mao Tse-tung and his supporters appear to have intended that full-time education should eventually move towards a part-time form, Liu Shao-chi's interpretation tended to stress economic considerations. Meanwhile the part-time and full-time systems continued to exist side by side, representing an unsatisfactory compromise between Soviet organizational structure and native educational philosophy.

The economic value of these institutions was certainly not to be underestimated. In the years from 1949 to 1958 the majority of middle schools were in the urban areas; part-time institutions now provided a very real service in the rural localities. Yet in scholastic achievement the part-time schools in no way approached the standard of full-time middle schools in the cities. While part-time universities enrolled graduates of full-time higher middle schools,[23] very few products of the part-time middle schools succeeded in entering full-time higher education. Furthermore, in the years which followed the Great Leap, enrolment in higher education decreased as large numbers of middle school graduates were sent to take part in productive labour in the countryside. Thus it can be concluded that part-time middle schools did not generally provide a means of upward mobility into higher education for workers and peasants.

It was on issues such as these that the clash between the two educational lines occurred. The main question was one of interpretation. To Mao Tse-tung, higher education should move towards the part-time form, which was valued for its own sake; to Liu Shao-chi, the part-time system was supplementary and instrumental, for it served certain limited economic goals. To Mao, education should be integrated with productive labour and directly related to the needs of society; in addition, and more importantly, this was the correct relationship between education and society. To Liu, part-time schools provided education for those who would not normally be able to afford it, and also produced urgently-needed technical personnel at various levels of production. Liu Shao-chi and his supporters were determined that the quality of full-time education should not be sacrificed. The September 1958 Joint Directive of the Central Committee of the Chinese communist party and the State Council had called for both popularization and élitism in higher education; Mao's principle was that élitism should be achieved on the basis of popularization. But by the early 1960s élitism was by all accounts being given the greatest priority. Liu and his supporters had reversed the order.

Once again it should be emphasized that the policies of Liu Shao-chi and his supporters were not a deliberate act of opposition to the ideals expressed in the 1958 Joint Directive on education. Both Liu Shao-chi and Mao Tse-tung had unconsciously inherited the legacy of the traditional relationship between education and society: that education should be directly related to the needs of the community. Both saw the integration of education with production as indispensable to a developing economy. Both recognized the necessity of popularizing technical skills as rapidly and as widely as possible. But Mao at every stage stressed the supremacy of politics: human relationships were of greater importance than the forces of organization, for both ideological and economic reasons. Liu Shao-chi on the other hand saw economic considerations as paramount: the élite-mass structure presented by the dichotomy between part-time and full-time education was necessary if the country were to reach the advanced scientific and technological levels of the rest of the world. Popularization and the creation of worker-peasant intellectuals were the final goal, but in the short term compromises had to be made. Certain patterns of élitism could not be avoided. Talent would have to be tapped, wherever it could be found: it was desirable to bring into the universities the most outstanding candidates from among the workers and peasants. But academic standards should not be sacrificed.

By 1956 Liu Shao-chi and his associates were said to have recommended the adoption of 'two educational systems': the full-time and part-time institutions were both to be retained.[24] The middle 1960s saw the formal advocacy of an élitist system of education. But the charges made during the Cultural Revolution that Liu Shao-chi and his supporters had closed the doors of higher education to workers and peasants is not supported by rigorous analysis. The élite-mass structure of higher education emerged not via deliberate revisionist opposition to university enrolment policies, but by a slow process of evolution; it came about initially through the contradiction between native educational philosophy and Soviet organizational structure, and later because of differing interpretations of the educational directives issued in 1958.

By 1965 all the signs pointed to the arrival of a new technocratic élite. If workers and peasants had succeeded in being admitted to it, this did not mean that the original aim of creating worker and peasant intellectuals had been achieved. Limited mobility had been taking place at the same time as increasing stratification. It little mattered that some of the new élite were of worker-peasant origin; in effect they had 'changed colour', and had become divorced from their proletarian origins. To Mao, the integration of education with production was an article of faith: it was through this that the students re-established their link with the masses. To the supporters of the so-called revisionist educational line, the primary purpose of productive labour in the educational process was to increase students' understanding of specialist curricula. The unity of mental and manual labour was to them essentially instrumental.

The stage was thus set for the clash between the two educational lines in the Cultural Revolution. The official Maoist victory saw the implementation of new university enrolment policies, involving a process of recommendation and selection of students by the workers and poor and lower middle peasants, under the guidance of the party. Before entering higher education, candidates would have spent a period of time in productive labour. In addition to the students from higher middle schools, tempered in production, meritorious workers and peasants were also to be chosen for universities and colleges.[25] The students would thus forge an unbreakable link with the masses, and the emergence of an academic élite divorced from the rest of society would be prevented. Academic organization was restructured to make productive labour an integral part of university curricula. Students were to work not only in factories set up within the universities, but also in enterprises outside. In the words of the Cultural Revolution, the worker, peasant, and soldier contingent 'entered the university, managed the university, and used Mao Tse-tung thought to reform the university', thus bringing the educational revolution to a new stage.

But subsequent events have demonstrated that these new educational policies have not yet meant victory for the proletarian educational line of Mao Tse-tung. The last few months have seen renewed emphasis on expertise.[26] The social composition of students does not appear to have significantly changed from pre-Cultural Revolution days,[27] and workers and poor and lower middle peasant students are being accused of having changed colour. The struggle is not yet over; but there is every reason to believe that the educational line associated with Liu Shao-chi has emerged victorious.

To suggest this is not to denigrate the vast achievements of Chinese communist education since 1949. At least Mao Tse-tung has attempted to grapple with a problem faced by most developing countries: the need to produce highly-qualified personnel for economic development, while at the same time ensuring that unacceptable inequalities do not emerge between an urban-based élite and the rural masses. He has faced the demand for élitism to be reconciled with popularization.[28]

Nevertheless the supporters of Liu Shao-chi appear to have addressed themselves to this problem with far greater candour and realism. Like Mao Tse-tung they have inherited the traditional Chinese relationship between education and society; but, unlike Mao, they have been willing to make adjustments to the changes which alien institutions and foreign technology demand. They have granted concessions to new centres of power and sources of talent in the form of economic incentives for highly-qualified personnel, and limited social mobility for outstanding students from the worker and peasant masses. For the requirements of a developing country the educational line of Liu Shao-chi makes economic as well as political sense. In adjusting to the demands of a modern industrial society, the gradualist and pragmatic policies associated with Liu Shao-chi have represented attempts to utilize available talent at suitable levels of expertise. If present policies, which represent an approximation of Liu Shao-chi's rather than Mao Tse-tung's education line, [29] continue to hold sway, they would seem more likely to achieve a reasonable balance between the need for social justice and the demands of a developing economy.

Notes

1 This quality of discernment has been described by one scholar as 'the evaluating mind'. For a full and lucid exposition of this theme see Donald J. Munro, *The Concept of Man in Early China*, Stanford University Press, Stanford, California, 1969, p. 48.

2 Mary C. Wright, *The Last Stand of Chinese Conservatism*, Stanford University Press, New York, 1957, and Teng Ssu-yü and John K. Fairbank, *China's Response to the West*, Harvard University Press, Cambridge, Mass., 1954.

3 The standard work on the May the Fourth period is Chow Tse-tsung, *The May the Fourth Movement*, Harvard University Press, Cambridge, Mass., 1960.

4 For information on the nature of Soviet aid to education see Cheng Chu-yuan, 'Role of the Soviet Union in Developing Scientific and Technical Manpower in Communist China', in Stewart E. Fraser (ed.), *Education and Communism in China*, International Studies Group, Hong Kong, 1969, p. 522.

5 Mao Tse-tung, 'On Practice', *Selected Works of Mao Tse-tung*, vol. i, Foreign Languages Press, Peking, 1967, pp. 295–309.

6 Teaching methods based on unity of theory and practice were formally adopted at the National Conference on Education, held in 1950. See *Jen-min chiao-yü*, July 1950, p. 9.

7 *Jen-min chiao-yü*, May 1950, p. 24.

8 *Hung-ch'i*, October 1970, p. 32.

9 *Jen-min chiao-yü*, July 1950, p. 13.

10 *Kuang-siung jih-pao*, 1 March 1954.

11 'Our Country's People's Education Serves Socialism: the Deep Transformation of New China's Higher Education', *Jen-min Jih-pao*, 23 September 1954.

12 The enrolment regulations for the summer of 1950 stated that various categories outside the educational system were eligible to apply for entry to higher education. These included, among others, past graduates of teacher training colleges who could show that they had been employed for two years since graduation and graduates of higher vocational schools or secondary vocational schools who could show that they had since worked for two years.

13 *Peking Review*, vol. v, no. 50, 14 December 1962, p. 23.

14 That is, a level of scholarship equivalent to that of higher middle graduation. This was designed to give eligibility to those who had formerly studied in vocational or technical colleges, and who had 'dropped out', but who had since conducted their own studies. A full explanation is given in special enrolment handbooks published by the Central Government. Certain categories of candidates who had graduated from higher middle schools a long time before were also included under this rubric.

15 The total number of cadres to be allocated was determined by the Central Government, and then a quota was allotted to each of the Large Administrative Areas into which the country was divided. These Areas in turn named a certain number for localities under their jurisdiction.

16 Candidates were examined in compulsory and optional subjects. They were also required to fill in personal preferences for departments and institutions. The number of choices varied from year to year and from area to area. After the examination papers had been marked the candidates were allocated to institutions and departments according to their preferences and examination performance. In this allocation process a candidate's selection of departments was exhausted, and then his choice of institutions. See *Jen-min jih-pao*, 26 September 1952, and *Wen-hui pao*, 21 June 1954.

17 This document, which appeared in *Jen-min jih-pao*, 20 September 1958, is reproduced in translation in Stewart E. Fraser (ed.), *Education and Communism in China*, pp. 554–66.

18 'Chronology of the Two Road Struggle on the Educational Front in the Past Seventeen Years'. *Chiao-yü ko-ming*, 6 May 1967; reproduced in *Chinese Education*, vol. i, no. 1, Spring 1968, p. 30.

19 *Peking Review*, vol. i, no. 40, 2 December 1958, p. 16.

20 *Peking Review*, vol. viii, no. 1, 1 January 1965, p. 28.

21 *Peking Review*, vol. viii, no. 50, 10 December 1965, p. 18.

22 The running of factories at a university is discussed in *Kuang-ming jih-pao*, 23 July 1970. For an account of the part-work part-study system at Ts'ingHua, see *Peking Review*, vol. i, no. 25, 19 August 1958, p. 5.

23 Fang Cheng, 'Reform Work in the Chinese Communist Educational System', *Tsu-kuo yueh-k'an* [China Monthly], no. 11, 1965; reproduced in *Chinese Education*, vol. iii, no. 4, Winter 1970–1, pp. 260–1.

24 For comment on the 'two educational systems' see *Hung-ch'i*, no. 10, 1971, pp. 37–8.

25 At the beginning of the Cultural Revolution, higher middle school students made recommendations to the Party's Central Committee concerning the reform of entry requirements in higher education. See 'Revolutionary Students of Peking No. 4, Middle School Write to Chairman Mao', *Peking Review,* vol. ix, no. 26, 24 June 1966, pp. 20–1.

26 Probably because of the excessive criticism which took place in higher education during the Cultural Revolution, there were cases where university teachers lectured on 'politics' and neglected 'expertise'. Recent articles in the press have sought to reverse this trend and emphasize 'expertise', presumably because the Party line on education has now been stabilized. For example, an article on this subject, relating to Liawning University, appears in *Kuang-ming jih-pao,* 10 January 1972.

27 For references to the social composition of university entrants, see *Kuang-ming jih pao,* 21 and 23 September 1970.

28 This is not to suggest that elevation and popularization are mutually exclusive. Economic development is likely to create a demand for the popularization of education, if only to impart a number of specialist skills needed for industrialization. Nevertheless the need for elevation in certain fields of expertise often requires a disproportionate amount of public funds and facilities. This may promote social stratification, since it often allows those with certain qualifications which are at a premium to bargain with society for the price of their services.

29 Other, but related, issues are developed in much greater depth in a study being prepared for publication at the Australian National University.

The Great Proletarian Cultural Revolution

S.A.M. ADSHEAD

In this paper my aim is to give a straightforward account of the Cultural Revolution. The survey falls into three parts. First, the antecedents of the Cultural Revolution between 1957 and 1965: the social and institutional changes in the preceding periods which made it possible. Second, the course of the Cultural Revolution proper from 1965 to 1969: the sequence of events which made it actual and defined its character. Third, the results of the Cultural Revolution: its legacy in terms of institutions and events from 1969 to the present. Before I commence, however, let me confess the prejudice which underlies the interpretation I am going to present. Many people, when they become interested in the Cultural Revolution, try to analyze it in terms of the aims of Chairman Mao or the intentions of the Chinese communist party. They see the Cultural Revolution as contrived, consciously planned, rational: a political purge or propaganda drive. For my part, however, I find it difficult to believe that events of such magnitude and complexity as the Cultural Revolution are really susceptible to this kind of analysis. Though some contrivance, planning, and rationality certainly existed, I see events in China between 1965 and 1969 as a genuine revolution: unplanned and unwanted, spontaneous in its generation, and irrational and unpredictable in its course. What I propose to give then is essentially an institutional and systemic analysis of the Cultural Revolution: the Cultural Revolution as a process rather than a plot.

I shall first discuss the antecedents of the Cultural Revolution between 1957 and 1965. This period is usually divided into first the Great Leap Forward from 1957 to 1961, and second, the Retreat from the Great Leap from 1961 to 1965. In both these

81

sub-periods combustible social material was accumulated which exploded in the Cultural Revolution as a result of accidental ignition. In particular, the ruling institution of China became on the one hand alienated from wide sectors of public opinion, and on the other divided within its own ranks.

The Great Leap Forward, 1957–61, was essentially Mao Tse-tung's application of his wartime strategy of revolution to the peacetime task of socialist construction. Mao found that the Soviet formula of economic development through centralized planning, capital intensivity, and expert management, with which he had experimented between 1949 and 1956, did not give satis-factory results in China. He therefore devised a new formula based on decentralization, labour intensivity, and popular mobilization: an instant industrialization through organization and ideology rather than through expertise and investment. The new system made sense in conditions of underdevelopment, but it was not operated well and produced two side effects which were factors in the genesis of the Cultural Revolution. First, the party became alienated from the mass of the people. During the Great Leap party cadres for the first time assumed direct economic management – in factories, transportation, and rural communes – and so the party became bureaucratized and impersonal. Even after 1961, when many economic leadership functions were returned to non-party factory managers and commune executives, branch secretaries and their attendant cadres remained enmeshed in red tape and paper-pushing, prone to the kind of behaviour communists describe as commandism. Second, the Great Leap divided the party internally by putting one faction permanently on top of another. Mao's programme of instant industrialization was supported and executed by the group which may be described as the party Reds: Mao himself, Liu Shao-ch'i, Teng Hsiao-p'ing, and P'eng Chen in the party; Lin Piao in the army. It was opposed by another group, the party experts: Chou En-lai in the Foreign Office; Li Hsien-nien in the Ministry of Finance; Ch'en Yü and Li Fu-ch'un in the State Planning Commission; P'eng Te-huai in the army. Although the division between the two groups was not irreconcilable, it was a sharp polarization, and the contention left behind it a deposit of ill-will for later circumstances to reactivate.

This ill-will was increased by the fact that while the next sub-period, the Retreat from the Great Leap, 1961–5, saw a reversal of policy and the victory of the ideas of the opposition, it saw no change in leadership. Liu Shao-ch'i, Teng Hsiao-p'ing, P'eng Chen, and the Red faction retained their dominant position. The change in policy was inaugurated at the Ninth Plenum of the Eighth Central Committee in January 1961. The Great Leap Forward, poorly executed rather than mistaken in principle, had failed to produce the result expected of it: indeed, it had brought about what Marxist economists said was impossible, a socialist slump. Faced with this situation, yet reluctant to go back to the unworkable Soviet formula, the party in fact adopted the programme of the opposition, while continuing to reiterate the ideas of the Great Leap in theory. Economic management was taken away from the cadres and returned to the experts in factory, farm, and central government; agriculture was given priority over industry and an attempt was made to reduce the size of the swollen cities; market forces were allowed to determine the shape of production alongside central planning and ideological exigencies. At the same time, however, the domination of the Red faction and the level of ideological fervour were maintained by three new mass campaigns: socialist education, 'Imitate Lei Feng', and 'Learn from the People's Liberation Army'. This distinctively dual system of the Retreat from the Great Leap, organization being expert but ideology being Red, suited China's circumstances and produced real economic progress. But like the Great Leap it stored up trouble for the future by causing further alienation from the public and more division within the party.

On this occasion the alienation was more of particular groups than of the public in general. The attempt to reduce the size of the cities especially hit three classes in the community: the second-generation urbanite who suddenly found his education cut off at middle or high school level and himself permanently rusticated; the first-generation rural immigrant into the city who was peremptorily returned to his village; and the elderly urban resident who might be unexpectedly superannuated to his native place in the country. At the same time the transference of economic management from Reds to experts led to the laying off of some junior cadres and loss of status for others. These people belonged to the most enthusiastic and ideologically-motivated segment of the party and hence easily developed a puritan resentment against the party leadership, which they felt had betrayed the ideals of the Great Leap Forward.

With the party too the Retreat from the Great Leap made a bad situation worse. To the old division between Reds and experts were added new divisions among the Reds over the means necessary to maintain their domination. In my view the best analysis of these rather obscure inter-party disputes of the early 1960s is that of Paul Cocks. He suggests that in 1962 Mao Tse-tung opposed the new mass campaign proposed by Liu Shao-ch'i and favoured instead reform through the party control committee: that is, a police purge on Stalinist lines. Later, however, finding that the control committee was heavily bureaucratized, Mao came round to a mass campaign and worked closely with P'eng Chen to produce in May and September 1963 the documents known as the *Early and Later Ten Points*. Finally, late in 1964, a new difference between Mao and Liu Shao-ch'i appeared as to how the socialist education campaign then under way should be intensified. Liu, in his *Revised Later Ten Points* of September 1964, wanted to rationalize the campaign by making it selective and more like a police purge, while Mao, in his *Twenty-three Articles* of January 1965, wanted to energize the campaign by making it more unpredictable and wide-ranging. Liu and Mao had in fact exchanged positions between 1962 and 1965 and the difference between them was still narrow and capable of being bridged, but the three-year friction had created a potential for a real split which was actualized during the Cultural Revolution. In addition to his differences with Chairman Mao, Liu Shao-ch'i was also in increasing friction with the Minister of Defence, Lin Piao. Both men belonged to the Red, ideological wing of the party, but Lin was the obvious alternative to Liu as Mao's successor, and the 'Imitate Lei Feng' and 'Learn from the People's Liberation Army' campaigns had brought the army into competition with the party over control of propaganda. In 1964 and 1965 Liu tried to reassert party hegemony by appointing local party bosses – notably in Shantung, Manchuria, and Szechwan – political commissars in the parallel military region, but this move only exacerbated party/army rivalry. All in all, the communist ruling institution confronted 1965 in a dangerous state of external isolation and internal division, though there was still nothing to suggest that malaise would escalate into revolution.

I now reach the second part of my survey: the course of the Cultural Revolution proper from 1965 to 1969. I propose to divide this into three sub-periods. First, a sub-period from November 1965 to August 1966 when the chief sphere of activity was in the committee rooms of the party and the Cultural Revolution was essentially a piece of factional in-fighting within the ruling institution. Second, a sub-period from August 1966 to August 1967, when the streets of the big cities became the chief sphere of activity and the Cultural Revolution turned into a social revolution of the have-nots of communist society against the haves – of the masses against the classes. Third, a sub-period from August 1967 to April 1969 when the chief centre of activity shifted from the streets to the camps and headquarters of the army and when the Cultural Revolution from a social convulsion became a military *pronunciamento*, an exercise in the *poder moderador*. Let me now try to analyze the structure of these three sub-periods.

The Cultural Revolution began in November 1965 as a limited inter-party struggle between rival groups of ideologists – 'monks squabbling', to borrow Leo X's phrase. On 10 November the Shanghai newspaper *Wen-hui pao* carried an article by Yao Wen-yüan, a noted Shanghai theoretician, which criticized an historical play by a leading academic, Wu Han, *Hai Jui Dismissed from Office*, for 'making veiled criticism of contemporary people through ancient people', describing it as a 'poisonous anti-party weed'. At first sight this was no more than an episode in the long rivalry between Peking and Shanghai ideologists: academics had been criticized before now; a recantation might be expected, but no heads need roll. Wu Han, however, was Vice-Mayor of Peking and Mayor P'eng Chen's lieutenant for education, and things became more serious when on 29 November the Shanghai attack was supported by *Chieh-fang chün-pao*, the organ of the army and specifically of the Ministry of Defence headed by Lin Piao. A small fracas between ideologists was turning into a major party/army encounter. About this time Mao left Peking for the provinces, presumably to avoid being caught in the crossfire. P'eng Chen, taken by surprise by the army attack, prudently gave ground: although number four in the party hierarchy, he was no match for Lin Piao and at his stage he was probably not supported by Liu Shao-ch'i or Teng Hsiao-p'ing. On 30 December Wu Han, doubtless at P'eng's direction, published a confession in *Jen-min Jih-pao* admitting historical inaccuracy in his play but rejecting the political charges. In the spring of 1966 Lin Piao returned to the attack. On 18 April an article in *Chieh-fang chün-pao*, 'Hold High the Great Banner of Mao Tse-tung's Thought and Actively Participate in the Great Socialist Cultural Revolution', introduced the term cultural revolution. It argued that bourgeois thought in art and literature was not just the work of misguided individuals – Wu Han was not mentioned – but represented a trend in Chinese society which must be fought against in the name of class struggle. A second article on 4 May, a significant date for Chinese intellectuals, which was tactfully entitled 'Never Forget the Class Struggle' after a speech of Mao's to the Tenth Plenum in September 1962, went further by suggesting that behind the bourgeois counter-revolution in art and literature were anti-party and anti-socialist elements in the party hierarchy itself. The propaganda institutions of the party were obliquely referred to, and P'eng Chen, Wu Han's patron and currently in charge of the socialist education movement, was clearly the target. An attack of this kind could not be averted by timely recantation. Lin Piao, seeing that the party bureaucrats were vulnerable to ideological criticism, had extended his objective from a local success over the Peking party machine to total victory.

What happened over the next month behind the closed doors of the party's committee rooms is not clear. All we know is the outcome. On 3 June it was announced that P'eng Chen had been dismissed from the mayoralty of Peking. The affiliation of his successors indicates that there had been a struggle between Lin Piao on the one hand and the party chiefs Liu Shao-ch'i and Teng Hsiao-p'ing on the other, and that the result was a draw. P'eng's successor as mayor was Li Hsüeh-feng, party boss of North China and a man with links to both Liu and Teng, while Wu Han's successor as Vice-Mayor was Wu Te, the party secretary of Kirin province, who was linked to Lin Piao through the Fourth Field Army. Probably Liu and Teng had not objected to Lin Piao's first attack on P'eng: after all he was their rival as well as his and they would not mind seeing a few feathers pulled from his tail; but when the second attack was launched, they rallied to his defence in the interests of party solidarity against the army. The defence was unsuccessful: Lin Piao was reinforced by Chou En-lai and the old expert faction and by T'ao Chu, the ambitious party boss of central South China, The fall of P'eng Chen, however, did not end the fight. Liu Shao-ch'i and Teng Hsiao-p'ing still held the greater part of the machine, and the period late May to late July 1966 was later referred to in Red Guard literature as the 'Fifty Days of White Terror'. The radicals – Lin, Chou, T'ao, and the ideologists – therefore turned to the only authority capable of outweighing Liu's, that of Chairman Mao himself. Acting through his former private secretary Ch'en Po-ta and his wife Chiang Ch'ing, neither of whom had any reason to like the oligarchs, the radicals persuaded Mao that his senior lieutenants had given way to revisionism and that he must act against them. On 11 July Mao entered the fray in style with his swim in the Yangtze, a gesture repeated five days later to underline his call for a new Long March against the enemies of the party within the party. On 1 August a new plenum of the central committee convened. On 8 August, by narrow and uncertain majorities, it adopted sixteen resolutions which first condemned 'those persons in authority who are taking the capitalist road' (namely, Liu Shao-ch'i and Teng Hsiao-p'ing) and second, called for mass action to break their control of the regional party machines. The radicals' margin of support in the committee rooms was too small for comfort so, on the advice of Chairman Mao himself – for who else would have dared to make such a suggestion? – they appealed to the streets.

The second sub-period of the Cultural Revolution lasted from the Eleventh Plenum in August 1966 to the so-called Wuhan incident in July-August 1967. For over a year China witnessed a social revolution, unprecedented in scale and violence since the revolution of 1911 and beyond anything envisaged by the radicals at the Eleventh Plenum. They had intended merely to use the streets to cleanse the committee rooms of their enemies. What they found occurring was an uncontrollable upheaval, to which the previous in-fighting in the party was largely irrelevant and which threatened to convulse the whole political system. In January 1967 the radicals had to appeal to the army to intervene to save their interests and to prevent the country sliding into anarchy.

The institution of this social revolution was the mass organization or Red Guard unit – as characteristic of it as the crowd in 1789 or the storm troops of Nazi Germany. Mass organizations – of trade unionists, students, democratic women, etc. – had long been a feature of communism in China, indeed were one of the secrets of its power, and Red Guard units had appeared in Peking in May and June 1966 as adjuncts to the top-level party in-fighting. The mass organizations and Red Guard units of the period following the Eleventh Plenum were, however, essentially new. Unlike the old mass organizations, they were not created from the top down but from the bottom up, or else by a kind of migratory wave of revolution: activists travelling round the main urban centres to spread the slogans and techniques of revolution. Unlike the first Red Guard units, the new ones were not instigated or controlled by the party leaders, but negotiated with them as independent forces.

The new mass organizations were established on a local occupation-employment basis by demobilized soldiers, lower party cadres, and schoolteachers, and though passionately interested in what was going on in the rest of the country, they seem to have had no formal links with similar organizations outside their own locality. Their first target was the party, and the various regional machines were overthrown in a series of dramatic confrontations or revolutionary *journées*: the Shanghai commune of 6 January 1967 which overthrew Mayor Ts'ao Ti-ch'iu; the Canton confrontation of 17-25 January which led to the arrest of the party boss T'ao Chu; the Chengtu riots of April and May which destroyed the power of the Szechwan party chief Li Ching-ch'uan. Having disposed of the party, the mass organizations then turned to fight among themselves and it was now that the essentially social character of the alignments became apparent.

This social character may be seen if one looks in depth at the Red Guard organizations in the area for which we have the best information, Canton, for the pattern appears to be similar in other large centres such as Shanghai and Sian. In Canton, after the overthrow of T'ao Chu, the various mass organizations polarized between two super-organizations, or 'large loose coalitions' as Ezra Vogel describes them, known as Red Flag and East Wind. Red Flag was radical in that it was on the offensive and aimed at a thoroughgoing change in Chinese society. It consisted of ten subsidiary mass organizations of which the more important were: first, the August First Combat Corps, 160 000 strong, consisting of 40 per cent demobilized soldiers, 40 per cent workers, probably unskilled, and 20 per cent middle school students; second, the Young Intellectuals to the Countryside Rebellion Headquarters, 120 000 strong, consisting of students assigned to the countryside who wanted to come back to the city, or at least to be allowed to travel inside China; third, the Canton Fighting Corps, consisting of 40 000 middle school students who feared that they would be assigned to the countryside instead of going on to high school and university: this group was responsible for most of the killing on the radical side in the street fighting in Canton; fourth, the Canton Railway Workers Headquarters, consisting of 50 000 unskilled railway coolies; fifth, Red Headquarters, consisting of 60 000–70 000 miscellaneous Red Guards organized mainly by middle school teachers. What all these people had in common was insecurity and vulnerability to the whims of party bureaucracy. All of them belonged to the margin of urban society and hence were affected by the deurbanization programme of the Retreat from the Great Leap. East Wind, on the other hand, was conservative in that it was on the defensive and did not want the revolution to go beyond the political level of a purge of the party machine. It consisted of nine subsidiary mass organizations of which the more important were the following: first, Ground Command, 100 000 strong, consisting mainly of state factory workers; second, Red Workers General Headquarters, 80 000 strong, again consisting mainly of state factory workers; third, Spring Thunder, consisting of 10 000 skilled workers, particularly railway workers; fourth, the Doctrine Guards, consisting of middle school children of party cadres, the *jeunesse dorée* of the city, who could be sure that they would not be rusticated: these were the big killers on the conservative side; fifth, the Poor and Lower-Middle Peasants' United Command, with a membership of 800 000 and control of the suburban rural commune militia which opposed the radical Red Guards' incursions into the countryside. What all these people had in common was security, a share in the modest affluence communist China was beginning to provide in 1965, and a reluctance to see it upset by social revolution. All of them were either definitely urban like the skilled workers or definitely rural like the farmers, and so accepted the clear demarcation of urban and rural functions of the Retreat from the Great Leap.

This then was the alignment of social forces at the height of the Cultural Revolution. On the one hand insecure classes: urban adolescents, demobilized soldiers – particularly prominent because of their leadership qualities – unskilled workers, the urban elderly threatened like youth by rustication, and the losers in earlier power struggles, such as, at Canton, the localists, the wartime guerrilla leaders purged in 1952, and, most strange of all, some of T'ao Chu's associates purged in January who now saw their only hope in a total *bouleversement*. On the other hand secure classes: party cadres which had survived the fall of their leaders, skilled workers in regular jobs, members of rural communes. What would have happened if the protagonists had fought it out, it is hard to say. The radicals had the advantage of momentum and enthusiasm, the conservatives of weight and number. The radicals could invoke the name of Mao Tse-tung, but the conservatives had behind them the *vis inertiae* of the party state. In fact, there was no fight to the finish. On 17 or 18 January 1967 Mao, worried by the growing anarchy and equally alarmed that the radical mass organizations might not emerge victorious or, one suspects, that they might, ordered the army to intervene on the Maoist side and to restore order. It was an ambiguous instruction and for six months the military commanders in only six out of China's twenty-nine provincial areas took much notice of it, but following a particularly flagrant disregard of party orders in July by the military commander at Wuhan, Ch'en Tsai-tao, the army found itself compelled to intervene decisively, though not always in the sense intended by the Maoist leadership. By August 1967 initiative in the Cultural Revolution had passed from the streets to the camps and headquarters of the People's Liberation Army.

The third sub-period of the Cultural Revolution, the phase of military intervention, lasted from the Wuhan incident of July-August 1967 to the Ninth Party Congress in April 1969. The army's attitude to the Cultural Revolution was determined by three of its own characteristics. On the one hand the army was the natural rival of the party. It occupied a special place in Mao Tse-tung's theory of revolution; it had been the generals who in 1935 had put Mao into the party leadership; and it was the army which offered in Lin Piao the strongest competitor to Liu Shao-ch'i, the party's candidate for the succession. Through the recruitment system the army stood close to the common people and understood their grievances against cadre commandism. Before 1965 the army had been in rivalry with the party propaganda organs for control of the mass campaigns and it resented the party's attempt to infiltrate its own regional organization through the political commissarships. As long therefore as the Cultural Revolution remained in the committee rooms – Lin Piao against P'eng Chen, Lin Piao against Liu Shao-ch'i, Liu Shao-ch'i against Mao Tse-tung – the army remained a radical Maoist force. On the other hand the army, like the party, was a well-established bureaucratic machine. The top generals had all held office for a long time; they were professionals; the regional commands were assigned and units positioned according to a well-institutionalized pattern of contained competition; and the promotion structure was likewise satisfactorily routinized. It was an ideological army, Mao's army, but also the army of an organization. When the Cultural Revolution moved from the committee rooms to the streets, once the issue came to be social revolution against social order, the army began to have reservations about the Cultural Revolution. As early as the Eleventh Plenum, before it was plain what Mao's appeal to the streets was going to mean, the army insisted, in Article 15 of the resolutions, that within its own ranks the Red Guard movement be under its own control. Finally, transcending these contrasting antibureaucratic and bureaucratic characteristics, the army was a single organism which wanted to maintain its own unity, in particular the careful balance it preserved between its five field armies. William Whitson has emphasized the importance of the field armies as the ongoing sub-élites and the effective constituents of the army. While in a sense in rivalry with each other, the field armies are in practice, he argues, more concerned with not letting such rivalry go too far and with maintaining their own internal cohesion and that of the army as a whole. In all phases of the Cultural Revolution the army had therefore an essentially crossbench attitude. It wanted China to be like itself: to compromise, to accommodate both radicals and conservatives, and to sacrifice factionalism in the interests of a greater unity.

The resultant parallelogram of forces brought the army closer to the battered conservative mass organizations, which were only too willing to compromise, than to the intransigent radicals, who were not, so that military intervention worked to the advantage of social order. Just what new institutional structure Mao originally envisaged as resulting from military intervention is not clear, but by March 1967 the Central Committee gave its approval to a semi-radical body which had first appeared at Harbin in January. This was the revolutionary committee which was to replace the old party bureaux and to consist of 50 per cent representatives of mass organizations and 25 per cent each of army officers and converted cadres. The army's task was to assist in the setting up of these committees; their composition and the army's role in establishing them have been studied in particular by Jürgen Domes. Domes shows that down to the Wuhan incident the army dragged its feet and showed little enthusiasm for active intervention, though the six revolutionary committees which were set up mainly reflected the radical interest, as Mao himself had intended. After the Wuhan incident the establishment of revolutionary committees speeded up but their character changed. The proportion of army officers and converted cadres was increased from 25 per cent each to $33\frac{1}{3}$ per cent each, while the representation of the mass organizations not only fell from 50 per cent to $33\frac{1}{3}$ per cent, but also began to be drawn from the conservative rather than from the radical mass organizations. This last change was particularly evident in Canton. Here it had been the radical Red Flag alliance which had been mainly responsible for overthrowing T'ao Chu in January 1967, but by February

Red Flag was at loggerheads with Huang Yung-sheng, the local military commander. In April, it is true, it received an access of strength from Chou En-lai's visit to Canton, and after the Wuhan incident had shown that the army could not show its dislike of radicalism too openly, it had another period of ascendancy. By September, however, the army was clamping down again. The August First Combat Corps, the nucleus of Red Flag, was placed under stricter controls and the Canton Fighting Corps was dissolved. Early in 1968 the army formed a workers' provost corps, ostensibly to help it keep the peace between the factions but actually drawn far more from conservative East Wind than from radical Red Flag. A similar pattern of conservative bias in intervention is revealed in other large centres. Thus the Wuhan incident, which looked like a victory for the radicals, in fact ushered in a general decrescendo for the Cultural Revolution. In August the leading radical involved at Wuhan, Wang Li, was purged and the following March the army chief of staff, Yang Ch'eng-wu, was replaced by Huang Yung-sheng, the conservative from Canton. The formation of revolutionary committees with only minority representation for radicalism continued and on the basis of them the Ninth Party Congress was elected and met in April 1969, with, as an Australian journalist put it, 'a smell of compromise, if not straight horse-trading, in the air'. The army had recreated China in its own image.

I now come to the last part of my survey: the results of the Cultural Revolution. I shall look at this in terms first of institutions and then of events. As regards institutions, the Cultural Revolution had a real but limited impact, as one sees if one analyzes it under its three aspects. First, as a piece of political in-fighting, the Cultural Revolution produced some changes in people and politics. Liu Shao-ch'i, Teng Hsiao-p'ing, and P'eng Chen disappeared from the political scene, as did their regional lieutenants T'ao Chu, Li Ching-ch'üan, and Liu Lan-t'ao, and the regional party machines which had dominated politics in the early 1960s were broken down and replaced by smaller, provincial units. New faces appeared: Chiang Ch'ing and the Shanghai radical bosses Chang Ch'un-ch'iao and Yao Wen-yüan; Chou En-lai increased his power; and the party gained a less bureaucratic constitution. Yet, as the dust settled, many old faces reappeared and one could wonder whether in an institution as large as the Chinese communist party bureaucracy really had been killed. Second, as a social revolution the Red

Guards certainly achieved one of their objectives: to elevate ideology unambiguously above organization. After 1969 communist China was as never before a Maoist state. Yet for the majority of those who took part in the mass organizations, life was much the same, was perhaps even worse, as rustication was enforced by the army. Just as the crowd in the French revolution became the cannon fodder of Napoleon's armies or the factory fodder of French industrialization, so the Red Guards have been swallowed up in China's struggle for ecological viability. Third, as military intervention, the Cultural Revolution was successful, but in a limited way. The army did not seek power for itself, and its small size – 3 million compared with the party's 20 million – made it impossible for it to substitute itself for the party. The army produced only a caretaker government, primarily at the provincial level, for at the centre the party radicals retained the initiative. Further, the system of economic management devised during the Retreat from the Great Leap – limited central planning by technocrats plus decentralization to factory managers and farm experts – remained in force after the Cultural Revolution. So did the economic policies of the early 1960s: priority for agriculture, deurbanization, emphasis on chemical fertilizers, and toleration of private plots in the rural communes.

If one turns from institutions to events, one has the same impression of real but limited impact. The two principal events in China since the Ninth Party Congress have been, I suppose, in the provinces the replacement of the caretaker revolutionary committees by regular party committees, and in the capital the mysterious coup which led to the disappearance of Lin Piao and the three service chiefs in October 1971. The composition of the new party committees, as analyzed in recent numbers of the *China Quarterly,* suggests the re-emergence of a party machine dominated not by Maoist radicals or youthful Red Guard activists, but by people of second or third rank in 1965 who managed to avoid too much trouble later. For example, in Shensi the chairman was Li Jui-shan, a former mayor of Changsha who opposed the Red Guards in Hunan in August 1966; in Honan he was Liu Chien-hsün, the former party secretary deposed in March 1967. In Shansi one of the secretaries was Chang P'ing-hua, the former party secretary in Hunan, who had been deposed in July 1966; in Inner Mongolia one was Chao Tzu-yang, formerly T'ao Chu's right-hand man in Canton. In Szechwan the two leading radicals on the revolutionary committee were dropped from the new party committee. At the provincial level then the course of events since 1969 suggests re-emergent conservatism and rebureaucratization. At the capital, on the other hand, the picture is different. The events of October 1971 are still far from clear, but if, as has been reported, Lin Piao, Huang Yung-sheng, the army chief of staff, and the two other service chiefs, Wu Fa-hsien and Li Tso-p'eng, have been eliminated from Chinese politics, this is best interpreted as a palace revolution by the Chou En-lai faction against the army, the Fourth Field Army in particular, which may have had little effect on politics in the provinces. Reports so far do not indicate that the fall of Lin and Huang, both Fourth Field Army men, has led to a general purge of the numerous Fourth Field Army men in positions of authority in the provinces: Ch'en Hsi-lien in Mukden, Tseng-Ssu-yu in Wuhan, or Chang Kuo-hua in Chengtu. Ever since the ending of the Cultural Revolution Chinese politics have manifested a curious dualism: conservatism in the provinces, radicalism in Peking. The events of October merely underlined this dualism, but which was appearance and which reality still remained an open question. How far subsequent events have resolved the matter I leave for the reader to decide.

Mao Tse-tung's Revolutionary Diplomatic Line: The Revolutionary Experience of the Chinese Communist Party and Its Role in China's International Relations

W.A.C. ADIE

When Premier Chou En-lai returned from seeing President Nixon off, he was hailed with slogans celebrating the victory of Chairman Mao's revolutionary diplomatic line. Observers concluded that reception of the imperialist chieftain in Peking had really been a policy of Chou En-lai, which was now being given the stamp of Mao's approval. In fact the three major Peking papers had referred to this diplomatic line back in August 1971,[1] when the military were still in a position to see that barely veiled doubts about ping-pong diplomacy and restatements of the leading role of the armed forces in the state found expression in the official propaganda. Lin Piao and other military leaders fell in September: according to the wilder rumours, after having tried to assassinate Chou En-lai or even Mao.

This extraordinary event confirmed the suspicions of those who, like the present writer, saw in the Mao cult propagated by Lin Piao a deviation from genuine Maoism.[2] But in order to reach any valid conclusions about the future development of China's diplomacy and defence policy, it is necessary to consider the historical origins of Maoist thinking on these matters. It cannot be assumed without question that all previous counter-productive foreign initiatives from Peking were the work of those who are now called political swindlers – Liu Shao-chi, Lin Piao, and company.

As long ago as 1949, on the eve of victory in China, Mao himself hinted at the essence of his diplomatic strategy when he told his cadres that they must learn to master diplomatic struggles *both overt and covert*. This instruction of Mao's was published towards the end of the 'Great Proletarian Cultural Revolution',[3] at the time when the agencies responsible for conducting China's foreign trade and other relations were regrouping for what was called Peking's diplomatic offensive.[4] The combination of overt and covert is a key to understanding Peking's diplomacy, since it follows from the dialectics of Mao Tse-tung's thought as a whole. Peking's *modus operandi* in dealings with all outside individuals and groups, whether Chinese or foreign and whether in authority or not, must be understood in terms of the inherited traditions and revolutionary experience of the present Chinese élite, as summed up in the published Thought of Mao, especially the military writings.[5]

As Mao himself implies by his frequent quotations from them, many of his ideas derive from the medieval Chinese romances as well as from the classical histories such as the *Tso Chuan*, and above all from the classic *Art of War*, attributed to Sun Wu of the Warring Kingdoms period, several centuries B.C. Quoting one of these traditional novels (translated into English under the title *All Men Are Brothers* or *Water Margin*), Mao illustrates what he means by dialectical materialism:

> In *Water Margin*, Sung Chiang attacked Chu village...and was twice defeated because he had no clear knowledge of the conditions and used the wrong methods...[then] he... succeeded in disrupting the alliance between the Li, Hu and Chu villages, and won final victory in the third battle after secretly infiltrating his own soldiers in disguise into the enemy camp, a stratagem similar to that of the Trojan Horse. There are numerous examples of materialist dialectics in *Water Margin*, of which [this episode] is perhaps the best.[6]

This passage illustrates several characteristics of Mao's thinking, such as the technique of disintegrating the enemy, and the importance attached to ruses and stratagems. Another important idea which is found in *Water Margin* and which is developed by Mao as part of his military-political technique is the tactic of presenting neutrals or enemies with a *fait accompli;* this commits them to join the rebel or bandit cause and enables them to rationalize their decision with some high-sounding, moralizing utterance. This technique of exploiting what might be called the 'Vicar of Bray syndrome' was combined with other traditional features of Chinese society (such as the methods of the secret societies and politico-religious sects) and with the tradition of Soviet communist police techniques to produce the system of 'rectification' or 'ideological remoulding'. This technique is applied within the communist party both at home and abroad and is an essential feature of the Maoist system. At the lowest level it can be seen at work when members of an adolescent gang use 'stick and carrot' methods to induce others to join them. The inducement may consist of bullying, the cessation of bullying, or 'lenient treatment' used after an initial fright has been given. This is what Mao calls treating the disease and saving the patient: 'We must first shake up the patient by shouting at him, "You are ill!" and then when he is sweating with fright, tell him gently that he needs treatment.'[7]

Mao understands that the aim of a military commander, like that of the thought police, is to alter behaviour in the target group, and this cannot be done entirely by or without the application of threat or force. Preferably the force should be that of circumstances rather than purely one's own.

> The *Art of War* says:
> When in chariot fighting more than ten chariots are captured, reward those who take the first. Replace the enemy's flags and banners with your own. Mix the captured chariots with yours, and mount them. Treat the captives well and care for them.
> Commentary: all the soldiers taken must be cared for with magnanimity and sincerity so that they may be used by us. This is called winning a battle and becoming stronger.[8]

Mao Tse-tung adopted exactly the same principles in his fighting against the Nationalists and the Japanese. These principles were again seen in operation during the 1962 clash with India:

> This army has a correct policy for winning over enemy officers and men and for dealing with prisoners of war. Without exception all members of the enemy forces who surrender, who come over to our side or who, after laying down their arms wish to join in fighting the common foe, are welcomed and given proper education.[9]

Militarily speaking, this is one facet of the policy of disintegrating enemy troops and an extension of the requirement to win over neutral as well as enemy forces – in other words, *all* enemy forces.

Mao Tse-tung's own writings demonstrate the extension of this method and principle from 'education' of enemy troops and officers to the winning over and indoctrination of personnel either in 'friendly armies' allied with him or already incorporated in his own forces. As he put it in one of his early works,

> the majority of the Red army soldiers come from the mercenary armies, but their character changes once they are in the

> Red army .... After receiving political education, the Red army soldiers have become class conscious, learned the essentials of distributing land, setting up political power, arming the workers and peasants.... Each company, battalion or regiment has its soldiers' committee which represents the interests of the soldiers and carries on political and mass work.[10]

As Mao explains in his important speech of 27 February 1957, 'On Correct Handling of Contradictions among the People', in 1942 he developed his methods of indoctrination into the 'rectification campaign', by which he eliminated as far as possible the influence of ideas and habits opposed to his own of rival commanders in the communist forces.

In the early days of the party, owing to the dispersed nature of its guerrilla forces and the 'mountain-stronghold mentality' often castigated by Mao, the situation was such that a dispatch of 17 August 1932 from the British Embassy in Peking pointed out:

> If there is any central control over the 'Red Armies', such as is claimed by the political bureau of the Chinese Communist Party, it is of the very shadowiest description. Each horde occupies its own particular area by right of seizure and would almost certainly hold it by force against any other horde which attempted to enter it.... it is said nevertheless that the main groups are in wireless communication with each other and it is probably true that there is some sort of cooperation between them in face of their common enemy.[11]

It was this sort of thing that Mao Tse-tung had in mind when he said some ten years later: 'What is now a serious problem in our Party and is found almost everywhere is the mountain stronghold outlook, which is a kind of mental blindness.'[12]

Having established an initial degree of control over these 'hordes' by 'rectification', as Mao explains, 'We extended this method beyond our Party.... after the liberation of the country we used this same method – "unity-criticism-unity" – in our relations with other democratic parties and industrial and commercial circles.' He explained that, although the use of this method went back to 1927, it was used more purposefully and with success during the anti-Japanese war – in other words, after he took over in 1935. In 1957 he put forward the proposition:

Our task is to continue to extend and make still better use of this method throughout the ranks of the people; we want all our factories, co-operatives, business establishments, schools, government offices, public bodies, in a word, all the 600 million of our people, to use it in resolving contradictions among themselves.

The method of unity-criticism-unity is simply a modern development of what was done in the fifth century B.C. with the enemy charioteers: that is, the use of group pressure exerted in 'study sessions', 'struggle meetings', etc. to force people to commit themselves and denounce others; in the process they become committed to a certain pattern of behaviour required by the revolutionists ('our side'). The technique, which seems to be particularly well adapted to Chinese political culture, has been applied far from China: for example, in Cameroon and the Congo. In vulgar terms, the communist method of conversion or rectification includes what is called brainwashing. As a perceptive Chinese who experienced the process has written,

> When something is done and cannot be undone, men will do all they can to justify it. . . . the contemplation of this psychological mechanism may make it easy to understand the effect of rallies, parades, slogans, confessions, discussions, speeches, meetings, songs, group dances, and even such a simple gesture as raising one's hand, not on those who see them, *but on those who partake in them.* Voluntary confession differs from forced confession only in that, in the former, repentance precedes and, in the latter, it follows confession. The incredulous reader here should imagine confession, not spoken in whispers to a confessor sworn to be an absolute confidant, but spoken to a large assembly consisting of one's colleagues, family, friends, and acquaintances and repeated if the instigators are not satisfied that it is sincere.[13]

By 1942, of course, the original guerrilla conception of 'spreading the net wide to arouse the masses' and drawing it in to engage the enemy, or splitting one's forces in two for conventional (or holding) and special (or winning) operations, had been raised on to a higher plane, thanks to the special situation created by Japanese aggression against China and in particular by the Sian incident of 1936. The Sian incident forced Chiang Kai-shek to enter into a united front with the communists, ostensibly to resist Japanese aggression. As Mao pointed out in 1928 in *Why Can China's Red Political Power Exist?*, the successful survival of the original communist armed bands was due to the unique geographical and political situation in the China of the time, a country divided under the control of motley military régimes, more or less supported by different outside powers. (In this respect, from the Chinese viewpoint, the situation resembled that in some parts of Asia, Africa, and Latin America today, and accordingly these countries are regarded as suitable for Maoist guerrilla warfare. See below.)

The advantageous effects of a Japanese invasion had been foreseen as early as 1927 in a letter to the Shanghai committee of the Chinese communist party from the party's secretariat: it called for 'a militant anti-imperialist movement in Shanghai' by students, shopkeepers, and workers, mainly against the Japanese. It explained:

> If we continue to insist on the confiscation of land and on the arming of workers and peasants, the result will be an immediate break with the Kuomintang, and an immediate break with the Kuomintang will mean the immediate liquidation of our party...we must not fear imperialist conquest and intervention in the territory of Chiang Kai-shek...for in the event of an imperialist seizure, we can raise a new anti-imperialist war. This war will lead directly to the necessity of arming peasants and workers and to the confiscation of land...this movement must come as an explosion of the people's wrath. It must be general and national in character...you must *expand and intensify the movement in the presence of the foreign power* [my italics]. The more this movement develops, the easier will it be to organize our forces; and the forces of the bloc [the proletariat, the peasantry, and the petty bourgeoisie] will crush the forces of Chiang Kai-shek.

Mao Tse-tung was not in command at the time and this resolution was rejected by the Comintern delegate, M.N. Roy, as a tactic of the purest opportunism.[14] Nevertheless, once Mao was in control of the communist forces, he switched the emphasis of their propaganda from social revolution in the countryside to nationalist opposition to the Japanese. His lieutenants Po Ku and Peng Teh-huai told American visitors at the time that the method of organizing rural Soviets had done them no good; only thanks to the Japanese invasion would it be possible to win, by raising the flag of nationalism.[15] Accordingly, the communists' political arm organized what came to be called the 'Ninth December Movement', after a demonstration by 10 000 students in Peking (then Peiping) against the Nationalist policy of subduing the communists before resisting Japan.

At the same time Mao took military action to embroil China and Japan in a war which would relieve him of the Nationalist pressure. In February 1936 he sent troops across the Yellow River to attack the Japanese, but they were headed off by Chiang. Turning this setback to propaganda advantage, Mao succeeded in working on the commanders of the Government's Manchurian and northwestern armies. Converting political influence into military power by the famous Sian incident (the kidnapping of Chiang by the northern troops), he brought about the united front which sealed Chiang's fate.

Preparation had been made to move on without interruption from the National War of Liberation to the Socialist Revolution. As Liu Shao-chi pointed out,

> Our party never forgot for a moment that our final goal was to carry out the Socialist Revolution and throughout the struggle for the Democratic Revolution it already paid close attention to the establishment and consolidation of the Hegemony of the Proletariat.[16]

The reference to the Democratic Revolution shows how the alliance of classes polarized on to the same side by the Japanese attack was rationalized under Mao's formula of 'New Democracy' and the 'New Democratic Revolution', which was another way of talking about the 'united front'.

After Mao's régime had been in power for some time it reached a crisis owing to the difficulty of adapting its methods to its peacetime tasks, and these were increasingly questioned or ignored by party leaders. The characteristics of the united front were therefore authoritatively summed up and restated in 1961 as follows (my italics):

1 *The United Front led by the Chinese Communist Party;*
2 The United Front based on the alliance of workers and peasants;
3 The United Front based on the *alliance with and struggle against* the bourgeoisie;
4 *The United Front with armed struggle as its mainstay* at the stage of democratic revolution and based on the struggle of the proletariat at the socialist stage;
5 The United Front shouldering the revolutionary tasks at the democratic stage *and* at the socialist stage;
6 *The United Front of self-education and remoulding;*
7 The United Front supporting great unity of the world's people.[17]

According to Mao's 'algebra of revolution', the Japanese attack polarized the majority of forces present in China on to his side. Under a temporary 'division of labour' (Mao's phrase) the Nationalist armies could act as his conventional force and tie down the attacking Japanese; at the same time the Japanese would help to defeat the Nationalists by driving them out of their strongholds, the cities. Meanwhile the communists would infiltrate a large proportion of their forces into the areas cleared of Nationalists by the Japanese and build new guerrilla bases. Thus, while acting supposedly as a special or guerrilla force for the Nationalists, the communists were also consolidating their own power in preparation for the inevitable retreat of the Japanese.

As Mao analyzed the situation, though Japan was strong, it was small; though China was weak, it was huge. Therefore the war was bound to go through three phases reminiscent of Mao's original sixteen-character formula. In the first phase would come the enemy's strategic offensive and the retreat of the Chinese. In the second phase the enemy would be forced to bring his advance to a halt, having over-extended his lines of communication and not having enough troops to occupy the vast conquered territory. Under the resulting harassment by Chinese guerrillas he would eventually be worn down and forced to retreat, whereupon the third phase would begin, the counter-offensive, with mobile and positional warfare adopted by the growing Chinese communist forces.[18]

In fact, of course, the Japanese were defeated by the Allies and the use of atomic weapons, but this is hardly recognized in Chinese communist doctrine. By the end of the anti-Japanese war Mao had by this method expanded his forces from 30 000 to 900 000, with a militia of 2 million in the base areas. Hence the transition from 'alliance' to open warfare with Chiang Kai-shek's forces was not difficult. Chiang, like the Chinese government of Wang Ching-wei set up by the Japanese, was in turn regarded as a puppet of foreigners, this time of the Americans, and the flag of nationalism and patriotism was raised against him with the same success.

Mao summed up the principles evolved in his campaigns and developed his theory of people's war further in *On Coalition Government* (1945). Of special interest in this work is the attention he gives to the disintegration of enemy troops and to remustering and remoulding them into the communist forces, as well as to united front work or political work in general. We see that the basic principle of the united front was to maintain the communists' own independence and autonomy within the front and so to win over the friendly troops and even pro-Japanese elements while pursuing dual tactics of unity and struggle with them. The means were provided by the three magic wands: the armed struggle, the united front, and the communist party.[19]

The dual policy, blurring distinctions between friends and enemies in order to reduce the effective strength of the latter to a minimum, is also explained in Mao's *On Policy* (1940). An article of 27 August 1971 in the *Peking Review* expressly points out the relevance of this essay to the current international situation.

After the turning point had been reached in the war against Chiang Kai-shek, Mao saw three possible patterns for elimination of the remaining enemy forces: peaceful reorganization into his own units, attack and suppression by military means, or leaving them aside until later. The same general approach characterized his outlook on international affairs when, after the liberation of China, he 'leant towards' Soviet Russia, which was essentially a more dangerous and important enemy than the United States. It must be borne in mind that in 1949 Mao had not really established central control over the country. Apart from the fact that it was divided into semi-autonomous areas of military control, there were not only Tibet and Taiwan to be incorporated, but also other large areas in the border regions which had never been effectively brought under the central control of any Chinese state. The methods used to pacify, sinicize, and revolutionize these areas inhabited by minority nationalities are essentially the same as those used later in target areas of the Third World, notably Africa.

Developed from the techniques effectively used by the Red army in winning over minority peoples during their guerrilla period, they included such methods as sending in medical teams, building roads and railways, and forming a united front with the existing 'bourgeois upper strata', while carrying on 'mass work' among the rest of the population and preparing for the introduction of 'socialist reforms'.[20] This dual policy of intimidation and 'hearts and minds work' (coercion plus enticement) was intended not only to develop and get control of the natural resources of these areas, but also to promote social transformation (sinicization) and in some cases to facilitate the settlement of Han Chinese.

The whole process has been dramatically represented in a famous revolutionary Peking opera, *Taking Tiger Mountain by Strategy*. Here, although the 'masses' to be mobilized are still Han Chinese, the *modus operandi* is the same as if they had been tribal mountaineers – just a little easier to execute. On the one hand the Red army infiltrates an agent into the stronghold of the pro-Nationalist 'bandits', wearing their uniform and knowing their customs and jargon. On the other hand the unit 'arouses the masses' politically and builds up their economic and hence their military strength by helping them to get a local railway running. Then it helps them to set up and arm a militia to take part in the final two-pronged assault on the enemy stronghold from without and from within. In this way the 'masses' are helped to relieve themselves of their original rulers. Any visitors from Tanzania and Zambia who have seen this opera performed could hardly fail to guess the message.

Starting from the original scene of such operations in China proper, this process of assimilation has been extended as and when expedient into the non-Han areas such as Tibet and over the cartographic border into the contiguous, opium-growing no-man's-land of Laos, Burma, and Thailand, notably in the form of a road into Laos protected by six battalions of Chinese troops (as at November 1971) and anti-aircraft artillery. But in a less obvious manner Peking's entire foreign policy, even in non-contiguous areas such as Africa, is an extension of the same policies for handling out-groups and minority peoples – which, after all, we non-Chinese all are.

In 1949 China became the 'Yenan of the world'. Regarding the international system of nation-states as analogous to the China of the 1930s, split up among divers warlords, several of Mao's colleagues made statements implying that his Thought would now have to be applied to repeating the process which had so far unified China. In November 1949 Liu Shao-chi said that the peoples of various colonial and semi-colonial countries must take the path followed by 'the Chinese people in defeating imperialism and its lackeys' – that is, they must use the three magic wands: armed struggle, united front, and party-building.[21] This was not mere rhetoric. The secret Chinese Army Work Bulletins[22] contain several authoritative directives from Marshal Lo Jung-huan, Marshal Yeh Chien-ying, and others on the 'international implications' of Mao's thought. Foreign Minister Marshal Ch'en Yi expressed the situation more accurately when he wrote in September 1964 that Mao's strategic and tactical thinking, together with the policies and general lines of the Party Centre, had been the principal guides for Peking's analysis of international problems during the past fifteen years.[23] At that time, we were told during the Cultural Revolution, Peking's policies and

Mao's thought had been distorted by Liu Shao-chi. In fact a case can be made out that during the early sixties the application of Mao's revolutionary strategy was distorted by attempts to turn Peking not into the Mecca of revolution, but into another Moscow, complete with its own apparatus of international front organizations and splinter pro-Peking communist parties. Concurrently and subsequent to the outbreak of the Great Proletarian Cultural Revolution there was evidence of adventurism in the application of a guerrilla style in international relations, links with youth groups, feudal elements, and various other non-communist armed elements being used to bring off Trojan Horse operations and to promote warfare and insecurity. It is quite likely that the leftist deviations will be blamed on 'political charlatans like Liu Shao-chi', a category which now (spring 1972) includes not only the ultra-leftists responsible for the Boxer Diplomacy of 1966–7, but also Marshall Lin Piao and perhaps the International Affairs Bureau of the People's Liberation Army.

While rival factions and bureaucracies in China may have interpreted Mao's strategy differently and obstructed each other's work in the field (as happens to other large powers), broadly speaking they differed only in emphasis. They retained the basic premise that in the initial period of military weakness political strength must be built up for conversion later into military or coercive power, while in the meantime it divides and embroils the opposition. As a basis for building up political strength, enough defensive military strength must be acquired to ensure survival – everything else grows out of the gun-barrel. Once secure in the 'base area', Mao's régime should not attack the encircling enemy on his own ground of military strength, but where he is weak – in politics, in social and psychological spheres, and in all areas where 'contradictions' are waiting to be exploited.

Symbolizing the world of nation-states which the Maoists rejected,[24] the United Nations Organization was regarded by the author of a briefing in the Army Work Bulletins as a pig-pen; joining it would be like joining a 'government of the northern warlords'.[25] This was why for years China sought to build up its own Third Force organization, a counter-United Nations of 'newly emergent' Afro-Asian and Latin-American forces. This policy foundered when the Second Bandung Conference, due to be held in Algiers in 1965, had to be cancelled because it became evident that China could not control it. As far back as the Suez crisis of 1956 and on several other occasions Peking had offered 'volunteers' in the hope of escalating and prolonging 'anti-imperialist struggles' in the Middle East and Africa. In 1960 at Conakry Peking delegates to the Afro-Asian Solidarity Conference tried to secure agreement for the setting up of an Afro-Asian volunteer army to fight the white régimes in Africa, and the Army Work Bulletins made clear that Africa was seen as a theatre for the application of techniques such as the people's war and the united front, modified in accordance with local conditions. In the absence of agreement on the 'volunteer army', Peking trained African cadres in China and in several radical African countries, and looked forward to the day when a revolutionary wave would roll up the continent.[26] In the Cameroons, the Congo, and several other African countries Chinese trainees took part in abortive insurrections during the sixties, but the Chinese army stressed the weakness of local revolutionary leadership, and took a long-term view.[27]

It was in the Middle East that Mao's strategy of provocation and united front was applied with the greatest effect in the sixties. Small-scale aid to the extremist Palestinian mini-groups helped to enable them to exert influence out of all proportion to their numbers on the multifarious commando 'organizations' and hence on the Arab governments. In turn, the Soviet Union was forced to go along with policies against its own interest, if only to retain the ability to stop things getting out of hand. Peking's aid to Al-Fatah began in January 1965. Combined with other moves, and thanks to Israeli retaliation for the guerrilla raids, it helped to bring on the June War of 1967. Like the Japanese invasion of China, this served to weaken and discredit what the commandos call 'Arab officialdom' and to give Arab public opinion the impression that only the exponents of guerrilla warfare were resisting aggression and incarnating the national spirit. It was obvious to King Hussein and many other rulers of successor states to the Ottoman Empire that the intention of the commandos was to use the pretext of fighting Israel to unite their territories in a new Marxist-Leninist super-state of Arabia, just as Mao's men had used Japan to restore the Manchu empire under their rule. Though the Palestinians were driven underground in Jordan, their power has not been broken. Meanwhile, since the early sixties the Dhofar Liberation Front, later the Front for Liberating the Arab (Persian) Gulf, has been built up with Chinese aid via Aden to threaten that strategically vital area.

Since the Chinese aid to Tanzania, Zambia, and West Pakistan put China in the forefront of aid donors in the communist world, it has become clear that, after initial attempts to promote armed struggles in Africa without sufficient preparatory work, Peking is now laying a firm politico-economic base in Africa, which could later be used to carry to its logical conclusion the process which has already been seen in operation in the Middle East: escalation of commando attacks on the 'diehard' white régimes; retaliation by them against the host countries; radicalization of the latter or take-over by the militant groups; growth of revolutionary movements transcending existing state boundaries, and so on. This process has in fact already begun, as I predicted some years ago.[28]

Now that Peking has entered the United Nations, probably earlier than it expected, the possibilities of 'walking on two legs' are immeasurably greater: it can turn military advantage derived from the guerrillas being a 'force to be reckoned with' into political advantage on the world scene, and use its political leverage in bilateral relations, making use of the veto if necessary, to secure military advantage. On the western flank of the Indian Ocean, the session of the Security Council in Addis Ababa has also shown how political influence can be used for essentially military purposes – to move towards the practical implementation of the militant united front which eluded Peking in 1965, this time using the Organization of African Unity and the United Nations itself as the front organization. Though the possibility of conventional military activity by the African guerrilla states against South Africa, Rhodesia, and Portugal seems chimerical now in view of the military balance, as Premier Chou has observed on occasion, the African situation is excellent for a Chinese-style combination of political and limited warfare, in which the enemy's use of his conventional military strength only drives the uncommitted forces into opposition. It is possible that, with the elimination of Lin Piao and his military-industrial complex in Peking, the application of Mao Tse-tung's 'revolutionary diplomatic line' may become a means of dressing up normalization of Peking's foreign relations in revolutionary rhetoric. This remains to be seen.

Notes

1 Joint editorial of *Red Flag, Liberation Army Daily*, and *People's Daily* (Peking), trans. in *Peking Review*, no. 32, 6 August 1971, pp. 7 ff.
2 See W.A.C. Adie, 'China's Second Liberation in Perspective', *Bulletin of the Atomic Scientists*, February 1969, vol. xxv, no. 2, p. 16. (This issue is now available as a paperback book from Vintage Press, New York.)

3 *New China News Agency* (NCNA), 24 November 1968.
4 *Le Monde Diplomatique*, December 1970, p. 26.
5 Mostly to be found in *Selected Military Writings of Mao Tse-tung (SMW)*, Foreign Languages Press, Peking (PFLP), 1963. See also Mao Tse-tung, *Basic Tactics*, trans. and with an introduction by Stuart Schram, Pall Mall Press, London, 1966.
6 Mao Tse-tung, *On Contradiction*, PFLP, 1958, p. 21.
7 Mao Tse-tung, *Oppose the Party Eight-legged Essay*, PFLP, 1960, p. 6. See also *Rectify the Party's Style in Work*, PFLP, 1955, p. 28.
8 Sun Tzu, *The Art of War*, trans. Samuel B. Griffith, Clarendon Press, Oxford, 1963, p. 76.
9 Mao Tse-tung, 'On Coalition Government', excerpted in *SMW*, p. 300.
10 Mao Tse-tung, 'Struggle in the Chingkang Mountains', *SMW*, 1963, p. 27.
11 'Documents on British Foreign Policy 1919–39', second series, vol. 10, *Far Eastern Affairs*, March-October 1932, pp. 690–1.
12 'Our Study and the Current Situation', PFLP, 1960, p. 6.
13 Mu Fu-sheng, *The Wilting of the 100 Flowers*, New York, 1963, p. 244. On the special factors in Chinese political culture which favour this process see Lucian Pye, *The Spirit of Chinese Politics*, MIT Press, Cambridge, Mass., 1968.
14 R.C. North and Xenia J. Eudin, *M.N. Roy's Mission to China*, University of California Press, 1963, pp. 363–4.
15 Nym Wales (Mrs Edgar Snow), 'Yenan Notebooks' (mimeographed), quoted in *China Quarterly*, no. 22, 1965, p. 197.
16 Liu Shao-chi, 'The Victory of Marxism-Leninism in China', PFLP, 1959, p. 9.
17 See Li Wei-han, 'The Characteristics of the Chinese People's Democratic United Front', *Red Flag*, no. 12, 16 June 1961, trans. in *Selections from China Mainland Magazines (SCMM)*, no. 268, Hong Kong, 3 July 1961; also 'The United Front Is a Magic Wand with Which the Chinese People Win Victory', *SCMM*, no. 266, 19 June 1961 (*Red Flag*, no. 11, 1 June 1961) and 'The Struggle for Proletarian Hegemony during the Period of the New Democratic Revolution' (Current Background, CB, no. 678, 5 March 1962 – People's Daily 9–11 February 1962). These articles stress that 'imperialism' forced 'the people' to counter-encircle it, and since they constitute 90 per cent of the world's population, 'The East wind has prevailed over the West wind', *SCMM*, no. 268, p. 23.
18 See section on the three stages of protracted war in Mao's 'On the Protracted War', PFLP, 1954, pp. 43–65. During the strategic defensive the revolutionary forces carry out small, quick-decision offensives. *Even in defence, attack is primary*. War is the politics of bloodshed, which sometimes demands an extremely high price; partial and temporary sacrifice is made for general and permanent preservation (p. 79). During the strategic stalemate, territory falls into three categories: enemy base areas, our base areas, and the contested or intermediate zone. In this stage, we switch a large proportion of our troops from the front to the enemy's rear to build up subversive forces; the enemy is worn down (a) by fighting (b) by spread of anti-war sentiment in their rear by our 'special forces'. Once this has gone far enough, we go over to the offensive. On the world scale, the intermediate zone consists of the small and middle powers, especially in Asia, Africa, and Latin America.
19 'The Question of Independence and Autonomy within the United Front', PFLP, 1954 (=*SMW*, p. 289).
20 George Moseley, Policy of the CPR towards Minority Peoples in South China, PhD Dissertation, Oxford, 1970.

21 Opening speech by Liu Shao-chi at the Trade Union Congress of Asian and Australasian countries, 'For a Lasting Peace, for a People's Democracy', 30 December 1939, p. 14; quoted in Tang Tsou and Morton H. Halperin, 'Mao Tse-tung's Revolutionary Strategy and Peking's International Behaviour', *American Political Science Review*, vol. lix, no. 4, March 1965, pp. 80 ff.

22 'The Politics of the Chinese Red Army', trans. Chester Cheng, Hoover Institution, 1966; original on microfilm at Chatham House, London. Hereinafter referred to as 'Bulletins'.

23 'Commemorating the Thirtieth Anniversary of the Publication of the *Shih-chieh chih-shih*', *Shih-chieh chih-shih,* 10 September 1964, p. 1; cited in Tang Tsou and M. Halperin, *op. cit.*, p. 83.

24 The Maoist attitude to our 'bourgeois' world system of international law, diplomacy, etc. has, understandably, been 'if we can use it, use it; otherwise, smash it and if possible replace it'. See W.A.C. Adie, 'China's Diplomatic Breakthrough', *Mizan*, London, October 1971, p. 65.

25 Bulletins, p. 480.

26 Ibid., p. 485.

27 The relevant passage reads in part:

> Among the independent countries in Africa, if only one or two of them complete a real national revolution, solving their own problem of resisting imperialism and reaching an internal...democratic national revolution, the effect will be very great, the time ripe for action, the revolutionary wave will swallow up the whole African continent... we should take a long-range view of this problem.

Here terms such as 'democratic national revolution' must be interpreted in the Chinese sense; i.e. a struggle led from the start by Marxist-Leninist-Maoists and proceeding without interruption to the 'building of socialism and communism'.

28 See W.A.C. Adie, 'China's Year in Africa', in Colin Legum and John Drysdale (eds), *Africa Contemporary Record*, London, 1969, 1970, 1971. See also W.A.C. Adie, *Conflict Studies:* no. 10, 'The Communist Powers in Africa', and no. 12, 'China, Israel and the Arabs', Institute for the Study of Conflict, London, December 1970 and May 1971.

Further Reading: on aspects of the matters treated here, see also Tang Tsou and Morton H. Halperin, 'Mao Tse-tung's Revolutionary Strategy and Peking's International Behaviour', in *American Political Science Review,* no. 59, 1965, pp. 80–99; Ralph L. Powell, 'Maoist Military Doctrines', in *Asian Survey*, April 1968; Michael Oksenberg, 'The Strategies of Peking', in *Foreign Affairs*, October 1971, pp. 15 ff.; David Mozingo, 'The Maoist Imprint on China's Foreign Policy', in *China Briefing*, University of Chicago Press, 1968, pp. 23 ff.

Sino-Japanese Relations in Flux

D.H. MENDEL

Now that the United States has returned Okinawa to Japan, China policy is the most crucial and divisive issue in Japanese politics. It divides the ruling Liberal Democratic Party (LDP) more than any other issue in the postwar history of conservative rule, and arouses more public interest and debate than it does in any other nation, because of the long contact between Japan and both mainland China and Taiwan. The Nixon visit to China early in 1972, after the United Nations voted to replace the Nationalist regime by its rival, the People's Republic of China, had a severe impact inside Japan, dividing almost every party and organization. With a world-wide swing toward Peking, how will the most advanced economic and democratic power in Asia adjust to the new environment? One thesis of this paper is the writer's belief that Japan's China policy has been dictated more by external than by domestic forces in the past two decades and that this is likely to be the case in the future.

Even the four opposition parties, which had accused the Sato Cabinet and its Liberal Democratic Party predecessors of shamelessly following American imperialist policy on China for a generation, changed about last summer in demanding that Sato should visit Peking because Nixon had announced his planned visit on 15 July 1971. The writer was spending that summer as usual in Tokyo and witnessed the confusion among both government and opposition ranks, not to mention the six Taiwanese independence groups in Tokyo whose leaders were even more uncertain how to react to the announcement. The writer, who has studied the China issue in Japanese politics since 1952, had never seen such confusion, concern, and demands for independent Japanese action, combined with a lack of consensus on what Japan should do. In the following year a pro-Peking, anti-Taiwan consensus began to emerge at all levels, but the initiative to influence eventual Japanese policy remains more in Washington and Peking than in Japan.

The writer is best known as a specialist in Japanese opinion polls on foreign policy and is often criticized by those who feel that only the executive elite decide foreign policy.[1] He has also been ostracized by many conservative members of the LDP for charging that the Cabinet ignored majority public opinion on American military bases, Okinawa, and China policy.[2] Yet in all polls the Japanese have been more ambivalent toward China and Taiwan than on any other international issue, reflecting perhaps its complexity and also Japan's unique past relations with China and Taiwan. Japanese public attitudes toward trade and diplomatic relations will be discussed later in connection with official policy, but it is appropriate to begin with the Japanese public images of China because they form the basis of more specific attitudes and even of government policy.

First, every domestic and foreign scholar emphasizes the Japanese cultural debt to Chinese civilization, beginning in prehistoric times when a majority of mainland immigrants whose descendants now populate Japan came from China via the Korean peninsula and the Ryukyu chain. Japan adopted her written language, Buddhism, many painting and art forms, and the Confucian ethic from the mainland between the fourth and ninth centuries A.D. She allowed Chinese trade during the Tokugawa seclusion centuries (1620–1854) but learned far more from contact with the Netherlands, the only other foreign nation permitted to send ships to Nagasaki. Respect for Chinese art, literature, and culinary talents has remained strong throughout the centuries to this very day, whereas in the nineteenth century Japanese came to look down upon Chinese political and economic weaknesses. Englishmen may still regard French cuisine as superior to their own, but they do not feel so superior to continental Europe in other areas of life.

Second, almost all Japanese today regret the actions of their prewar military forces in China, if not in Manchuria, especially in the second Sino-Japanese war of 1937–45, and wish to apologize for past injury in any way possible. Peking's charges of Japanese remilitarization are based on this recent past, and every Japanese visitor to the People's Republic is reminded of his nation's crimes. But, though the people of mainland China suffered most from Japanese imperialism, the People's Republic has benefited, and its rival, the Kuomintang in Taipei, has suffered. Hence every Japanese visitor to postwar Taiwan has been told by his Nationalist hosts to repent Japan's prime responsibility for causing the KMT to lose the civil war on the mainland and to be grateful for the KMT's postwar support of the Japanese imperial system and for its refusal to demand reparations. Native Taiwanese on the other hand praise Japan for its half-century of colonial rule over Taiwan and have reason to demand nothing but support of their right to independence. How does a Japanese feel after visiting both mainland China and Taiwan? His confusion is understandable and helps to explain the mixed image of the two Chinas in all Japanese opinion polls.

National polls for every month since 1957 showed that China is the second least-liked foreign nation, although the degree of dislike declined during 1971. Typically about 20 per cent of Japanese named China as their 'most-disliked nation', second only to the Soviet Union, in the *Jiji* Press monthly surveys which began in 1957, while the percentage naming China as 'best-liked nation' rose from 2 to 10.[3] By contrast the United States' image as 'best-liked nation' has dropped from 50 to 20 per cent in the past decade, mainly due to the Vietnam war. Dislike of Peking's nuclear policy has been a major factor in Japanese attitudes to China, especially as every political party (except the Communist party for a brief period) condemned China's nuclear tests. Pacifism has been the dominant theme in all Japanese opinion surveys since 1945, so that one would expect a majority of Japanese to oppose the People's Republic's attacks on Nationalist offshore islands as much as Nationalist threats against the mainland or United States actions in Vietnam.

The Cultural Revolution (1965–8) also antagonized most Japanese, because of both the attacks on innocent Japanese in China and the tendency of Japanese radicals to use Maoist tactics in their very unpopular civil disobedience movements.[4] Moreover Peking's charges that the Sato Cabinet was reactionary and militarist drew mixed reactions from Japanese who were increasingly opposed to the Sato regime but did not agree with Peking's extreme criticisms.[5] Few Japanese named China as a foreign country they would like to visit, but most wanted Tokyo to recognize both Peking and Taipei diplomatically and to end all restrictions on trade with the mainland and on travel. In short the Japanese people, who are surveyed more efficiently than the people of almost any other nation, like Chinese culture and want to have both economic and political relations with the Peking regime, but they dislike its militaristic policies. As Peking moderates its foreign policy image by its reconciliation with Washington, Ethiopia, Iran, and other conservative governments, the Japanese people's resentment of the People's Republic's past policies may be overcome by the basically positive desire to cement friendly economic, cultural, and trade ties with Japan's most important neighbor. As on other issues, the public will follow its leaders' policies, but on the China issue the ambivalence of public attitudes toward China and Taiwan gives the political elite more options than on the issue of United States bases, to which public opinion has been strongly opposed for a generation.[6]

Japanese policy toward China and Taiwan was determined by the nature of the San Francisco peace treaty of 1951 when the United States and its allies did not invite either Chinese regime to participate but the American government strongly urged the Japanese government to sign a bilateral treaty with the Chinese Nationalists. Premier Yoshida acceded to this urging partly because the United Nations recognized the Taipei regime as China and condemned Peking for aggression in Korea. Moreover the Yoshida regime was very pro-American and anti-communist, traits passed on to Yoshida's protegés (Ikeda and Sato) and even successors (notably Kishi), who hated old Yoshida. Few of the two hundred members of the Japanese Diet interviewed by the writer since 1952 really considered that the Chiang clique on Taiwan represented China; and most of them favored maximum trade with both Chinese regimes and looked forward to the eventual establishment of relations with the People's Republic. 'But we must await a change in United Nation and American policy' was the usual conservative attitude, while most opposition politicians were openly pro-Peking.

Also no Japanese of any political stripe thought that the People's Republic would long remain allied with Russia because they considered Chinese and Russians to be historic enemies despite their common ideology. They predicted the Sino-Soviet split long before it erupted publicly: one of the writer's best informants was Yoshio Shiga, veteran Japanese Communist Party (JCP) leader purged for voting for the Test Ban Treaty, and spurned by his Soviet friends who knew that the JCP mainstream would eventually become anti-Peking.

Postwar Japan faithfully supported Taipei's representation in the United Nations throughout the 1957–71 period, going down to defeat with the United States, Australia, New Zealand, and other pro-Nationalist delegations who favored the two-China compromise at the 1971 United Nations General Assembly (UNGA) vote. Many LDP factional leaders warned Sato not to support the United States compromise resolution which they knew would fail. Some of the writer's friends in the Japanese Foreign Ministry noted the dismal past record of the Italian study committee resolution as proof that anything less than expulsion of the discredited KMT regime would fail in the United Nations Assembly, especially after the announcement of Nixon's trip to Peking and of United States support for a seat in the United Nations for the People's Republic.[7]

Officially Japan espoused a policy of separating trade from politics in its dealings with Peking and Taipei. This would maximize trade, the keystone of postwar Japan's foreign policy, and minimize her involvement in the Chinese civil war. Peaceful settlement of all disputes was the other theme of Japan's postwar policy and public opinion strongly opposed any military commitment overseas or even major rearmament at home, so that every Japanese Cabinet has spurned suggestions from Washington, Seoul, and Taipei to join in a Pacific Defense Pact or convert the Asian and Pacific Council (ASPAC) towards that end.[8]

Trade and investment deserve major attention in this paper because until 1972 Taiwan provided Japan with more profitable economic opportunities than mainland China did. Table 2 shows the comparative trade statistics for 1960–71 and demonstrates graphically why no Japanese government wishes to sacrifice trade with either partner. It does not show that Japan has investments of over $100 million in Taiwan and many other economic ties resulting from its fifty years of colonial rule before 1945 and a major share of American postwar economic aid ($1·7 billion economic and $2·5 billion military) to postwar Taiwan. Even in trade alone Japan made $500 million profit from Taiwan in 1971 after six years of a progressively wider gap between her exports and imports to her former colony. Some Japanese argue that the Taiwan market is more lucrative than the mainland market, but others retort that the mainland has much greater potential for the future if only Japanese skills are applied to People's Republic development programs.

Tokyo permitted two credit sales to mainland China before 1963 and then bowed to Nationalist Chinese objections by having former Premier Yoshida send a private letter to Nationalist officials promising that no more government credit would be used to promote exports to the mainland. The 'Yoshida letter' has been one of the

TABLE 2

Japanese Trade with China and Taiwan 1960–71

(in US$ '000)

	PEOPLE'S REPUBLIC OF CHINA		REPUBLIC OF CHINA (TAIWAN)	
	Exports	**Imports**	**Exports**	**Imports**
1960	2 726	20 729	87 208	63 485
1961	16 639	30 895	104 027	60 881
1962	38 460	46 020	106 777	57 896
1963	62 417	74 579	97 095	118 420
1964	152 739	157 750	140 418	140 076
1965	245 036	224 705	206 054	151 631
1966	315 150	306 237	230 447	141 716
1967	288 294	269 439	314 679	134 794
1968	325 438	224 185	423 828	151 898
1969	390 803	234 540	489 233	178 853
1970	568 878	253 818	582 050	235 550
1971	577 575	322 168	767 352	267 039

Source: *Far Eastern Economic Review* (Hong Kong), 4 March 1972, pp. 44, 68.

most controversial issues in Sino-Japanese relations since 1964, as Peking demands its retraction and the Tokyo Cabinet equivocates in order to appease Taipei, Washington, and its own right-wing elite, while recognizing that a majority of the Japanese opposition parties and the public favor almost unlimited trade with the mainland. Two former Japanese foreign ministers assured the writer that Washington had exerted private pressures against Japanese credit sales to Peking, but this has been denied by all American officials. Ambiguity and hypocrisy may be typical of Japan's China policy just as Britain was accused of having perfidious tendencies in an earlier age: 'No permanent enemies or allies, only permanent interests' is a law of world politics.

Peking and Taipei both opposed Japan's efforts to separate trade from politics and attempted to extort diplomatic concessions for trade privileges, but this attempt has been ineffective because both Chinese regimes need their trade with Japan more than she does. Moreover 'face' is far more important to a Chinese regime than to

Japan. But the contradictory pressures created intense debate within the LDP majority and its business allies. The twin shocks of 1971 (the United Nations vote on China and Nixon's trip to Peking) intensified domestic debate in Japan and the pro-Peking pressure to make diplomatic concessions to Peking. That is why the LDP censured its former foreign minister, Fujiyama, for having approved Peking's demand for abrogation of the 1952 Japan-Nationalist peace treaty despite widespread LDP sympathy for Fujiyama's position. LDP factional competition to succeed Sato as party leader and premier in 1972 made the factional leaders more likely to use China policy as a political football inside the party.

Peking has always tried to divide the LDP and lure the Japanese opposition parties (except the Communist party) by claiming that the current LDP prime minister is hostile to the People's Republic and that only a change in cabinet would facilitate better relations.[9] As all Japanese see mainland China chiefly from an economic point of view, Peking can demand political concessions in return for expanded trade whenever Japanese businessmen or politicians visit there. The fact that the People's Republic has not prevented the dramatic increase in Sino-Japanese trade shown in Table 2 should show visiting Japanese that its threats carry little weight, but it has failed to do so. Many more Japanese firms reduced their Taiwan investment after the summer of 1971, and leaders of the Socialist, Democratic Socialist, and Komeito parties all told Chou En-lai of their 'One China' support. Anti-Sato factional leaders, including former Foreign Minister Miki, also became visibly more pro-Peking in an attempt to earn domestic political prestige in the post-Sato era; the national press moved in the same direction.

The writer is a specialist in Japanese public opinion and has followed the results of dozens of polls on China policy, including several that he has sponsored since 1958. As in American polls on China and Vietnam, the results are ambiguous, depending on the timing and the question.[10] On the issue of recognition of mainland China, for example, about 40 to 50 per cent expressed support during the 1960s and probably more would do so today. Yet only one-tenth of those who wanted to establish diplomatic relations with Peking also wanted to cancel relations with Taiwan. In other words the majority of the Japanese people want to have relations with both the People's Republic and Nationalist China just as its leaders want trade and friendly contacts with both regimes. Even late in 1971, when Chinese representation at the United Nations became a

116

critical issue, the polls showed a majority in favor of Japanese support for a seat for Taipei and Peking.[11]

It is impossible to detail the poll results here, but Table 3 gives some of the more significant data on the Japanese preference for amicable relations with both China and Taiwan. It also shows their reluctance to accept Peking's terms for 'One China' politically and economically and the widespread support by native Taiwanese for an independent Taiwan. Peking claims that only the Sato clique favors Taiwanese separatism, and the public stands of all four opposition parties and most LDP factions tend to substantiate that claim. No nation has a better system of opinion surveys or a more literate public than Japan, however, so the degree of support for a Taiwan free of mainland rule is impressive. But this question has been avoided in almost all native Japanese polls due to the extreme sensitivity of Taipei and Peking to the 'independent Taiwan' issue which inhibits Japanese supporters of either regime from raising the question.[12]

Equally important, the Japanese public is opposed to any use of military force in East Asia: by either China to attack the other, or by United States or Japanese forces to protect South Korea, Taiwan, or any country in Southeast Asia. Thus, though most of the attentive, educated public in Japan favor a free Taiwan, few would want their government to give material support to make Taiwan independent, even to prevent Taiwan from falling into communist hands. The same reluctance would be found in any American opinion poll after the Vietnam experience.

The Nippon Hoso Kyokai (NHK) poll of September 1971 showed only 11 per cent favoring the position that Taiwan is a part of China and hence that Japan should cancel her relations with Taiwan in order to accommodate the People's Republic. But another 28 per cent showed themselves willing to cancel those relations if necessary, compared with 39 per cent who wanted relations with both the mainland and Taiwan. A subsequent national survey by the *Jiji* press agency in November 1971 also showed a reduction of those favoring ties with both Chinas and an increased willingness to cancel relations with Taiwan in order to meet Peking's terms: 58 per cent wanted to normalize relations with Peking 'as soon as possible' and one-third of them were prepared to sever ties with Taiwan. This was an increase over a similar survey made in April 1971, and all indications point to further public acceptance of the pro-Peking position.[13] Moreover the same *Jiji* sample was asked if Japan should

TABLE 3

Japanese Political Views of China and Taiwan[a]

1 'Japan now has diplomatic relations with the Republic of China on Taiwan but not with Communist China (the People's Republic). Should Japan recognize Communist China or maintain its present policy?'

Recognize Peking 44%   Keep status-quo 20%   Don't know 37%
(Feb. 1970, N = 2 255)

(*If favor recognition*) What should we do about relations with Taiwan?
Keep as now 78%   Cancel 6%   Don't know 15%
(N = subtotal of 44% above)

2 'Should Taiwan in the future be an independent Taiwanese nation, part of Communist China, or ruled now by Nationalist China?'

	Dec. 1962	Nov. 1966	Feb. 1970
Independent Taiwan	33%	27%	31%
Communist Taiwan	6	3	5
Nationalist Taiwan	20	18	24
Don't know	41	52	40
Sample size	2 003	2 258	2 255
Plurality for independence[b]	+7	+6	+2

1970 sample subgroup pluralities for Taiwan independence:

Men over 50	0	Prof. occupations	+22
Univ. education	+11	LDP voters	− 2
		JSP voters	+ 2
	Univ. educ. opposition voters	+27	
	Pro-Japan defense buildup	+ 9	
	Fear of USSR attack	+15	

118

3 'Should Japan permit US forces to defend Taiwan if it is attacked by Communist China?'

    Yes 15% No 38% Don't know 47% Total 100%

                                      (Feb. 1970, N = 2 255)

4 'Should Japan give military aid to protect Taiwan if Communist China attacked it?'

    Yes 8% No 53% Don't know 39% Total 100%

                                        (Feb. 1970, N = 2 255)

5 'If Japan established diplomatic relations with China, our relations with the Nationalists on Taiwan would be a big problem, so what should we do about those relations?'

Cancel them because Taiwan is a part of China	11%
Keep relations with Taiwan while building them with China	39%
Not important to protect Taiwan relations to get China relations	28%
Other 3% Don't know 19%	(Sept. 1971, N = 2 523)

6 'Are you very interested in the China representation debate now going on in the United Nations?'

    Yes 23% Slightly 46% No 21% Don't know 10%

[a]Data in items 1–4 taken from the writer's sponsored surveys in 1962, 1966, and 1970; items 5 and 6 from NHK Japan national radio-TV network survey, 26–7 September 1971, on the eve of the United Nations debate.

[b]Plurality derived by subtracting pro-Peking and pro-KMT opinion from pro-Taiwan percentage. Mendel data in *Asian Survey*, December 1970, pp. 1046–69; NHK data in *Yoron Chosa* (monthly), December 1971, pp. 40–5. This excellent government journal is available from the Japan Government Service Center.

apologize or pay reparations to mainland China for damage inflicted in the Sino-Japanese war (1937–45): 57 per cent said an apology was necessary, 27 per cent favored reparations, and 32 per cent opposed them.

The trend of Japanese opinion is obviously in favor of concessions to Peking on the Taiwan issue, credit-based trade, and even reparations. Only one-tenth of the Japanese consider Peking an invasion threat, but three times as many are worried about Chinese military power in general.[14] The Japanese conservative elite, both political and economic, is more concerned about retaining its profitable economic relationship with Taiwan than with maintaining the Japan-Nationalist China peace treaty of 1952 or 'with other aspects of political relations. They note that Taipei is moving to broaden its trade by seeking contacts with Eastern Europe and other areas not previously considered friendly. If Taipei loses confidence in Washington, as Peking hopes it will, it may welcome non-political relations with almost any other nation, especially Japan. In March 1972 Professor Edwin Reischauer told a symposium on the future of Taiwan that continued United States and Japanese economic relations with Taiwan were most vital, because diplomatic relations may be sacrificed in the drive toward reconciliation with Peking.[15]

This makes even more relevant the 1971 prediction of the Japanese consular official in Hong Kong that Peking will continue to tolerate privately more Japan trade and investment in Taiwan and South Korea than it will approve publicly. The Japanese enjoyed more trade than ever before with both Chinas during most of the 1960s despite vigorous insistence by Peking and Taipei that they would not separate trade from politics. Now that Peking rather than Taipei has more international initiative, perhaps Taipei will accept a trade relationship without a diplomatic one, as Peking has done in the past. The Taipei record since 1972 bears this out.

Japanese governments have tolerated the presence of hundreds of Taiwanese independence activists for the past twenty years, despite demands from Taipei to suppress, punish, or deport them. Japanese immigration policy normally refuses to permit an alien to acquire Japanese citizenship if his native country objects, as both Chinas and Koreas do, so that most of the 25 000 Taiwanese resident in Japan are either nominal Chinese aliens (with permanent resident status if they resided prior to April 1952) or stateless persons (if Nationalist China denounced them or they renounced their Nationalist passports). The Sato government has deported two or three Taiwanese in the latter category to Taiwan at her request, and would have deported more if the Japanese press, courts, and academic world had not objected strongly. In the future some of the approximately 500 Taiwanese activists will follow those who voluntarily returned to Taiwan in 1971, while others will seek a freer political life in the United States or reduce their activity in Japan. Few have ever violated Japanese law or employed the kind of violence typical of the two extremes in Japanese politics, but from now on it will be Peking's pressure on Tokyo, rather than Nationalist pressure, that forces any Tokyo regime to minimize its own sympathy for the Taiwanese and warn them against embarrassing political activity.

Recent pressures on Japan to recognize Peking as the only China, with Taiwan as part of that China, have come mostly from abroad: for example, from Nixon's new China policy and from Peking's own drive for world recognition. Domestic pressures, as has been usual since 1945, have played a lesser role because the dominant Liberal-Democrats can afford to ignore opposition voices most of the time. Therefore it was less the pro-Peking stance of the four opposition parties (with the possible exception of the JCP) than the split in LDP ranks away from Sato's pro-Taiwan policy that caused the government dilemma. Business leaders, usually LDP supporters, were more attracted to China after 1969, and several LDP faction leaders made pilgrimages to Peking. The press, called part of the establishment by some observers but not by this writer, added its voice to the pro-Peking chorus. The public had always favored a rapprochement with the People's Republic, especially for economic, cultural, and disarmament reasons, and had never supported any militant anti-communist crusade even when LDP Cabinets paid lip-service to the anti-communist policies of Washington and its Far Eastern allies.

The normal erosion of intraparty and public support for a prime minister after six years' tenure of office reduced Sato's power and made him vulnerable to LDP factional attacks after the two Nixon shocks of 1971. China policy was always a time-bomb in the LDP majority party, and Peking astutely played on Sato's weakened position inside his own party and in opinion polls. Non-interference in the future status of Taiwan, admission that the People's Republic is the internationally-recognized China, and approval of government credit for sales to China are the three major concessions of the Sato Cabinet since the United Nations vote late in 1971. Sato's successor

Tanaka followed world and domestic trends and made further moves towards the 'One China-Peking' policy now demanded by a near-majority of the Diet and press, including even the abandonment of political relations with the embattled Nationalist regime in Taiwan and with its native majority.

Notes

1 See the writer's *The Japanese People and Foreign Policy*, University of California Press, 1961, reprinted by Greenwood Press, 1971, and Edwin O. Reischauer's foreword to that book, which was contested by Donald Hellmann in his study of *Japanese Domestic Politics and Foreign Policy: The Peace Agreement with the Soviet Union*, University of California Press, 1969. Hellmann contends that only the Prime Minister's mainstream faction of the LDP controls foreign policy.

2 See, for example, the writer's 'Japanese Views of Sato's Foreign Policy: The Credibility Gap', *Asian Survey*, vol. vii, no. 7, July 1967, pp. 444–56. Related articles include 'Japanese Defense in the 1970s: The Public View', *Asian Survey*, vol. x, no. 12, December 1970, pp. 1046–69, and 'Japanese Views of the American Alliance in the Seventies', *Public Olinion Quarterly*, *(POQ)*, vol. 35, winter 1971–2, pp. 521–38.

3 D.H. Mendel, 'Japanese Views . . .', *POQ, op. cit.*, and every monthly issue of *Shukan Jiji* (Weekly *Jiji*), Tokyo. According to the 20 February 1972 *Jiji* poll 9 per cent liked China best and 15 per cent named China as most-disliked nation, a marked improvement over past years' results when over 25 per cent cited China as most-disliked. By contrast the 1972 sample named the USSR (25 per cent) and North Korea (20 per cent) as the least-favored nations.

4 Several Japanese businessmen and newsmen were arrested and physically abused during the Cultural Revolution, and two JCP visitors were beaten by visiting Japanese youth at Peking Airport so that they had to be carried aboard a waiting North Korean plane. Ultra-leftist groups in Japan seized universities, occupied

major transport terminals in Tokyo, and even killed some of their renegade members in early 1972. The moderation inside China since 1969 greatly improved her image in Japan.

5 A *Jiji* poll conducted from 10–13 November 1971 and reported in *Yamato Shimbun*, Tokyo, 27 November 1971, showed only 12 per cent agreeing that Japan was remilitarized (42 per cent disagreed and 20 per cent partly disagreed). *Jiji*'s early 1972 samples opposed the Sato Cabinet by a 58–22 margin.

6 See the writer's articles cited above for majority public opposition to any United States military bases in mainland Japan or Okinawa. Japanese views on Taiwan are given in the writer's *The Politics of Formosan Nationalism,* University of California Press, 1970, one chapter of which was summarized in 'Japanese Policy and Views toward Formosa', *Journal of Asian Studies,* vol. xxviii, no. 3, May 1969, pp. 513–34.

7 The writer's friends on the Policy Planning Council of the State Department agreed with this viewpoint, citing the dismal UNGA treatment of the Italian Resolution for a study committee to solve the Chinese representation deadlock. (The United States and Japan voted for it, but most pro-Peking and pro-Nationalist delegations opposed what would have been a good move.) Both Chinese regimes denounced any attempt to divide the Chinese seat, much less to create a separate Taiwan seat, a move which would have been anathema to them.

8 The late Kawashima Shojiro, deputy Prime Minister in the mid-1960s, told the writer that Japan could never permit ASPAC to evolve into a military alliance, and Taipei chastised Tokyo for cowardice in the face of the Asian communist threat in many official statements and press editorials. Taipei always favored independence for Okinawa rather than its reversion to Japan, feeling that Tokyo would not permit continued United States military bases on that strategic island.

9 Chou En-lai has told every visiting Japanese group that Sato must go before he will welcome a Japanese prime minister, claiming that Sato is more anti-Peking, pro-militarist, and reactionary than Richard Nixon. The difference is rather that Nixon heads a superpower regime, while Sato's days are numbered and most potential successors are more sympathetic toward the PRC. Chou may also anticipate far more economic development aid from Japan if he continues the past cold line toward Tokyo.

10 Many Japanese press polls use complex alternatives from which the respondent must choose; they also tend to report mainly the pro-Peking opinions and play down the many cool responses toward Chinese nuclear tests, the military stance generally, and the 'One China' demand.

11 Most Japanese poll results show a preference for compromise and for avoiding extreme choices.

12 Most Diet members, China specialists in the Tokyo press, and officials at the Japanese consulate-general in Hong Kong confirmed this to the writer in the summer of 1971. Despite three years' effort by the writer and dozens of influential friends, no Japanese publisher would risk even a subsidized Japanese translation edition of his 1970 Formosan nationalism book.

13 *Yamato Shimbun,* 27 November 1971, gave the *Jiji* results: in April 1971 only 9 per cent favored severing relations with Taiwan, compared with 19 per cent in November, and there was a similar rise in the percentage of those who felt that it would be necessary to sever Taiwan relations before Peking would permit reconciliation. Japanese veteran newsmen of the *Mainichi* who attended the March 1972 Taiwan symposium in New York confirmed this pro-Peking trend to the writer.

14 Results of a *Jiji* poll on military threat, conducted in February 1972 and reported in the April 1972 issue of *Yoron Chosa,* the monthly journal of the Public Information Office, Prime Minister's Office, Tokyo. The writer's 1970 survey on invasion fears was reported in the *POQ* article cited above.

15 United States-Japan Symposium on the Future of Taiwan, Biltmore Hotel, New York, 25 March 1972, sponsored by President Kagehisa Toyama of Radio Kanto, Tokyo, who favored a union of Taiwanese and mainlanders on Taiwan to create a 'Republic of Taiwan', with foreign observers to report results of a Taiwan plebiscite on whether or not to join the mainland. Reischauer told the group that independence was the best and most probable future of the island, if only the KMT would reorganize its regime to make it a genuine popular democracy or even if the status quo *de facto* separation could be preserved for another generation.

New Zealand's China Policies:
A Review and a Prospect

W.T. ROY

Domestic and foreign critics of New Zealand foreign policy frequently make the glib statement that until fairly recently New Zealand had no foreign policy at all. This clearly reflects either an attitude of mind that mistakes gibes for arguments, or (to be more charitable) failure to appreciate a fundamental characteristic of New Zealand's experience as a nation: namely that, owing largely to circumstances unlikely ever to be duplicated, her history bears little relation to her geographical position.

From time to time states have attempted to isolate themselves from the main currents of world events by fostering autarchic policies, in the belief that their resource base was good enough to ensure their success. Indeed the Chinese empire has at times provided a good example of this attitude. Alternatively isolation has sometimes been achieved at the rather daunting cost of rejecting improvements in standards of living: the hermit-crab policies of Tokugawa Japan (1639–1853) come readily to mind as an example. However, most states relate to their neighbours in fairly predictable ways, and international relations theorists seem in general to agree that the main objectives of foreign policy are: first, the preservation of political independence; second, the improvement or at very least the maintenance of living standards; and third, the protection of the cultural identity of the nation or society against corruption by alien values and ways of life. New Zealand has in fact pursued these very objectives, but in an oblique manner rendered possible only by her unique historical circumstances. To ignore those circumstances, or to judge that manner by twentieth-century criteria of what constitutes the prudent pursuit of self-interest by a state, inevitably gives to New Zealand policies in the nineteenth century an appearance of absurdity that they do not really merit.

In the first place New Zealand was settled by colonists almost exclusively of British stock at a time when Britain was a near unchallenged global power. Secondly her economic development was based on an unparalleled endowment for the rapid production of pastoral commodities on an industrial as distinct from a subsistence scale. Thirdly an urbanized, industrialized Britain provided a steady market for these products, especially after the introduction of refrigerated cargo ships (1882). All three factors combined to produce a high degree of dependence on a distant metropolitan centre, linked only by long sea-lanes and a cultural tradition which was cherished by New Zealanders a good deal more than the British – particularly the ruling classes – believed. In effect New Zealand adopted a ludicrous posture and behaviour, based on the illusion that she was an offshore island of Great Britain instead of a remote antipodean dependency singularly vulnerable to coercion by any maritime power stronger than Britain. Nevertheless, since no such power appeared in the South Pacific until the closing years of the nineteenth century, a 'foreign policy' of dependence on Britain was not as absurd as it would have been in different circumstances. Indeed the policy served quite adequately to fulfil the first two objectives of foreign policy noted above.

It is in analyzing New Zealand's pursuit of the third objective, the protection of the cultural identity of the nation, that we find clues to the development of distinctly independent policies towards her Asian neighbours, and consequently the germ of a 'China policy'. Notwithstanding her basic acceptance of a cosy dependence on Britain, she did from time to time indulge in imperial fantasies in which she saw herself as the agent of British hegemony in the South Pacific. Angus Ross[1] gives ample evidence of the enthusiasm for such policies exhibited by notables like Sir George Grey, Sir Julius Vogel, and R.J. Seddon. B.K. Gordon cites the example of Charles Buller prophesying in 1845 to the House of Commons in declamatory tones that the new dominion 'might give laws and manners to a new world, upholding subject races, and imposing your will on the strong'.[2] Of course Buller was speaking from the security of Westminster, and successive British governments quickly quelled the extravagant ambitions of this brash South Seas colony, but the existence of support in New Zealand for such policies shows a zanily chauvinistic frame of mind that partly explains the nature of her first relations with China. Frustrated imperialism abroad was compensated for by frankly racist immigration legislation at home, and its prime target was the Chinese.

Restrictive immigration legislation was sparked off by the entry of Chinese gold-miners to New Zealand in the 1860s. Uncritical, hostile attitudes to these newcomers were not locally generated, but adopted from Australian and British immigrants to the Otago and West Coast gold-fields. These immigrants arrived in New Zealand with a ready-made set of prejudices, which projected a highly unfavourable stereotype of the Chinese and aroused widespread agitation against them. Seddon in particular was the most persistent architect of restrictive immigration laws, directed where possible against Asians in general and the Chinese in particular. The Immigration Acts of 1881, 1888, 1896, 1899, and 1907 incorporated humiliating regulations governing the entry and exit of Chinese. New Zealand not only received protests from the Chinese government, but also came under some pressure from Britain to moderate her legislation. For example, at the Colonial Conference of 1897 Joseph Chamberlain, then Colonial Secretary, hinted strongly that New Zealand legislation should not embarrass Britain in her relations with China. In short the early record of New Zealand's relations with China was anything but happy and mainly of her own making.

After the turn of the century hostility towards the Chinese slowly turned into indifference, relieved occasionally by sympathy for a people in anguish from the ravages first of their own warlords and later of the Japanese invaders. But no special notice was taken of the revolution of 1911, nor even of the Japanese invasion of Manchuria in 1931. China was after all far distant and seemed no longer the 'Yellow Peril'. Indeed that sobriquet had by then been passed on to the Japanese and New Zealand was increasingly preoccupied with the growing threat of Japanese maritime power in the Pacific. Thus it came about that, although immigration of Asians was still restricted in practice, the Immigration Act of 1920 introduced the ritual of granting entry by the exercise of ministerial discretion. This paved the way for the gradual abandonment of the specifically anti-Chinese provisions of the earlier acts, but it must be emphasized that the process was very clearly a piecemeal one and can in no way be thought of as deliberate policy. Thus after 1934 the poll tax on Chinese entering New Zealand was no longer imposed, although it did not disappear from the statute books until the Finance Act of 1944 was passed. After the Japanese invasion of China in 1937 the wives and children of Chinese resident in New Zealand were permitted to enter. The Nationality and Citizenship

Act of 1948 conferred New Zealand citizenship on all aliens cast on these shores by the fortunes of war, and this included some Chinese. Abroad New Zealand had supported the Chinese case at the League of Nations since 1937, which can hardly be taken as anything but a friendly gesture. Nevertheless by 1948, when Mao Tse-tung came to power, no clear overture of friendship had been made to China, no policy settled, and no links established.

Since 1948 New Zealand's attitudes to the People's Republic of China have formed an integral part of a revamped policy aimed overall at substituting United States protection for traditional British protection. This change of policy might be regarded as a prudent safeguard were it not for the fact that attitudes developed during New Zealand's 'where-Britain-goes-we-go' days have also carried over. In fact the self-image of being somebody's brave and resourceful little brother eager to prove his loyalty, coupled with a proneness to trust too much to the Lafayette syndrome[3] (a folksy belief that Americans remain true to traditions forged during their War of Independence and never let down an ally) has led to New Zealand's overcommitment to the United States cause. Thus the then Prime Minister, Sir Keith Holyoake, speaking on 6 March 1969 in Wellington, said:

> We can only have good allies by proving ourselves a good ally. A good ally is not subservient: he has judgement and a voice and uses them: but he is also prepared to take up his share of the burden. Our voice can be all the more effective by having an accepted place with our close friends rather than sitting on the sidelines.[4]

In the opinion of a growing number of New Zealanders we have not only set out to be a good ally – we have overdone it!

Having joined ANZUS (1951) largely as insurance against a revived Japan (this is a rather over-simplified view), New Zealand then became entangled in SEATO (1954), and in doing so has accepted rather uncritically two views of the international consequences of the rise of the new China. The first is the assumption that the People's Republic has unlimited designs for expansion and for the achievement of world hegemony. The second, by derivation, is that the 'domino theory' is entirely credible. The consequences of holding these views have been threefold.

First, New Zealand has continued to reinforce the tradional belief that to gain protection from a presumed threat it is necessary to be an ally of a great power. To quote T.B. Millar (though he was speaking in an Australian context), 'We can lose nothing by insuring against the possibility of Chinese aggression. We could lose everything by not doing so.'[5] New Zealand therefore adheres closely to her connection with the United States. Second, she continues to cherish the traditional military doctrine of an over-the-horizon defence perimeter. Gordon has noted that as early as 1939 New Zealand Chiefs of Staff agreed that '. . . the defence of New Zealand's interests lie outside New Zealand'[6] and that Singapore was the most vital point for the defence of those interests. More than twenty-five years later, on 28 May 1965, the Prime Minister, Mr (now Sir) Keith Holyoake, defending the commitment of New Zealand troops to Southeast Asia, said in parliament: '. . . the *fact* that confronted us was that New Zealand's first line of defence is in Southeast Asia', thus promoting an assumption to the status of a generally accepted and incontestable fact. Third, the presence of New Zealand in Southeast Asia and Vietnam has come to be regarded by the government of the People's Republic as an act of unprovoked hostility and imperialism by association. Though the New Zealand government may protest that New Zealand made up its own mind on these issues and acted accordingly, her record for the 1950s and 1960s must, to any foreign observer, have every appearance of waiting on signals from her American protector.

Perhaps none of these consequences would matter very much (even if New Zealand's assumptions were incorrect) had the status quo remained unchanged in every respect. However, the international situation has been in a state of flux since about 1970, culminating in the seeming Sino-American *détente* (which no observer would have predicted confidently even five years earlier), and a consequent move towards a Russo-Japanese *entente*. This makes it imperative for New Zealand to re-examine her policies, starting with the premises on which they are based. Only then will it be possible to devise rational China policies with some possibility of them being carried out.

The first premise to re-examine then is that the People's Republic is a threat to New Zealand's way of life or even to her sovereign status. Is China such a threat? Here we find a wide spectrum of opinion ranging from that of M. Halperin, who claims: 'With growing power [China] will pose an increasing threat to Western interests and to Russian interests in the forseeable future',[8] through N. Maxwell: 'China is not expansionist, aggressive, reckless and dangerous',[9] to A. Huck, who goes so far as to say that the Chinese see themselves as vulnerable, encircled, and threatened.[10]

On balance the Chinese record to date has indicated that they are unwilling to take any risks, and have not been overtly expansionist except towards territories, such as Tibet, to which they believe they have historical claims. In brief, pragmatism (to use an over-fashionable word) seems to be the touchstone of Chinese foreign policy. However, it would be unwise indeed to ignore the ideological emphasis that the Chinese themselves give to their motives, thus proclaiming themselves the missionaries of a universal secular faith. In addition notice must be taken of their avowed intention to apply the strategy of the protracted war to the international situation by classifying states into world cities and world villages, and of their belief that historical inevitability will lead to the triumph of the latter. But it must be remembered that one of the chief protagonists of this view was the late Lin Piao and the other is the aging Mao Tse-tung himself. With the passing of the revolutionary Old Guard, it seems at least likely that the missionary motive will be de-emphasized and revolutionary fervour perhaps modified – a process some observers see as taking place already. If that is so, then moves in China's 'ping-pong diplomacy' since 1971 may be taken as indications of a desire to assure China's neighbours of her peaceable intentions. While it would be imprudent to accept this image unquestioningly, it is clearly possible for New Zealand to modify her long-held assumption that she faces an immediate and grave threat from the People's Republic.

The second premise to re-examine is that of belief in the unfailing reliability of New Zealand's chosen protector, the United States. There is some evidence that Americans, distracted by turmoils at home and failures abroad, are increasingly disenchanted with the role of world policeman and that a new isolationist tide is running quite strongly. Editorials in the *New York Times* of 7 July and 16 July 1968 spoke of the need for the President to redefine the United States' vital interests. Presidential adviser McGeorge Bundy warned that: '...the American commitment anywhere is only as deep as the continued conviction of Americans that their own interests require it',[11] and President Nixon, speaking in Bangkok on 29 July 1969 conceded: '...if domination by the aggressor can destroy the freedom of a nation, too much dependence on a protector can eventually erode its dignity'.[12] If these statements indicate current American thinking, it would be wise for New Zealand to reconsider the doctrine of American reliability and, while giving it some credence, to remember that it is clearly not of the 'come-hell-or-high-water' variety that she has fondly imagined it to be.

The third premise requiring re-examination is that of the suitability of an over-the-horizon strategy for New Zealand's defence needs. Clearly the discussion of this strategy would make a whole paper and it cannot be treated in depth here. However, it is evident that it has some viability in the context of British withdrawal from the Indian Ocean, eventual United States withdrawal from mainland Asia, and forward moves by Soviet Russia in the vacated areas. The present arrangements may well prove to be short-lived, since Malaysia's Premier Tun Razak is openly propagating a non-aligned stance, notwithstanding the five-power defence agreements of 1971 (ANZUK) to which Malaysia is a party. Indeed, if New Zealand outwears her Malaysian host's welcome (and this is by no means a remote possibility), her forward defence strategy would become untenable. The alternatives open to her: for example, non-alignment and unilateral disarmament; 'Fortress New Zealand'; a Pacific-Polynesian perimeter held jointly with Australia, are outside the scope of this inquiry, but it is fairly clear that there is a strong likelihood of her withdrawal from an extreme forward position in the fairly near future.

Briefly, if it is possible or even likely that a reassessment of the premises on which New Zealand's China policy is based produces a more favourable image of the People's Republic, a looser connection with the United States, and the withdrawal of the military irritant from Southeast Asia, then New Zealand has a new basis for negotiating a rational relationship with the New China. But, although the advantages of establishing cordial relations with this great power, without sacrificing existing relationships with another great power, are pretty obvious, other obstacles to such a connection and also other factors favouring it must still be taken into account.

Probably the main obstacle was New Zealand's continued recognition of Taiwan.[13] Nevertheless it would be difficult at this stage for her to sacrifice a thriving trade with Taiwan as part of the price to be paid for approval by the People's Republic. The same argument may apply to her economic and diplomatic relations with Japan, particularly if Sino-Japanese relationships deteriorate in the future. Again, New Zealand's record at the United Nations in matters affecting the People's Republic, both before and after its entry to that body, may prove a stumbling block.

Factors working in favour of the new relationship are that neither China nor Japan sets much store by New Zealand's importance as a trading partner, so it could well be possible for her to continue trading with both these countries and with Taiwan into the bargain, especially now that her diplomatic post at Taipei no longer exists. Again, posturings at the United Nations are not taken too seriously by any of its members, and pragmatists like the Chinese can readily ignore past offences if it suits their present convenience. If it does not they can equally readily make capital of any slight infraction of their *ex post facto* (retrospective) rules of desirable conduct in order to hold up closer association, and New Zealand could do little about it.

In short it is high time that New Zealand made serious efforts to get on better terms with the People's Republic, and now the way seems a good deal clearer in the light of the Sino-American *détente*.[14] The best choice would seem to be a pragmatic approach, leading to negotiated solutions of individual issues, with the overall goal of improved relations to be ratified by accepted and acceptable diplomatic interchange. If New Zealand can shake off her encumbering historical attitudes it will be quite possible to operate these policies and thus to serve her national interests better in the confused and critical years ahead.

Notes

1 Angus Ross, *New Zealand Aspirations in the Pacific in the Nineteenth Century*, Oxford, 1964.
2 B.K. Gordon, *New Zealand Becomes a Pacific Power*, Chicago, 1960, p. 10.
3 The author is indebted for this felicitous phrase to Dr Harry Gelber of Monash University.
4 K. Holyoake, *A Defence Policy for New Zealand*, New Zealand Institute of International Affairs, Wellington, 1969, p. 13.
5 T.B. Millar, *Australia's Defence*, Melbourne, 1965, p. 51.
6 B.K. Gordon, *op. cit.*, p. 111.
7 New Zealand Parliamentary Debates, 1965, p. 342. The italics are this writer's.
8 M. Halperin, 'China's Strategic Outlook', in A. Buchan (ed.), *China and the Peace of Asia*, London, 1965, p. 108.
9 N. Maxwell, 'The Threat from China', *International Affairs*, vol. 47, no. 1, January 1971, p. 44.
10 A. Huck, *The Security of China; Chinese Approaches to Problems of War and Strategy*, London, 1971.
11 T.R. Reese, *Australia, New Zealand and the United States*, London, 1969, p. 56.

12 Quoted by B. Grant in *Foreign Policy in the 1970s*, Wellington, 1970, p. 49.
13 Now that this has been withdrawn, the way to better relations with the People's Republic should be clearer.
14 The first steps have been taken by the Labour Government elected in November 1973, which has established full-scale diplomatic interchanges. This has resulted in a closer relationship already, as can be seen from the exchange of trade and cultural missions. Nevertheless it would be prudent to advance at a measured pace instead of imitating the headlong approach of the Australian Federal Government under the leadership of Mr Gough Whitlam.

China and Eastern Europe:
The Rumanian Example

J.H. JENSEN

When I was in Rumania in 1971, the brand names that were moving on the grocery shelves were Chinese. Chinese tinned meats, Chinese tinned vegetables, even Chinese ţuica (brandy) provided a colourful backdrop to the patient queues of Rumanian housewives. In Constanţa on the Black Sea coast, when I turned back the bright plaid blanket on my hotel bed, I found a Chinese label. The electrical equipment in the new display block at the Bucureşti Centre for Technical Documentation for the Transportation Industry – again, made in China.

Since my return from that trip I have followed the development of economic relations between these two members of the world community of socialist nations in the pages of newspapers and magazines I receive from Rumania; these periodicals chronicle the development of Rumanian industry and transportation. They include the newspaper of the Ministry of Construction and Construction Materials, the *Railway Review*, and the Ministry of Transport *Review*. In the August 1971 number of the Rumanian *Railway Review, Revista Cailor Ferate*, I found a summary of these relations, which has been developed further in brief news items since. Of course my news from these sources is always a few months out of date, but western European sources of very recent date have confirmed this continuity in policy.

The occasions for this summary of economic collaboration were:

1 the visit of the Rumanian delegation, led by Nicolai Ceauşescu, First Secretary of the Rumanian communist party, to Peking in June 1971;

2 the holding of a Chinese Industrial and Trade Expedition in the new pavilion in Herăstrau Park in Bucureşti.

This was the third such Chinese display in Rumania since the begin-

134

ning of Sino-Soviet disagreements; the first two were held in 1959 and 1965 – the dates are significant, as we will see. It was followed up by a Rumanian show in Peking in October 1971.

From 1965 to 1970, according to the summary, Sino-Rumanian trade had grown by about 200 per cent. This was from a very small base, but the figures were becoming significant in Rumania's total foreign trade balances by the end of that period. As we will see, this sort of development offered some important advantages for the Rumanian government in its efforts to build a balanced pattern of foreign trade, and to deal with some sensitive problems in the relations between its own economic development and its consequent reliance upon certain foreign suppliers and markets. At the beginning of 1971 a new trade agreement was concluded between the two countries to cover the period 1971–5; it envisaged a slowing down in the growth rate of exchanges between the two countries, but a broadening of the participation of different sectors in the two economies. By this process more sophisticated industrial products would be exchanged, and Rumanian dependence upon European suppliers, both eastern and western, would be lessened. During the trading year 1971–2, the proposed growth rate for Sino-Rumanian trade was 30 per cent.

At the same time, in this economic survey and in other incidental reports on relations between the two countries, a good deal of attention has been given to the non-commercial and even doctrinal element in Sino-Rumanian collaboration. For example, there has been emphasis on Chinese contributions to the aid fund for the relief of victims of the flood disaster along the lower Danube in 1970, and to the process of reconstruction which followed. It was the Chinese communist party as well as the Chinese government which gave this aid, and it was given free. This emphasis suggests an invidious comparison with the Soviet Union which the Rumanians have not needed to spell out. China's willingness to provide a low-interest loan (with no strings) of US$200 million for industrial development has also been given wide publicity, and it would be a very dull Rumanian indeed who could not see this against the backdrop of Soviet exploitation of Rumania through the infamous 'mixed-company' system of the late forties and the early fifties.

The Rumanian government has also given explicit approval to the communal approach to agricultural development in China. This system, they say, has expressed the 'vital, brave, intelligent, persevering spirit' of the Chinese people; it has fitted their special national conditions, and their understanding of Marxist doctrine. While Rumania has shown no intention of following China's path, this in no way lessens her support for China in this very important area of Marxist explication. This support is in perfect accord, as we might expect, with Rumanian insistence on many national roads to socialism, and with their rejection of any effort by a brotherly communist party to interfere in the private concerns of another party. The Rumanian party rejects the Brezhnev doctrine of general Soviet supervisory control over members of the socialist camp. Hence it welcomes evidence that national communist parties will find national roads to their own future. Pluralism is the essence of the Rumanian viewpoint and it is built into their comments on China – even in the newspapers of the Construction and Construction Materials Ministry, and in the Rumanian *Transportation Review*.

This economic and ideological collaboration with China is part of the positive side of Rumania's policy of independence vis-à-vis the Soviet Union. We are aware of other examples of such independence: Rumania's reception of President Nixon two years ago; her links with western European economies and with western European communist parties like the Italian party which has been critical of Soviet leadership during the past five years; her continued ties with Israel; her African and Near Eastern policies; her friendship with Yugoslavia, and, more recently, with Albania. The negative side would include her lack of interest in Warsaw Pact military obligations; her resentment of any efforts to change Comecon, the east European equivalent of the European Economic Community and her condemnation of Soviet intervention in Czechoslovakia in 1968. The positive and negative sides of Rumanian policy come together in her refusal to work with the Soviet leadership in efforts to rebuild communist unity and in her pretensions to act as the honest broker in bringing the People's Republic of China and the Soviet Union together to discuss and reconcile their differences. Six years ago, when this policy was only partly developed, and when Rumanian independence was still largely a matter of stubbornness about her right to economic growth on her own terms, observers tended to explain her policy solely in terms of a very cautious and local reaction to Soviet initiatives in this same sphere. The argument then was that Nikita Khrushchev had started it with his 1959–60 plans for tightening up Comecon, and that Rumanian refusal to cooperate was the result of her party's unwillingness to face the Rumanian people with a policy which would doom Rumania to remaining the 'farm and petrol-filling station' of eastern Europe. But the consistency with which Gheorghiu-Dej and his successor Nicolai Ceauşescu followed and enlarged their independent line focused attention upon other and earlier aspects of Rumanian party experience. And the study of the larger dimensions of Sino-Soviet disagreements has provided evidence which suggests that Rumania, along with other eastern European states, was being exposed to the dissension between Moscow and Peking as early as 1956.

To go back in time with the Rumanian communist party is to become aware of Titoist elements there as early as 1944. The issue was between 'natives' and 'Muscovites', between Rumanian communists who had struggled against the Nazis and against the Antonescu regime during the war years, and communists of Rumanian nationality who returned in the baggage of the Soviet armies after years of residence in the Soviet Union. The struggle began even before the country was liberated, when the natives ousted a party leader, Ştefan Foris, who was imposed from abroad by Stalin. With the Soviet army on the scene the natives had to be more circumspect. Muscovites like Ana Pauker and Vasile Luca (one Jewish and the other of Hungarian origin) were able to hold Gheorghiu-Dej and his colleagues to a rigidly pro-Moscow line. The difference between Yugoslavia and Rumania in 1948 was the presence of the Red Army. In 1952, in the dust raised by new excitement in Moscow where Stalin was preparing new purges of his own, the Rumanian natives were able quietly to eliminate Ana Pauker and her Muscovite allies. During the years that followed, Rumanian party leaders were able to begin to steer their country away from the Soviet carbon-copy course dictated earlier; by 1956 a much more equitable economic relationship had been established and the Rumanian economy had been relieved of some of the worst Soviet pressures. Rumania escaped the troubles of Hungary and Poland in 1956 through a combination of this relief and tight police controls. In 1958 the leadership managed to negotiate the withdrawal of Soviet occupying forces. In 1959 they began their stubborn and at first largely passive resistance to eastern bloc economic integration; in 1961 their resistance began to come out into the open – and the rest is history, in the sense that western observers have gained increasing insight into the differences between Rumania and the Soviet Union. The part played by Rumanian governments in wrecking plans for developing Comecon, and then in helping to bring about Khrushchev's fall, have focused attention upon this little east European state.

China played an important part in eastern Europe during those years (1956–7) when Khrushchev was trying to hold on to Soviet influence in Poland, Hungary, and the Soviet Union's other western borderlands. It is well known that the Chinese analysis of differences between the problems of Poland and Hungary was accepted and acted upon by Soviet policy-makers and, significantly, by Khrushchev. Poland was not about to break out of the socialist camp; there was evidence that Hungary was. Poland was hedged in to the west by East Germany and Czechoslovakia, while Hungary was open to the west, and was being increasingly influenced by the Yugoslavian example. Poland's communist party, army, and people were united in their support of their new party leader, Gomulka; the lines of loyalty in Hungary were far from clear, and the army especially seemed to have turned against the communist party. China advocated a conciliatory attitude towards Gomulka and firm repression in Hungary. The Chinese leaders were correct on both counts, in terms of practical politics, and Khrushchev had reason to be grateful for the guidance and support he received – notably from Chou En-lai, who made a flying trip to Moscow and Warsaw to explain China's position to the protagonists.

The lessons of 1956 were not wasted on either Khrushchev or his Rumanian neighbours. Khrushchev took from them a bitter aftertaste compounded of Chinese intervention in an area of exclusive Russian interest; of his own dependence upon Chinese support in a period when he was being challenged in Moscow by the anti-party group and in Hungary and Poland by the 'new course' national communists; and of his recognition that a long hard period of rebuilding lay ahead if the Soviet Union was to reassert her permanent interests in Europe and in the world communist movement.

The Rumanian leadership in its turn took away the impression that the cardinal sin would be to give cause for a charge that they were trying to ease their party and state out of the socialist camp. So long as they paid lip-service to socialist unity and allowed no evidence to emerge which suggested that anti-communist elements in their society were gaining the upper hand – or even freedom of action – they should be able to claim a considerable degree of autonomy in policies which dealt with issues of vital Rumanian concern. Of course, as the world communist movement grew increasingly fragmented, it would become more and more difficult for any critic to demonstrate that a particular policy line by one national party would lead that party out of the world movement. Polycentrism gives freedom of action and allows, within practical limits, for shifts between great power protectors by smaller and weaker parties, whether in power or out.

The Rumanians have played these games with increasing precision and imagination ever since. But they have never strayed far from their original analysis of the implications of the Polish and Hungarian affairs of 1956. It is necessary to emphasize at this point that there are domestic limits to the freedom of action of the Rumanian party. Rumania is not yet a communist country in the sense that her leadership can rest confidently on the loyalty and adherence of her people. The régime's legitimacy is enhanced by an anti-Russian bias, but problems still remain. The rigidity of her police controls emphasize this point. The régime has not succeeded in moving as far as Yugoslavia or Poland in this regard, and the last two years have shown how shatter-prone are these two best-based eastern European régimes. So there are practical reasons why the Rumanian party has maintained its own unity and its own firm grip on opinion and on political action within the country. Later on I want to comment on the impact of the Soviet invasion of Czechoslovakia in 1968, and of the Brezhnev doctrine, on Rumanian policy in these matters. For the moment let us note only that both the former leader, Gheorghiu-Dej, and the present leader, Ceauşescu, have been consistent in their efforts to stay within the broad confines of the world communist movement in both foreign and domestic policies.

How did Khrushchev respond to China's intervention in European communist affairs in 1956–7? With his Soviet power-base assured after his elimination of the anti-party group in 1957, with the post-sputnik prestige which the Soviet Union enjoyed, and with the temporary *détente* in Soviet-United States relations at the time of the Camp David meeting in 1959, he proceeded to tighten control of the Warsaw camp and of the Comecon system. The process began with the Moscow Conference of November 1957, when the eastern European parties were required to support a very firm statement about unity in the face of capitalist imperialism, and also in the face of 'dogmatism' and 'revisionism'. The Soviet Union's guidance of the movement was strongly reaffirmed and the eastern European parties found themselves under increasing pressure from Moscow in the years that followed. Khrushchev did reverse the flow of economic assistance between the Soviet Union and eastern Europe, to the latter's advantage, in the several years which followed. This worked to China's disadvantage and was one of the major factors driving the two greatest communist states apart. But Khrush-chev was also moving by these and other means towards tighter control of the parties in power on Russia's western flank, and he was playing these states off against one another. The northern half of the eastern bloc: Poland, Czechoslovakia, and East Germany, were to gain at the expense of the less-developed lower Danubian states; Rumania and Bulgaria were to compete with each other for the favours of the advanced northern states. And the Soviet Union was to profit ultimately with assistance for her own foreign trade and aid programmes in the Third World. The end result was to be Soviet leadership – in Southeast Asia, the Near East, and Africa, as well as in eastern Europe – at the expense of China. The concurrent break in Sino-Soviet economic and technological cooperation was another aspect of the concentration of Soviet attention where it was likely to be most productive. Khrushchev did not scruple to use the German question, especially the Berlin question, to press his eastern Europe-an allies into the desired dependence upon Soviet leadership.

Things seemed to be moving satisfactorily in these directions from Khrushchev's viewpoint when, in 1959–60, he moved even more firmly to recover Soviet leadership of the world communist move-ment. His activities were Russian-centred and European-centred, and emphasized the growth of material well-being and the inevitable victory of socialism through peaceful co-existence. The Chinese positions on economic development and world revolution were now equated with Trotskyism; the commune system was the product of ideological blindness and 'conceit' (Hungarian Party Congress, December 1959); and a Warsaw Pact meeting in Moscow early in 1960 was informed that the Soviet Union had no intention of giving nuclear weapons to China in view of the wrong policy line followed by the Chinese communist party.

This was the background for the Rumanian Third Party Congress (Bucureşti) in June 1960, and for the November 1960 meeting of eighty-one communist parties in Moscow. At Bucureşti, Khrushchev tried to isolate and discredit the Chinese party. The Chinese delega-tion came prepared to carry on with critical but muted comments about Soviet inconsistencies and failures; under strong Soviet pres-sure they claimed the right to give new leads to the world movement. At Moscow in November they refused to let the Soviet Union avoid its responsibility for past incorrect leadership. The Soviet communist party, they said, was still the leading party, until some other party took over this position. But, in the meantime, 'in relations between parties there is no reason to demand that the minority should submit to the majority, for between parties there are no superiors and inferiors: each party is independent . . . . ' This was a virtual declaration of war between the two great centres of the world movement; the history of this split is reasonably well known up to the present.

I hope that this brief review of Sino-Soviet entanglements in the eastern European communist movement as well as in the movement in the rest of the world has made clear that the European sector remained paramount in Khrushchev's thinking. This was the controllable power-base from which further advances could be made. In the remainder of my paper I want to emphasize Rumania's use of this developing split in her own hazardous progress towards independence. She had already profited; shifts in Soviet military and economic policy in the years between 1955 and 1960 had worked to her advantage. The Soviet army was gone from her territory. Could Rumania continue to enlarge her sphere of freedom of action without stimulating a Soviet over-reaction? This is the issue before and after August 1968, and this issue must always be seen in terms of the Soviet priority of concern about eastern Europe.

The Rumanian party opened its drive for independence in a Central Committee plenum towards the end of 1961. Here the idea of a division of labour among the socialist countries, which could lead to unbalanced development for less-developed countries like Rumania, was criticized as 'an erroneous theory'. Then, early in 1963, at a Comecon Executive Committee meeting in Moscow, the Rumanians rejected Moscow's economic integration proposals. And, during the spring of 1963, the Rumanian party carried through a national (and nationalistic) campaign of discussion of its policies vis-à-vis the Soviet Union, and was able to gain a unique degree of popular support on this issue.

This groundwork for economic independence was closely linked to a more autonomous line in the Sino-Soviet differences. Rumania did not join in the blasts of anti-Chinese rhetoric which Moscow elicited from the other Warsaw Pact countries. Rumania refused to maintain her support for the anti-Albanian campaign with its obvious anti-Chinese overtones. In April 1963 the Rumanian ambassador was sent back to Tirana, though other eastern European representatives were not. When Khrushchev (and his successors) tried to organize eastern European solidarity against China, the Rumanians refused to cooperate. This became clear in 1963 when meetings like the East German Party Congress (January 1963) were boycotted by the Rumanian party. This policy has been followed up to the present. Rumanian representation at Comecon, Warsaw Pact, and more informal gatherings of eastern European leaders has become so erratic that we now ask why they attend (if they do) rather than why they are absent! And the Rumanian party began as early as March 1964 to offer itself as a mediator (often very unwelcome from the Soviet standpoint) between the two giant parties. We may suspect that her actions in this direction have contributed to the United States-Chinese dialogue of 1971–2.

Then, in April 1964, the Rumanians made their clear statement of the autonomy they demanded within the eastern European regional associations, and within the world communist movement.

Why was this statement issued at this particular time by the Rumanian Central Committee? We might speculate about domestic political considerations, but it would remain speculation. In the international sphere the following considerations seem to have been in play. First and foremost was the unsatisfactory aftermath of Rumania's successful withdrawal from eastern European economic integration. Soviet contracts and technical assistance were failing, and bilateral treaties between the Soviet Union and Rumania's eastern bloc partners were creating a ring of cooperative systems which threatened to isolate her. A Rumanian delegation which had visited Peking early in 1964 (and had failed to get anywhere with its mediation plans in Moscow on the return journey) had been filled with Chinese comments about the Soviet Union's use of its economic and technological muscle in such 'fraternal' cooperation. Rumania's interest in Chinese and western economic links also required some such statement of policy. And so it came in April 1964.

It contained three basic elements. First the statement contained a renewed rejection of 'a joint plan and a single planning body . . . of inter-state technical-productive mergers of branches of industry . . . of supra-state schemes which would turn sovereignty into a notion devoid of any content.' Rumania would trade, would seek and offer aid, where she pleased. Secondly, the statement offered a lesson in Marxism-Leninism to justify these policy decisions. It emphasized that Marxist states and parties must respect the equality and national sovereignty of all their colleagues. The only basis for unity in the world movement was respect for the unique conditions prevailing in each nation, conditions which could be properly evaluated only by its own body. No supra-state or supra-party could lay down the law for the entire movement. Finally the statement meted out impartial justice in bringing the Soviet and Chinese parties to order. It called for an end to polemics which could only weaken the movement. It asked all parties to join in planning a new world communist conference which would meet without any prior commitment to criticize any single party. This last was a direct slap at Soviet plans to organize a world conference which would rebuff China's efforts to lead astray the 'truly Marxist-Leninist parties'.

It is now clear that Rumania has paid a price for her independence. Although not subjected to the sort of economic and diplomatic blockade that faced Yugoslavia in 1948 or Albania in the early sixties, the Rumanian party has been kept under pretty intensive pressure. On the home front this has meant belt-tightening. We have already seen that Soviet cooperation with the other eastern bloc countries in the mid-sixties was not extended to Rumania. Rumania did negotiate a bilateral economic accord with the Soviet Union in 1965, a year or more after such agreements were worked out with the other bloc countries. But she has been partly frozen out of the network of multilateral agreements designed to encourage joint development plans: for example, in the metallurgical industry. She has gone it alone with her own new iron and steel complex at Galati, but she has not been helped in this by the Soviet Union (as was, for example, Bulgaria with her similar project at Kremikovtsi). She has not been satisfied about arrangements for buying iron ore and coking coal in the Ukraine. Russian contracts for these materials have been fulfilled slowly or with poor quality material, or have remained unfulfilled. This has been a major factor in directing Rumania's attention to potential suppliers in North Africa and even further afield. In the process, the Soviet Union's share in Rumanian trade has declined from over 40 per cent in 1964 to less than 25 per cent in 1971. The Soviet Union has moved rapidly to cut off Rumanian oil markets in the northern states of the eastern bloc by pushing a pipeline across from her new petroleum fields in the Urals to Poland, East Germany, Czechoslovakia, and even Hungary. Rumania has turned to western markets, and to joint enterprises with Yugoslavia. The great Iron Gates electric power complex is the most important of these efforts.

Political pressure has also been intense. This was not so apparent in the mid-sixties, but it has increased sharply since 1968. Bucureşti has been engaged in a delicate balancing act for the past four years, reconciling a minimum participation in Warsaw Pact activity with the summer troop concentrations just across her frontiers to the north. The balancing act has extended to domestic policies generally. Nicolai Ceauşescu must reconcile his plans to lighten the weight of his police state with the need to prevent a 'Prague Spring' which could bring Soviet tanks. He has stood up to the Russians, but this could release nationalist and racialist passions embarrassing to his party. He has released political prisoners, rehabilitated the victims of past purges, and given greater elbow-room to writers and intellectuals. But he has had to do this very cautiously. We must remember that he has had to establish his claim to lead after the death of the long-ruling and efficient Gheorghe Gheorghiu-Dej. He has had to operate in an atmosphere of Russian pressure, where his rivals for power could always exploit his handling of the Russians or of domestic dissent if he once slipped. And these rivals have always had the option of working with the Russians to do him down. This too is a pattern of Russian policy. How much could Chinese approval help a Rumanian leader faced with these problems? And could China be of practical assistance if Russia turned nasty?

Rumanian policy during the past five years has been based only partly on her Chinese connections. It has grown naturally out of the diversification of her economic connections abroad. It has reflected the partial alignment implicit in the Rumanian ideological position laid down in the mid-sixties. Finally it has grown apace with the urgent need for political links that would give some kind of reassurance in the face of Soviet threats. We have already noted Rumania's own assumptions about the principles which should govern an independent foreign policy line for a communist state. The Soviet invasion of Czechoslovakia, and the Brezhnev doctrine which followed, struck at the roots of these assumptions.

Economic diversification is essential for Rumania's balanced development. She seeks more advanced technology from western Europe and the United States; she looks for markets for her own special products (like petro-chemical plant) in developing countries; she needs reliable sources of iron ore and coal; and she faces awkward exchange problems if she deals too exclusively with the eastern bloc countries or with western Europe. She wants the favourable arrangements which are possible through trade connections with African or southern Asian countries, or with China, where political considerations are likely to sweeten the deals she can make. As we have already noted, between the early sixties and early seventies her trade percentages with the Soviet Union have declined from over 40 per cent to less than 25 per cent (in 1955 they were almost 70 per cent), while her trade with other eastern bloc states has declined more slowly from about 30 per cent to about 20 per cent. At the same time her trade with western Europe and the United States has grown from about 30 per cent to over 40 per cent of her total imports and exports. From near zero her trade with the rest of the world, including China, has gone up to over 15 per cent of the total. China's share is now around 5 to 6 per cent of the total, and approaches the figures for Poland and Czechoslovakia. A number of things could be said about the magnitude of these changes, keeping in mind the very rapid changes in the Rumanian economy itself in the past decade, but I would emphasize that Rumania is experiencing some of the inflationary balance of payment problems which bedevilled Yugoslovia a decade ago, and that finding a better mix of trading partners is one way of avoiding deeper trouble of this kind. These considerations lie behind her fostering of trade with China, though it is clear that the high points in the development of this trade, from its beginnings in 1959, through its acceleration in the mid-sixties, to its relatively mature levels in 1971, have all been related to Rumania's need to draw close to an economic partner who could also offer political support.

I think that there is little need to review Rumania's ideological arguments for national communism. The intense diplomatic activity of Nicolai Ceauşescu and his colleagues since the spring of 1969 has emphasized the width of Rumania's circle of friends, her appeal to extra-European states, and her insistence on making her own connections with other communist parties as well as with other states. Among these new friendships, the exchange of visits by Ceauşescu and President Nixon, the attention paid by Rumania to the Arab and the Israeli sides in the eastern Mediterranean chronic crisis, and the community of views that the Rumanian communist party shares with, say, the Italian communist party all represent insurance against a Soviet decision to pressure her as Czechoslovakia was pressured into line in 1968–9.

The Rumanians can never again enjoy the confidence which was theirs before August 1968. But they can do their best to guard against the confusion and isolation and the frantic search for sympathy that characterized Czech reactions then. The friendship with the People's Republic of China mentioned at the beginning of this paper is an obvious part of this process. So long as the Soviet Union is sensitive to pressure along the Amur and in Central Asia, she will move cautiously against Rumania. And as the People's Republic of China has sought other friends in southeast Europe, Rumania has also tried to tighten her links with Yugoslavia and Albania. R.V. Burks has suggested that, in the early sixties, Bulgaria was near to the path that Rumania took. She then drew back but she could well move in that direction again. This is the more likely as Rumanian-Yugoslavian friendship grows, and as the Lower-Danube region moves increasingly out of the Soviet orbit. And into the Chinese? We can only surmise. I would hesitate to suggest possibilities for further movement in this direction for Hungary or Poland, let alone Czechoslovakia or East Germany. But let us not underestimate the importance of the treaties ratified by the West German parliament in May 1972. None of these eastern bloc states will stop being communist in the next little while, but it will be increasingly difficult to see them as part of an 'eastern bloc'.

What is China's gain from what looks like a very altruistic policy of aid and loans, of diplomatic and ideological pressure expended on behalf of friends half way round the world? If we take John Fairbank's analysis (*Foreign Affairs*, April 1969), these links are useful as deflecting Soviet attention from Chinese strategic priorities in Central Asia. They emphasize a Eurasian landmass strategic conception (ignoring sea power), which is familiar to the policy-makers of Peking. The third element in this analysis, 'the superiority of China over the barbarian rest of the world', also finds an echo in this policy. How flattering for the Chinese communist party, after its difficult years of international criticism and domestic uncertainty, to be courted by European communist parties and states!

A summary of the Rumanian experience, however, should not give priority to China's role. Her pressure on Moscow and her ideological stance in the early sixties provided the occasion for Rumania's 'new course'. During the mid- and late sixties, in the years of China's Cultural Revolution, Rumania had to go it alone almost entirely and she played her cards shrewdly and well. The Czech affair in 1968 upset all her calculations, and her renewed courtship of China is part of her search for a power line-up which will discourage the Soviet Union from applying the Brezhnev doctrine in Rumania's own case.

Trick and Treat Diplomacy?

W.A.C. ADIE

*The new era in China's foreign relations, and the changing
alignments in the Pacific and Indian Oceans*

President Nixon's new shock treatment for the world's chronic
ailments, and the reactions of Peking and Moscow, are still rattling
the political kaleidoscope not just in the Pacific region, but throughout the world. Not so long ago international conflicts were thought
to be so outdated by the nuclear balance that the human race was
settling down to civil strife as a more exciting substitute for over-
mechanized warfare; but now the assumptions and alignments
which have prevailed since World War Two must come under
'agonising reappraisal'.

When World War Two's untidy aftermath congealed into the
cold war, three provisional, anomalous, and increasingly ana-
chronistic situations were perpetuated and linked, so as to engender
or exacerbate repeated international crises. These centres of conflict
have been the Berlin problem, the problem of Palestine and Israel-
Arab conflict, and the Taiwan problem with• its ramifications in
Korea and Indochina. In all three the two superpowers were
committed, and dared not make concessions in one without trying
to secure concessions in the others; often their policies were determined or their options limited by their clients or satellites, or even
by extremist groups able to exert pressure on these allies or on their
own public opinion. Now, suddenly, Moscow seems as keen as
Washington to defuse Berlin, while Washington is as keen as
Peking to defuse Taipei. As for the Middle East, a reopening of
China's ancient trade routes is foreshadowed by the Sinkiang-
Pakistan highway which opened in February 1971, and by the
opening of Peking's diplomatic relations with Iran and Turkey. It
is the emergence of China and Japan on to the world scene which is
creating a new, multipolar world and profoundly altering the situation in the Pacific, perhaps in the Indian Ocean too – areas which

147

some observers see as the focal points of world politics in the coming years.

George Kennan, founder of the United States State Department's policy planning staff, wrote in *Foreign Affairs* in July 1947:

> It is clear that the main element of any U.S. policy towards the Soviet Union must be that of a long-term, patient but firm and vigilant *containment* of Russian expansive tendencies...designed to *confront* the Russians *with unalterable counterforce* at every point where they show signs of encroaching upon the interests of a peaceful and stable world. [my emphasis]

This was the rationale of the Truman Doctrine, announced to Congress on 11 March 1947 after Britain had warned the United States that it could no longer hold the line in the eastern Mediterranean. After the victory of the communist armies in China and the outbreak of the Korean war, the United States found itself obliged to 'contain' and 'confront' what appeared to be 'expansive tendencies' of China as well. George Kennan's article was signed 'X'; writing over his own signature in the same journal in October 1967, Mr Nixon said:

> Any American policy toward Asia must come urgently to grips with the reality of China. This does not mean, as many would simplistically have it, rushing to grant recognition to Peking, to admit it to the United Nations and to ply it with offers of trade – all of which would serve to confirm its rulers in their present course...the primary restraint on China's Asian ambitions should be exercised by the Asian nations in the path of those ambitions, backed by the ultimate power of the United States.

As the Asian nations demonstrated their capacity to defend themselves, argued Mr Nixon, the Peking leaders would turn their energies inward rather than outwards; then a dialogue with China would begin. In the short run, therefore, a policy of 'creative counterpressure' was required. Dealing with Peking was something like trying to deal with 'the more explosive ghetto elements' in the United States: 'Aggression has to be restrained while education proceeds.'

Advocating such a positive 'psychiatric' policy at a conference held in Munich in mid-1966, the present writer pointed out that it was a logical extension of Mao Tse-tung's own method of dealing with China.[1] And, indeed, it was largely because the Peking leadership of the early sixties was frustrated in its designs that the Cultural Revolution broke out and swept it away; while the resulting military régime met 'creative counterpressure' from the Soviet Union. Instead of the United States containing both China and Russia, both were now set to 'contain' each other – one with 'ping-pong diplomacy', the other with 'collective security' pacts, bases, and the Red Fleet.

Mr Dulles once said: 'If the communist government of China in fact proves its ability to govern China without serious domestic resistance, it too should be admitted to the United Nations.' That was in 1950. What is most worthy of attention in the subsequent history of Sino-American relations is not the fact that they are now at last, apparently, moving towards normalization. It is how they were prevented from doing so before. It is also instructive to note how the obstacles were overcome; not by methods President Woodrow Wilson would have applauded, but more in the Robin Hood style of Chairman Mao. With elaborate secrecy and deception (deception especially of his own side), while Vice-President Agnew made a seemingly pointless tour abroad, President Nixon sent his court sophist or persuader,[2] Dr Kissinger, to convince Premier Chou En-lai that the interest of China's rulers lay in agreement with the then United States administration. This dramatic move, when revealed to the naïve astonishment of the world's politicians and media, obscured the fact that it was merely the culmination of years of frustrated crypto-diplomacy – frustrated sometimes by the uncontrollability of multifarious events, often by the protagonists' own apparatus of conventional defence and diplomacy.

It had for years been obvious to analysts of international relations that the conjuncture called for a Sino-American rapprochement; within twelve days of taking office, President Nixon put Dr Kissinger to work on it. China scholars in the United States had long been arguing publicly for a more flexible policy,[3] while other 'western' leaders had set the example, starting with General de Gaulle in January 1964. French diplomacy, latterly aided by other intermediaries such as Rumania, was very active behind the scenes in the cause of bringing China on to the world scene, with such aims as securing American withdrawal from, and neutralization of, Indochina (permitting the restoration of a certain French *présence*), making the Soviets more amenable in Europe and its Islamic periphery, and disrupting the French Left. But these initiatives could not bear fruit until after the Great Proletarian Cultural Revolution in China had toppled successive Chiefs of Staff, officers commanding the Peking garrison, and leading cadres of the propaganda apparatus, and even the Secretary General of the Party and Chairman of the Government themselves. Truman dismissed General MacArthur. Mao dismissed his Chinese equivalent, Marshal P'eng Te-huai. . . . [4] And in the last few months, his chosen heir Lin Piao and the cream of the military élite also disappeared.

It was of course the Korean war that had first prevented normalization of communist China's foreign relations and created the conditions for the two Indochina wars. Some believe it was started by Stalin to pit America against China and to give him a free hand both there and in Europe. Since the Korean war the situation's complexity continued to snowball, centring on Taiwan (Formosa). Though things showed signs of moving in 1955–6 and again in 1963–4, internal stresses and upheavals in China and the exigencies of United States domestic politics, as well as extraneous factors, always intervened to arrest any promising development. But from the outbreak of the Sino-Soviet dispute in April 1961 a Sino-American *détente* was always on the cards.

Before his election Mr Nixon, like Mr Trudeau, had publicly indicated his intention to do something about Peking. He wrote a carefully-phrased article in *Foreign Affairs Quarterly,* while Mr Trudeau more bluntly, and less logically, announced in May 1968 that if elected he would take steps towards recognition of Peking because of increasing Sino-Canadian trade. This trend was noted in Peking. As China emerged from the Cultural Revolution and a thoroughgoing self-criticism on foreign policy, the official media republished an instruction originally issued by Mao in 1949: the Party should learn 'how to wage diplomatic struggles against the imperialists. We must learn how to carry out overt struggle against them, we must also learn how to carry on covert struggle against them.'[5] This directive was propagated in more dramatic form by the immensely publicized Peking opera *Taking Tiger Mountain by Strategy*, the message of which was that while China was weaker than its enemies it should adopt Trojan horse tactics and send agents into the enemy stronghold, while mobilizing the masses below for the final assault.

This parable may be taken as rationalizing the results of a review of foreign policy which was made after attempts collapsed in 1965–6 to mobilize a militant 'third force' in Asia, Africa, and Latin America, led by China and perhaps embodied in a revolutionary counter-United Nations.[6] It was evidently decided to take the line that China should enter the existing 'bourgeois' United Nations in order to 'use, restrict, and transform' it, according to the usual formula of what is called 'united front work'. At the same time China should secure as much advantage as possible in bilateral political and trade relations with certain vulnerable countries, from the creation of a 'bandwagon' atmosphere on the question of United Nations membership.

Did this line merely give face-saving revolutionary cover to a sincere desire for normal international relations, or does it mean that China stoops to join the world only to conquer it? Such questions are metaphysical; only from the outcome can the 'real intentions' be deduced, and the outcome depends largely on the realism or naïveté of other governments. What is certain is that China at present retains the option to use the tactic of 'united front from above' (exchange of trade and other delegations, even of ambassadors) simultaneously with that of 'united front from below' (informal instruments of foreign policy, ranging from 'people's diplomacy' to support of rural and urban guerrillas, alienated students, wildcat strikers, and other disruptive forces). For example, Peking buys Malaysian rubber, but still supports the communist guerrillas in that country. Far from being contradictory, these overt and covert instruments of foreign policies are complementary. The 'diplomatic offensive' came as much from the West as from Peking. In January 1969 the then Italian Foreign Minister Sig. Nenni announced that Italy had decided to recognize the People's Republic of China. In May Sino-Canadian talks on recognition began in Stockholm.

Chinese reaction to the western approaches was typically cautious and canny. The signals were often smoky, but signals there were, such as agreement to open the Warsaw talks in the spring of 1969. I wrote at that time that the consequent opening of a triangular geopolitical chess game between Nixon, Brezhnev, and Mao could not be taken as proof that Peking had decided to switch alliances altogether. What the Chinese gambit would turn out to have meant would depend very much on how the Nixon team moved in reply.[7] In July 1969 President Nixon relaxed restrictions on United States citizens travelling to China and buying Chinese goods. Further such moves were made in December 1969, in April and August 1970, and in March and April 1971, mainly in the direction of free Sino-

American trade. Already by mid-1970 it was clear that a political deal was on the way, though in order to fit into Peking's ideological universe it had to be represented as a victory of 'struggle', especially of armed struggle, by the masses of the world, including the American people against United States imperialism and its running dogs.[8] For those able to decode the jargon, this was the main significance of Mao Tse-tung's denunciation of the Cambodian operation in May 1970.

From the secret Chinese Army 'work reports' which fell into American hands in 1961, it was known that Mao and his dauphin, Lin Piao, were thinking in terms of an eventual settlement of all outstanding quarrels with the United States, in one package. Although criticized during the Cultural Revolution and now out of office, Foreign Minister Marshal Ch'en Yi privately expressed the same idea in 1964, according to his ultra-leftist Red Guard critics: 'We hope Sino-American relations can improve...perhaps one can say that an improvement of Sino-American relations would be the final improvement of relations throughout the world.' Indeed the evidence suggests that from the mid-1950s at least part of the ruling élite on the Chinese side sought some favourable accommodation with the United States, as Mr Chou noted during President Nixon's visit to Peking. But the history of the difficulties which the Chinese 'doves' encountered, as did their opposite numbers in the American camp, illustrates the warning Dr Kissinger himself wrote in *Foreign Affairs Quarterly,* January 1969. International reefknots – such as the Vietnam war – could not be undone by a single 'dramatic gesture'. Korea not only perpetuated the 'serious resistance' of Chiang Kai-shek in Taiwan, it also determined United States policy on Indochina and raised a spectral trident of potential counter-revolutionary intervention from those three encircling bases. Hence the tendency towards what the Chinese call 'erroneous military lines' (hardware solutions) in both China and the United States.

When the first Indochina war was wound up at Geneva in 1954, a congruence of interest between Moscow and the West (especially with M. Mendes-France) cheated the Vietnamese communists of their apparent victory and set the stage for the second Indochina war. Now, it seems, the intention is to end this war too at the expense of the stubborn hopes of the Vietnamese communists and anti-communists, or factions of them, thanks to the new congruence of interests between Washington and Peking.

The reaction of Peking's allies and 'allies' to President Nixon's blockbuster of 16 July 1971 was, predictably, to lay a smokescreen. Radio Peking itself broke the news in a curious manner, omitting the usual quotation from Mao Tse-tung (e.g. 'People of the world, unite and defeat the United States aggressors and all their running dogs' – as it announced on 17 and 19 July). The normal 6.30 p.m. news was interrupted after the ninth item (French parliamentary delegation meets Kuo Mo-jo and other members of the National People's Congress). After giving the full text of the Sino-American communiqué without comment, the bulletin continued: Kuo Mo-jo meets a group from Sweden.... Tass waited seven hours before reporting the announcement, and ten days before carrying any substantive comment. Then Moscow warned Peking and Washington not to combine against the Soviet Union – an intention expressly disclaimed by President Nixon. In Paris Mme Binh said in effect that Peking would never let her side down. With greater realism, the official organ of the North Vietnamese communist party, *Nhan Dan,* ferociously warned President Nixon that he had gone to the wrong place and would gain nothing from a compromise between big powers. 'The time when the imperialists could dictate their will to the world has definitely gone. The time when a big power could bully a smaller country has also ended for good.' *Pravda* later supported this line. In other words, if it could, Hanoi would sabotage a 'more Asian' Geneva held at its expense. So, perhaps, would some elements in Saigon. There is also a paradoxical congruence of interest, as well as of mythology, between the Chiang and Mao régimes which the Nixon-Chou communiqué recognized; both maintain that Taiwan is a 'province of China', meaning a territory of their respective states, though a majority of its fourteen and a half million people may well think otherwise; they were not asked.

How to end the Vietnam war is fortunately only one among many considerations which have brought Washington and Peking together; reduction of Moscow's power in Asia in order to make the Soviet Union more amenable on other issues, containment of Japan, maintenance of internal stability,[9] the lure of the 'China Trade' and its political exploitation are others. Chances therefore exist for getting clear of the Vietnam tangle in the manner of all insoluble disputes – by its becoming irrelevant to the main issue. On the other hand the record of both Soviet-American and Sino-American efforts towards *détente,* at summit meetings or lesser moves, shows how initiatives from the top can again and again be frustrated by incidents provoked or inopportunely publicized by the respective

153

military, diplomatic, and intelligence bureaucracies. We all know how the U2 incident wrecked the Khrushchev-Eisenhower Paris summit. Further Red Guard-type revelations and Pentagon papers may reveal whether similar contretemps occurred in Sino-American relations because the officers concerned were not in the know, or because they were. The Chinese have let it be known, for example, that a senior Foreign Affairs official, held responsible for the aberrations of 'Boxer diplomacy' such as the burning of the British Mission in Peking, has been tried and sentenced to exemplary punishment. At that time he was denounced by Chou En-lai for doing irreparable harm to China's foreign policy. On the other side, to quote one instance, resumption of the Warsaw talks in February 1969 was apparently sabotaged by United States agents whisking a defecting Chinese diplomat, Liao Mo-shu, from Holland to the United States. At least this incident provided Peking with an excuse to postpone talks. On another occasion, military tactics (the Cambodian operation) cut across the higher diplomatic strategy which was concerned with the same issue. The Sino-American talks were again called off, but Peking did not slam the door. Thanks to the Cultural Revolution, things there were more or less under control. 'Nobody here but us moderates', as *Time* put it.[10]

Reaction from some United States allies to President Nixon's announcement was confused. In Japan and Australia, for example, a spate of political comment about 'missing the bus' missed the point that a symbolic undertaking such as 'I shall go to Korea' or 'I shall go to Peking' has an entirely different significance depending on who makes it, and in what circumstances. The issue was further complicated by wild talk about 'trade with 800 million Chinese', ignoring the facts that China's present trade – all controlled by the authorities – is about four-fifths that of Hong Kong, and that Japan's trade with Taiwan is larger than that with the mainland, is far more profitable, and increased by more than 20 per cent in 1970. (Japan also has about $100 million worth of investments in Taiwan.) China has great potential for internal development but economists and well-informed business sources point out that it has shown no inclination to build up an extensive international trade (at present it amounts to 3 per cent of GNP). China seeks autarky in machinery and until its new five-year plan gets under way it is unlikely to be a large buyer of commodities.

When the ping-pong games started, the present writer argued that a major aim of Peking should be to detach allies from America by giving them the impression that they should immediately get on the Sino-American bandwagon; the bandwagon could then have disappeared, for example by Peking's imposition of less acceptable conditions for President Nixon's visit, and Peking would have gained much and lost nothing.[11] As Head of State visiting China's Premier, who was merely an official, President Nixon had 'lost face' in Chinese terms before he arrived. It might have been thought that he faced such pressure from uninformed public opinion expecting miracles to be worked at a 'summit', and from groups such as anti-war demonstrators, strikers, and Afro-American guerrillas, that he would be forced to make concessions to save the visit. In spite of his claim that the week in Peking had changed the world, it was not immediately clear what overt gains for the United States the visit had achieved, though the possibilities of secret agreements and repercussions in Soviet-American relations were obvious. Who, in fact, stood to gain more from holding the trip? Many well-informed Americans opposed it. It clearly paid China, among other considerations, to settle Taiwan with departing America rather than with resurgent Japan, and to settle Indochina with America rather than allow the domination of all the four states by North Vietnam, perhaps with increasing Soviet and Japanese influence as well. Mr Chou, like President Nixon, would at this stage prefer a polycentric Asianization of East Asia to a replacement of the United States by Japan as hegemon, or a Soviet-Japanese condominium. By going direct to the United States over the heads of other nations, China has already achieved extraordinary disarray in Japan and has obtained a toehold in the politics of several other countries. It seems unreasonable to expect that Peking should forego entirely the use of 'mass struggles' in order to reinforce diplomatic and other pressure on all possible countries, including the United States itself, to secure Taiwan and other objectives. Among the many analogies one may draw with the first Geneva, one is particularly disquieting: as the curtain fell on the first Indochina war, the scene shifted to Algeria. Now, even if King Hussein and the Lebanese were to leash the Palestinian commandos, others are deployed to continue the struggle with Peking's covert support, from Ankara to Oman. From its position in the United Nations, Peking will be able to exploit this situation with its 'overt' diplomacy, and veto if need be any arrangements which the superpowers may have had to delay making until after the United States elections.

Although Peking has proved that it will deny overt support to

'Maoist' bands when inexpedient, as it has done in East Bengal and Ceylon, it has not altered the aims of its foreign policy.[12] Nor has it changed its method, which is based on the adaptation to the world scene of the tested scenarios of guerrilla warfare. (In stage one, avoid battles you cannot win, seek psychological rather than territorial advantage, divide the opposition and ally with those afar to combat those near, and so forth; when the time is ripe, the low posture can be abandoned.) As long as Peking's leaders think the revolution must defeat its enemies in order to survive, they must loyally plan for stages two and three. It is pathetic to see people who once exaggerated the threat of China as 'aggressive and expansionist', in the conventional sense of grabbing bits of territory, swinging over to euphoric relief as they at last learn they were wrong. Peking's present method of indirect defence by exploiting the 'internal contradictions' of its adversaries is in fact cheaper and more effective than conventional politico-military methods, and therefore potentially more dangerous. It not only provokes inapposite reactions on the part of powers directly and indirectly affected, but it also strengthens the hand of those who blame genuinely local disorders on the hand of Peking, and who are tempted to try and solve domestic social and economic problems by a military 'pre-emptive defensive strike' against the supposed source of the trouble. It cannot be denied that Peking *has* extended its hidden hand to exploit latent 'contradictions' in many remote parts of the world, especially racial tensions and troubles arising from the generation gap; thoroughly-documented cases abound.[13]

The great question raised by President Nixon's visit is whether, once China has gained sufficient international 'face', it will abandon the crypto-diplomatic or covert activities designed to make itself a 'force to be reckoned with'. During the internal upheavals of 1971 which culminated in the disappearance of Marshal Lin Piao and the cream of the Chinese military-industrial complex, articles appeared in the Peking media which suggested that what was called 'Chairman Mao's revolutionary diplomatic line' (the dual tactics, including the approach to Nixon) had been one of the bones of contention between the factions. The Great Proletarian Cultural Revolution got rid of Liu Shao-chi and his line, which consisted essentially of beating the Russians at their own game by imitating and sinicizing their methods – setting up a world-wide apparatus of communist ('Marxist-Leninist') parties, international front organizations, and similar bodies. While Lin Piao had the upper hand, in uneasy combination with those who have now been purged as 'ultra-leftists', the military played an important part in the conduct of overt as well as covert foreign affairs; in the previous period there is reason to believe that their activities were not coordinated with those of the regular diplomats and foreign trade apparatus and were even designed to interfere with them. At the time of writing, the Lin Piao men and exponents of the 'guerrilla style' (rather than the Bolshevik style) are gradually being eliminated, though some are still apparently holding out in parts of China; but in foreign relations there is no evidence that support for guerrilla movements and other disruptive forces, regardless of their own ideology[14] – behaviour which was typical of the post-Cultural Revolution period – has actually been discontinued. It would be difficult for Peking to retain its image in competition with the Soviets if it should so 'abandon its internationalist duty'. The most that can be expected is for clandestine operations to be played down and/or run through proxies, while state, trade, and cultural contacts are built up to provide a platform which can, if and when expedient, be used for launching clandestine operations again on a bigger scale.

In Leninist terms, to abandon the option of carrying on illegal, clandestine, revolutionary activities and to rely only on legal and open campaigning would be 'parliamentary cretinism'; on the global scale, to rely only on the United Nations and ambassadors would be 'diplomatic cretinism'. Conversely, to rely *only* on the arts of crypto-diplomacy – for example on guerrillas, secret agents, pro-Peking student groups, or trade unionists – would be 'infantile leftism'. A single country, in the same way, would be stupid to stick only to secret work when open activities were also possible; each reinforces the other. Old soldiers all know the technique: while one half of the squad gives covering fire, the other moves into a better position; then the roles are reversed. Sun Tsu, the ancient Chinese strategist, wrote: 'Use the normal force to engage; use the extraordinary to win.' Chairman Mao, the modern Sun, told his cadres in 1949 that they must learn how to carry on diplomatic struggles, both overt and covert; his instruction was republished in November 1968 to usher in his 'diplomatic offensive'. During the anti-Japanese and civil wars in China, Mao used to spread his net wide to arouse and win over the masses, then draw it in to fight the enemy. Now he casts his net over distant Africa and Latin America to win new friends and to mobilize them at the United Nations into a collective power which can oppose the superpowers on various popular issues.

Where the net is cast wide, the work of the revolution is carried on by political rather than conventional military means. The result is the building up of a favourable balance which can later be 'cashed' in military terms, for example by 'liberation' of territory. In the present phase the object is not to gain territory but to disintegrate the enemy, to reduce and take over his effective strength, and it is then expedient, as it was during the anti-Japanese war, to ally with a long-term enemy against a short-term one. In his writings of the period, such as his essay of 1940 *On Policy*, Chairman Mao explained that such a temporary alliance must combine unity with struggle: 'In the struggle against the anti-communist diehards, we must take advantage of the contradictions among them in order to win over the majority to oppose the minority and crush our opponents separately, and follow the line of justifiability, expediency, and restraint.' The policy in government-controlled and enemy-occupied areas, he went on, must be 'maximum development of the united front, while at the same time concealing our identity and simplifying our structure in organization and struggle, building up our strength and biding our time.'

In August 1971 the *Peking Review* printed an important article explaining how this essay of Mao's applied to the present international situation. The contradictions to be exploited were those between Russia and America, and between the superpowers and the rest; there were even hints that the 'principal contradiction' was not between the imperialist camp and the world masses struggling for liberation but between the imperialists themselves. Corresponding to the large areas of China occupied by the enemy or held by the Nationalists in wartime were the many small and medium-sized countries, which the superpowers wanted to drag on to their side. Leaders of many of these countries calculated that by making a direct diplomatic approach to China they could get rid of problems of internal subversion which China's crypto-diplomats helped to create in the first place. China of course welcomed this maximum development of the 'united front from above'. But it is hard to see why it should then abandon the other half of the formula, the clandestine work from below, just when its effectiveness had been proved by the 'diehards' as they came round to recognizing the Peking government.

In remoter regions like Africa and Latin America, whoever has emerged on top after the recent upheaval in Peking's military circles may well favour government-to-government relations at the expense of ineffectual insurgents; in areas closer to China, however, 'walking on two legs' is required by the logic of the situation. The Shah of Iran's overtures to China last year (followed by opening of Sino-Iranian diplomatic relations announced on 17 August 1971) were associated by some commentators with his desire to stymie local 'Maoist' terrorists, several of whom have recently been shot.[15] The sensational visit of the Emperor of Ethiopia to Peking may be linked with his less-publicized visit to Sudan, which the 'Eritrean Liberation Front' (ELF) has been using as a base for its Chinese-supported terrorism inside Ethiopia. In return for the extradition of eight Sudanese pro-Moscow communists involved in the recent abortive coup against President al Nemery, the latter agreed with Emperor Haile Selassie to expel the ELF; at a press conference in their new headquarters in Beirut an official of the Front said it was no longer supported by China, whose policy was now to widen international relations. If true, this is totally at variance with Peking's continued propaganda support for such movements, and with the evidence of stepped-up communist activity in Thailand, West Malaysia,[16] and elsewhere. What Peking has done is to make it possible to maintain the fiction that these insurgencies have nothing to do with Peking, by making its propaganda broadcasts from pseudo-clandestine stations in China instead of through Peking Radio in the normal way.

To take one example of what we should expect: Peking's opening of diplomatic relations and entry into the United Nations have already enabled it to exploit the situation in Africa, and to use the session of the Security Council in Addis Ababa to promote the race war and the 'united front'. As far back as 1960 Chinese delegates to an Afro-Asian solidarity conference in Conakry were pressing for the creation of an Afro-Asian volunteer army – ostensibly to fight the whites but in reality to revolutionize Africa. The sagacious Premier Chou En-lai may not favour such schemes today; his troops are only building a railway in Africa and training a few guerrilla leaders. But China's present diplomatic success is paradoxically related to continuing domestic uncertainty. A recent visitor to China, who helped to set up the visit to Peking of Mr Whitlam, then the Leader of the Opposition in Australia, has recently written:

> Of course, as China grows in power, her ambitions will increase. She will go, when she is able to, from 'strategic defence' to 'counter-offensive'. China will not always be in a

> condition of relative weakness...having 'stood up', China
> is likely to 'stretch out.'[17]

It is true that China's policies are conditioned by a feeling of weakness; the present generation of leaders is likely never to get rid of it, nor did they expect to get into the United Nations so quickly. They can hardly grasp the fact that the West is not implacably hostile to China, that it is not dedicated to defeating the bogeymen it used to believe in; in fact, apart from the Taiwan question, there has never been as much conflict of interest between the United States and China as there has been between Japan and China, and especially between China and the Soviet Union.

Chou En-lai has always stressed that President Nixon's visit was Chairman Mao's idea. No one in Peking seems to have had a very clear idea how it would go, and its main significance may well prove to lie in the way in which both sides have used it in dealing with internal politics, as well as with their allies and their bureaucracies. Rumour has it that the order has gone out to the agents of America's CIA: 'Don't do anything, just stand there.' It is greatly to be hoped that Peking will be ready and able to cut down its own CIA-type activities abroad; but until concrete evidence appears Pacific nations will continue to assume that China retains its revolutionary dual policy. First reactions to President Nixon's Peking visit in Indonesia, Thailand, etc. showed more realism than those of the United States and Australia.

On landing at Peking the President was confronted with a pair of quotations from Mao, the gist of which was that 'the logic of the imperialists' is to make trouble and to fail until their doom; not shown was the rest of the passage, which says that they will never 'lay down their butcher knives and become Buddhas'. The people, however, are bound to triumph.[18] Unless President Nixon's disclaimer of any secret arrangements is to be taken with salt, and subject to the surprises Dr Kissinger has doubtless planned for the second and presumably more important part of the package tour – in Moscow, the net result of their television appearance in the hitherto Forbidden City would appear to be gains on the home front for both sides, but more obvious gains for Chou's China in international affairs. As the rearrangement of the kaleidoscope proceeds, however, this conclusion will probably require modification. In the first place, as Mr Bundy put it,[19] given American conditions the visit itself was in large part the villain, since it created vast quantities of ignorant and trivial comment and false expectations. It would, however, be in accordance with Dr Kissinger's style to harness the in some ways new and irresponsible power of the media to Mr Nixon's electoral juggernaut. Beyond this, in spite of ominous signs of rapprochement between Japan and the Soviet Union, and between Japan and North Vietnam, at the end of the day it is still possible that what has been described as 'American Gaullism in action' will be revealed even as a sort of American Maoism – letting the ocean barbarians pacify each other and so facilitating the reduction of American commitments abroad. The new America, like the Chinese, in confronting a foe with more weaponry than ideas is shifting the emphasis to another sphere of conflict – to the creation and management of world public opinion. For many years it has been at a disadvantage in this sphere. It remains to be seen how far the requirements of the new image will dictate American policy instead of serving it.[20]

Notes

1 See R.A. Rupen and R. Farrell (eds), *Vietnam and the Sino-Soviet Dispute*, Praeger, New York, 1967, p. 98.

2 Professor Kissinger's role of crypto-diplomat was probably more congenial to the Chinese than conventional diplomacy, resembling as it did that of the persuader in traditional Chinese statecraft. Cf. *Chan-kuo Ts'e*, trans. J.I. Crump, Clarendon Press, 1970.

3 For example, I wrote that it was up to the outside world to help China deal with its diehards 'by approaching China with fairness and tact and overcoming its isolation' (*Spectator*, 1 November 1963, p. 557).

4 Space precludes a listing of the other civilian and military personnel, concerned with defence and foreign relations on both sides, who have significantly changed their jobs – or their minds – in the last few years. It is not entirely facetious to argue that a sort of 'Cultural Revolution' also aided this process in the United States. See *Far Eastern Economic Review*, 29 May 1971, pp. 47. ff.

5 NCNA, 24 November 1968.

6 Mentioned by Chinese leaders at a banquet for Soebandrio, Indonesia's Foreign Minister, 24 January 1965, and at a banquet for President Kaunda of Zambia, 14 June 1967.

7 'Chinese Checkers; Three Can Play', *Interplay* (New York), March 1969.

8 'The World Chessgame; More Gambits, More Players', *Interplay*, October 1970.

9 See 'A Setback for the Democrats', *Newsweek*, 26 July 1971.

10 26 July 1971, p. 8. This, of course, encapsulates a most serious misconception. The dismissal and disgrace of Chinese leaders who hoped to manage Russia by involving her in a Koreanized Vietnam war, and who had committed themselves to policies of world revolution which proved counter-productive, means only that the present leadership proposes to pursue the aims of the revolution in a more effective manner, not to give them up. Similarly, as the Chinese put it, Washington is only pursuing its aims in a more 'cunning' manner than before.

11 *Canberra Times*, 6 May 1971.

12 A recent book, '*Revolution and China's Foreign Policy*', by Peter Van Ness has discussed the question of Peking's *overt endorsement* of armed insurrections, but this is not the same thing as *support* in the normal sense of the word.

13 *Times*, 15 March 1968, p. 10.

14 In his famous article on world-wide People's War (*Peking Review*, no. 36, 1965, p. 26) Marshal Lin Piao provides theoretical justification for the idea that a war of this kind need not necessarily be led by communists. Indonesia and Algeria were cited as examples; it was in these countries that evidence later emerged of Chinese involvement with army or armed groups distinct from the local communist parties. In these and several other Afro-Asian countries China provided arms for and encouraged the formation of a 'fifth force' to counterbalance the army, navy, air force, and police; in the light of criticism of policy in these countries revealed by the Red Guards, it appears that a military apparatus (*hsi-tung*) was using military methods (in the Maoist sense) to carry out what would normally be the task of civilian diplomats, i.e. the conduct of foreign relations. The usurpation of civilian functions by military personnel and organs was already noticeable

162

in internal Chinese affairs in 1965, though at this stage the 'military' included groups later revealed as opponents of Lin, notably the associates of Lo Jui-ch'ing with his secret-police background, dismissed as Chief of Staff by the end of 1965.

15 Cf. G. Cooley in *Christian Science Monitor*, 19 May 1971, and *Canberra Times*, 13 May 1971, p. 2. Talks on the establishment of Sino-Turkish diplomatic relations began in Paris in May 1971 (*Peking Review*, no. 20, 1971).

16 See the Malaysian Government White Paper 'The Resurgence of Armed Communism in West Malaysia', 2 October 1971. At his end-of-the-year press conference General Prapas said in Bangkok that in spite of its improved relations with Rangoon, Peking had *not* promised to withhold support from communists in Burma; this was a warning for Thailand. (*Far Eastern Economic Review*, 15 January 1972, p. 8.)

17 Ross Terrill in *Bulletin* (Sydney), 5 February 1972, p. 26.

18 I had argued that Peking's rulers are committed to the proposition that their foreign opposite numbers will never 'lay down their butcher knives and become Buddhas' until *compelled* to do so. See 'China's Diplomatic Breakthrough', *World Review* (Brisbane), July 1971, p. 20; the present paper incorporates ideas and material originally treated in the *World Review* and in *Quadrant*, November/December 1971, pp. 26–37, q.v. On the implications of President Nixon's trip to Peking, see W.A.C. Adie, '"One World" Restored?', *Asian Survey*, May 1972. Briefly the lesson is – self-reliance.

19 *Newsweek*, 27 December 1971, p. 52.

20 The foe in question is of course the Soviet Union, which is obviously moving in the Middle East and Asia to 'contain' China, just as China is moving into the Middle East and even the Mediterranean and the Balkans to 'contain' the Soviet Union. In some areas Russia replaces Britain more thoroughly than the United States ever did; in others, Chinese influence ties down the Soviets, thereby contributing among other things to the defence of Europe (cf. *Times* leader of 6 May 1970).

Sino-American Relations:
From Right to Left

D.H. MENDEL

Few people, least of all this specialist in Japan and Taiwan affairs, expected President Nixon to relax American policies toward the People's Republic of China or that regime to open its arms to the American president who built his career on anti-communist slogans. Yet, since 1969 the Nixon administration has dismantled all trade and travel barriers maintained since 1950; made an official visit to China; and accepted Peking's claim that the status of Taiwan is a domestic issue to be settled between Taipei and the mainland. One might almost say that Richard Nixon shocked his conservative Republican supporters of the past generation as much as Charles de Gaulle disappointed his right-wing allies by granting independence to Algeria. 'No Democratic president could have switched our China policy as quickly as such a proven anti-Communist cold warrior as Richard Nixon,' commented Seymour Topping of the *New York Times* in November 1971.[1] Professor Allen Whiting and others contend that the thaw in Sino-American relations was initiated more by Peking's desire to obtain maximum leverage against its Soviet antagonist, and obviously the historic Nixon visit to Mao and Chou signified a mutual desire for *détente*. What were the American and Chinese motives, how did they emerge after two decades of intense hostility, and what are the prospects for a genuine Sino-American rapprochement?

Richard Nixon's motives were foreshadowed by his article in the influential *Foreign Affairs* magazine in October 1967, a year before his election to the presidency. He wrote then that 'any American policy toward Asia must come urgently to grips with the reality of China.' Perhaps he recalled President Eisenhower's alleged statement after entering the White House in 1953 that 'it is going to be damned difficult to conduct a foreign policy based largely on the delusion that China is an offshore island'. President Eisenhower continued that 'this piece of idiocy had been built into American policy and no man, not even a President, dared challenge it'.[2] He did, however, challenge his Republican hawks on the Korean issue and on the more complex problem of dealing with Senator Joseph McCarthy, as well as with his veto of American air support of the French garrison at Dien Bien Phu. Moreover President Nixon must recall Secretary John Foster Dulles's releasing of Chiang Kai-shek's forces in his agreement with George Yeh in 1954 at the time of the United States-Republic of China security treaty. In short, past Republican policy had been to protect Taiwan from mainland attack but never to assist the Nationalists to conquer the mainland.

More significant, according to many who have access to both the White House staff and Chou En-lai, was President Nixon's decision to withdraw from the Vietnam engagement. This factor influenced Peking as much as, if not more than, Washington, because Hanoi is an ally of the People's Republic of China and the Kennedy-Johnson administration's escalation of aid to Saigon worried China more than President Nixon's abortive thrust into Cambodia which was overshadowed by his ground-force withdrawal from South Vietnam. If President Nixon wanted to cut United States losses and pursue the doctrine of self-reliance (one of Mao's favorite theses), he would have to establish better communications with Peking, which is the source of aid to several Asian insurgency movements. During the Johnson administration Dean Rusk often pointed to the People's Republic of China as the real enemy whose influence in Vietnam must be checked.[3]

Another motive favored by Moscow and Taipei was President Nixon's hope that his overtures to Peking would assist his re-election campaign as a peace hero in 1972. Richard Nixon is a political man anxious to adjust to the winds of popular change, not an ideologue determined to remain true to his ideals at any cost. Just as the Vietnam operation had proved counter-productive, so the United States' China policy of blind support for the refugee Nationalists must have appeared unprofitable as the United Nations moved to rectify its China policy and Chou En-lai's post-1968 foreign policy raised the prestige of the People's Republic of China around the world.

There must be other motives for the shift of United States policy, but motives are most difficult to detect in foreign policy. Actually, despite the surface hostility between the United States and the People's Republic of China since the Korean War (1950–3), we can see only very limited American support of its Nationalist ally. Neither Peking nor Washington ever relished a real confrontation and Washington made that clear several times during the Warsaw ambassadorial talks.[4] Peking's foreign policy has been far more violent verbally than in action, but Washington also showed significant restraint during the Quemoy crisis of 1958 and the prolonged bombing of North Vietnam in 1965–8.

Peking's motives are even more ambiguous. One of them must be the traditional Chinese tactic of friendliness toward distant nations and hostility toward neighboring ones, or of using the power of a distant nation to counterbalance the threat from its neighbors, Russia and Japan. Significantly Chou En-lai refused even to accept a letter from the Japanese governing party brought by Tokyo Governor Minobe, while he was most hospitable to anti-Sato Japanese politicians (except the Yoyogi communists), to the arch-reactionary, President Nixon, and to Dr Kissinger.

Chinese fear of its more powerful Soviet neighbor cannot be doubted, whether or not we believe it is justified. The belief that danger exists is far more important than the actual fact of danger. Moreover one of Peking's major aims has been to split the United States from its close alliance with Japan and Nationalist China. Peking wants to sow seeds of discord between Tokyo and Washington, a task accomplished more by American economic forces – the second of the Nixon shocks I witnessed in Tokyo in 1971. Peking tells some visiting Americans that she prefers to have United States troops remain in Japan and Okinawa to deter Japanese rearmament, but assures all visiting Japanese, in accordance with majority Japanese opinion, that she wants total withdrawal of these troops. Does Peking think that Washington can restrain Japanese militarism and expansionism? It is more logical to believe that the leaders of the People's Republic fear Japan than that they think President Nixon would restrain Tokyo from playing a containment role under the Nixon Doctrine.[5]

The reactions around Asia and inside the United States to the Nixon opening to China are also instructive. The anti-Peking regimes in Seoul and Taipei were very critical, whereas North Korea and North Vietnam were more restrained than their Soviet allies in denouncing the Sino-American rapprochement. Within President Nixon's own party, only a minority led by Congressman John Ashbrook openly denounced their leader, while Senator Barry Goldwater and the majority of conservative Republicans advised against any anti-Nixon campaign that would benefit the Democrats in an election year. Taipei also muted its objections by hoping that the president would live up to his pro-Kuomintang record, but encouraged rumors of an approach to Moscow as it had encouraged rumors of a separate peace with Japan during World War Two.

Perhaps the one common factor in Chinese and United States policy has been an emphasis on secrecy and big power elitism which some observers attribute to the Kissinger tradition. Elitist control of policy is a mode of Communist and Nationalist China as well as of the Soviet Union, but Mr Nixon has always distrusted the United States foreign service. His appointment of Dr Henry Kissinger as his special assistant was in line with previous presidents' use of personal foreign policy advisors in order to bypass the State Department. 'That was a good idea,' said one of my close friends in the Department's Policy Planning Staff in April 1972, 'because the bureaux of this Department are self-appointed custodians of past policy and only the President could break the China policy freeze. Only he could correct old myths and recognize the real China.'[6] Inside China, it was Chou En-lai, the realistic veteran of so many diplomatic endeavors, who had to contest with the blind ideologues of Maoism and past anti-American policy.

Before discussing the probable future course of Sino-American relations, we should draw a balance sheet of factors favorable to and hostile to a genuine rapprochement. The Taiwan issue has always been the primary stumbling block which deserves extended discussion later. First, what are the factors favorable to rapprochement? One is the record of United States relations with China over the past two centuries when the United States was the least imperialistic of all the foreign powers active in China. Despite charges of American economic and military aggression between 1890 and 1941, Britain, Russia, and Japan were the guiltiest parties, especially in their territorial incursions into the decadent Manchu Empire and, after 1911, into the struggling Republic. True, the United States played a junior partner role to the British and American businessmen and missionaries in China. However, the latter enjoyed the protection of British power far more than their own Yangtze River patrol. It is also true that Washington's verbal attacks on Japanese aggression did not deter Tokyo until after Japan attacked American forces directly in December 1941. But even the People's Republic of China must recognize that American forces, not Russian or Chinese, defeated Japan and expelled her from China in 1945.

Moreover the record of American policy toward the civil war in China after 1946 was sufficiently ambiguous to cause President Truman's critics to charge his administration and the State Department with the 'loss of China to Communism' after 1949. That charge was false, but many Nationalists and their dwindling number of American friends still echo it and even accuse President Nixon of following the same course today. Surely the overall record of American public and private actions in the century before 1949 presents no obstacle to good future relations between the United States and the People's Republic of China. American policy from 1950 to 1970 is another story of course.

A second factor favoring good relations is the United States' capacity to assist in the economic and social development of mainland China. André Malraux probably exaggerated Peking's desire for such aid, because Japan is more willing and more likely to serve as China's principal donor, but the time may now be ripe for the kind of proposal made by Professor Marion Levy Jr at a Princeton seminar early in 1949.[7] Peking's experience with Soviet aid and her intense nationalism will cause her to diversify her sources of outside credits, technical aid, and other assistance. She will seek to maximize the number of her trading partners.

A third factor is the growing popular respect for the People's Republic of China among the American public. Disillusion with the Vietnam war and the inflated villain image of Peking propagated by Washington between 1950 and 1970 is partly responsible for China's better image in the United States. President Nixon himself was correct in pointing to the need to bring China into disarmament negotiations and other international talks now that it is a thermonuclear power and likely to expand its military capacity. The prospect of profitable trade and travel contacts with China is far more operative on the private level than in official Washington thinking, which is why the writer did not list economic motive as impelling Nixon toward better relations with the People's Republic of China. Despite Marxist and neo-Marxist theories, American policy in Asia since 1941 has not been predicated on economic issues, although trade competition and protectionist tendencies loomed large in the 1960s and may increase.

Finally, the influence of the pro-Kuomintang China lobby on United States policy-makers has declined steadily since the Kennedy era. The reaction of the American public to President Nixon's trip to China, to Congressman John Ashbrook's challenge to the President in party primary elections, and to the United Nations vote in 1971 to replace Nationalist Chinese by People's Republic of China delegations shows the trend dramatically. In fact Professor Edwin O. Reischauer insists that the United States 'always overreacts to China'; but after all the real China has finally been recognized by Washington after two decades of make-believe.

The unfavorable factors to better Sino-American relations seem to loom far larger in Peking's view than in Washington's. Peking has always charged the United States with being a major imperialist threat ever since the bloody confrontation in Korea. Chinese intervention in the Korean war had a traumatic effect on American public opinion far out of proportion to the Chinese intent though China remains a firm ally to North Korea in words if not in deeds. But China fought the United States and United Nations forces to a draw in Korea, and may not object to the continued division of that peninsula as long as the United States does not threaten North Korea and continues to reduce its troops in the south.

United States obstruction to the very end of the representation of the People's Republic of China in the United Nations was bitterly attacked by Peking, but how much did Washington really fight to keep a separate seat for the Nationalists in 1971? After President Nixon's relaxation of trade and travel restrictions, and especially after his use of the name People's Republic of China and his travel announcement of 15 July 1971, could anyone really doubt that his administration was reconciled to the passage of the Albanian resolution that China should be admitted to the United Nations? Washington had to make a public show of support for the Kuomintang, and may have hoped for a two-China compromise, but my sources in official circles always felt otherwise. 'We have to put up a front for Chiang Kai-shek and his friends here,' some Washington advisors commented in 1971 and 1972. Peking deprecated the value of the United Nations during the Cultural Revolution (1966–9) although officers at the Japanese-United Nations mission claimed even then that she was eager to take the Nationalist seat. As soon as the United States signalled its willingness to see Peking in the United Nations, most American allies, except Japan and a few others with reasons of their own, switched to Peking's side. I was reminded of the long Indonesian struggle to expel the Dutch from West Irian (New Guinea): the Dutch delayed so long that the United States and other parties conceded the issue. If the Netherlands had promoted a compromise (such as United Nations trusteeship or independence) in the early 1950s, it might have succeeded. If the Nationalists and others had supported a compromise (e.g. the Italian United Nations resolution), a separate seat for Taiwan might have been possible up to 1968.

American policy in Vietnam, Laos, and Cambodia must have been a severe shock to Peking, because the Vietnam bombing and other escalatory steps between 1965 and 1968 sorely strained the Peking-Hanoi alliance. The American incursion into Cambodia in 1970 led Peking to host Prince Norodom Sihanouk, as it has hosted the free Lao group throughout the secret American intervention in that sad land from 1954 to the present. President Johnson often reassured Peking that he had no intention of toppling the Hanoi regime or endangering Chinese security despite the heavy bombing of North Vietnam. Peking and Moscow had shown little concern for Hanoi's interest at the Geneva talks in 1954, according to Bernard Fall's account of the 17th parallel decision, and one wonders how much Peking worries about its Vietnamese ally today. If Seymour Topping is correct in quoting Chou En-lai as being convinced early in 1971 of President Nixon's sincerity in planning to withdraw fully from Indochina, that would explain Chou En-lai's welcome to President Nixon in February 1972. One wonders, however, how far Peking can ignore American military actions in Southeast Asia.

Finally, American support of Chiang Kai-shek's regime on Taiwan is the biggest obstacle to Sino-American rapprochement. Any nation in Europe, Africa, Latin America, and Asia (except Japan), or in other regions could ignore the Taiwan issue when seeking to establish relations with Peking. Britain, the only nation to have a consulate in Taiwan and an embassy in Peking, finally closed its Taiwan consulate in 1972 to maximize relations with the People's Republic of China in the wake of the United Nations vote. Washington considers its ties to the Nationalist regime as merely a continuation of its World War Two alliance (which was never formal) and its post-1950 support of Taiwan as a separate matter. The United States-Republic of China security treaty of 1954, under which Washington provided over $2 billion military aid to the Nationalists (after the $1·6 billion economic grant aid ended in 1965), was reaffirmed by Washington in 1971. But Peking did not demand abrogation of that pact as it did of the Japanese peace treaty of 1952 with the Nationalists. Perhaps the cessation of patrols by the United States Seventh Fleet in the Taiwan Straits reassured Peking that Washington will not support a Nationalist attack against the mainland – a reassurance every administration in Washington has reiterated since 1954. Washington has not provided nuclear or strategic arms to Chiang Kai-shek's forces, but its attitude to Nationalist operations on Quemoy and Matsu continues to be ambivalent.

American policy toward Taiwan is the subject of several recent books.[8] Basically it has been a defensive not an offensive posture, permitting President Nixon to include in his Shanghai communiqué the hope that the two Chinese regimes would settle the issue peacefully. The writer gave a seminar at the University of Washington in June 1971 outlining the complaints that Nationalist China had against American policy, from relaxation of trade and travel to ping-pong diplomacy and tolerance of political activities by Taiwanese in the United States. Some visitors to Peking in 1972 claim that the regime is most worried about the danger of a Taiwan independence movement receiving foreign aid (Japanese and American). Peking accuses Tokyo more than Washington of aiding and abetting the Taiwan independence movement, but neither did so.

What is the policy of the United States toward the native majority on Taiwan (14 million of the 16 million population)? Secretary of State William Rogers claimed in a 1969 speech that 'self-determination' is the world-wide goal of American foreign policy, but it has never been applied to West Irian, Bangladesh, or other non-communist areas. The writer has spent ten years studying the native Taiwan issue and can attest to the lack of governmental support in Japan or the United States for the Taiwanese majority. Many Japanese and American diplomats, military officers, and other officials privately sympathize with the Formosan cause but fewer will express such support today than in the 1960s. Nor will either government intervene on behalf of the Formosan majority, as President Nixon's and Prime Minister Sato's statements showed in 1971. Unlike Prime Minister Sato, no United States president has ordered the return of any Taiwanese to the Chiang regime, but the future is more uncertain as Washington tries to reassure Peking of the territorial integrity of mainland China. After all, in 1943 at Cairo the United States agreed that the island of Taiwan belonged to the People's Republic of China. (George Kennan termed that the biggest diplomatic mistake of World War Two.)[9]

The Taiwan issue was more or less ignored during President Nixon's visit to China in 1972, but Edwin Reischauer interpreted the Shanghai communiqué as shelving the issue indefinitely: China renouncing the use of force to liberate Taiwan because it hopes for a peaceful merger after Chiang Kai-shek's death, and Reischauer hoped that the extension of the status quo over Taiwan would lead to Peking's eventual recognition of separate status for Taiwan.[10] Chou En-lai has often invited refugee Nationalists to return home to mainland China without penalty or to remain in a reunited Taiwan whose economy would be preserved. But Peking's record on autonomy for Tibet and other 'autonomous regions' cautions against any expectation that it would respect Taiwanese autonomy. This writer and many China experts in the State Department have always felt that the Nationalist elite might rather turn Taiwan over to the mainland then to the natives of the island, but a transitional status retaining mainlander control of a Republic of Taiwan could be acceptable.

The United States has always recognized Taiwan as a part of China, at least since the Cairo declaration of 1943, even though the legal officers of the State Department maintain to this day that the island's status is undetermined in international law. Possession is nine-tenths of international law, however, and the fact that Washington has supported the 'One China' thesis of the Nationalists for two decades makes it very difficult to deny Peking the claim to regard Taiwan as part of China. When Prime Minister Sato told a Diet interrogator that the People's Republic of China is the only legal government of China, that Taiwan is a province of China, and hence that Taiwan is part of the People's Republic of China, he was stating what the British government admitted by withdrawing its consulate from Taiwan and exchanging ambassadors with Peking.

For the past decade the United States has devoted much treasure and human life to defend the principle of self-determination for the people of South Vietnam. That effort may have been hopeless, but it would seem equally unwise to ignore the right of the 16 million people on Taiwan to determine their own future. Taiwan has none of the strategic problems of South Vietnam, nor do many of its people really yearn for communist liberation as Peking claims. Would Washington barter Taiwan for a rapprochement with Peking, or at least abandon its security treaty with the Nationalists and encourage them to patch up their dispute with the People's Republic of China? At this point preferences must part company with predictions because this writer has a strong commitment to a Free Taiwan, preferably a democratic regime in which the natives would have full political rights but, if that is impracticable, to a continuation of the status quo. The Quemoy-Matsu offshore island complex should have been evacuated years ago: it belongs to the mainland and Nationalist possession has obstructed progress toward Taiwan separatism.

But these are the writer's own preferences; predictions are another matter because both Chinese regimes denounce and fear Taiwan separatism more than anything else. James Reston told the American consul-general in Hong Kong on his return from talks with Chou En-lai in August 1971 that Chou En-lai feared the Taiwan independence movement as much as Soviet power. At any rate there are enough proofs of Chinese opposition to Taiwanese separatism to deter any United States official from expressing support for that cause or lending assistance to it. 'After all the coat-carrying and politeness displayed by Kissinger and Nixon in China, how could they raise the little issue of the Taiwanese?' a veteran American foreign service officer now employed by my university asked in April 1972. Later in the year interviews in Washington, Tokyo, and other places with American specialists on China policy confirmed this opinion.

American experts disagree on how important the Taiwan issue will be in Washington-Peking relations, because they disagree on Peking's real intentions. Is Peking more anti-Kuomintang than anti-Taiwanese, or is the Taipei elite more anti-communist than anti-Taiwanese? These will be vital questions for the future status of the island, because no foreign power will aid the Taiwanese majority and the writer has never predicted a native revolt.

In the wake of President Nixon's trip to China, he escalated United States bombing of North Vietnam. Prime Minister Chou En-lai said that this would not deter China from pursuing closer relations with the United States. Washington is likely to continue its military disengagement from Taiwan and its pressure on the Kuomintang regime to settle its differences with Peking. The security pact with Taiwan will be maintained to discourage mainland use of force, but the pact may lose its meaning if Washington's hope for a Peking-Taipei *détente* is realized. On the other hand, if the Kuomintang is realistic and transforms its government into a Republic of Taiwan, evacuating the offshore islands, the United States may persuade Peking to accept a neutralized, non-threatening Taiwan. If Taipei makes a deal with Peking to incorporate Taiwan into the mainland as an autonomous region, that would also meet American approval.

Neither China nor the United States expects much trade with each other, compared, for example, with Sino-Japanese trade, but the two-way volume may rise to US$1 billion annually in a few years' time. American travel to China will also increase as fast as Peking permits, but again Japanese travel is likely to remain more significant. In all respects the initiative rests more with the People's Republic of China than with Washington, and Chinese foreign policy depends heavily on shifts in the domestic power elite, which has undergone enough change in the past three years to caution us against predicting the future. We can hope for greater rationality and compromise on the part of both Great Powers so that their reconciliation will not damage the interests of smaller states in East Asia.

Notes

1 Comment by Mr Topping at the United States Military Academy Student Conference on United States Affairs, West Point, New York, 19 November 1971. Topping also expressed support for Taiwanese self-determination, although he said it was bitterly opposed by Chou and other CPR leaders. The *New York Times* carried its strongest pro-Taiwan editorial on 10 March 1972, entitled 'The Forgotten Taiwanese'. The *Times, Washington Post*, and *Christian Science Monitor* have usually favored a free choice for the Taiwanese, citing United States traditional espousal of self-determination of peoples.

2 Richard Rovere, 'Letter from Washington', *The New Yorker*, 4 March 1972, p. 105. Rovere ignored the issue of the native Taiwanese majority, as did Eisenhower in referring to Taiwan as an 'offshore island', when in fact it is five times farther from Asia than England is from the European continent. The trend of world politics is to ignore the Taiwanese as irrelevant to the higher-priority China question.

3 My World War Two colleague, Robert Scalapino, often defended the Vietnam war during the Johnson administration as a necessary disproof of Peking's theory of liberation wars to deter the Soviet Union from adopting the same militant line around the world if it succeeded in Vietnam.

4 See Kenneth Young, *Negotiating with the Chinese Communists: The United States Experience, 1953–1967*, McGraw-Hill, for Council on Foreign Relations, New York, 1968. Young claimed that Kennedy's assurances in 1962 that the United States would not support a Kuomintang counterattack during a low period of mainland fortunes was the most important message. The content of the talks has remained as secret as the Nixon talks with Chou En-lai in 1972, but United States officials in Warsaw confirmed the Young report to me during conversations in April 1970.

5 Most of my contacts in Japan who have visited the mainland in recent years claim that their Chinese friends have vivid memories of the Sino-Japanese war, 1937–45, and expect Japan to give material proof of its reformation. Nixon, on the other hand, has always favored Japanese rearmament, calling the constitutional clause which forbids military potential 'a mistake' in 1953 and urging every Japanese Cabinet since that time to buy more American weapons, to welcome United States forces, and to assume a role in defending United States Asian allies (such as South Korea) as the United States withdraws.

174

6 Conversation with the most veteran member of the Policy Planning and Coordination Staff, 3 April 1972. The same officer, who has been in government service since 1950, told me in 1971 that State Department support of Okinawan reversion to Japan won out over Defense Department opposition – 'a rare example of our victory over the much more powerful DOD'.

7 Professor Levy proposed a $10 billion or bigger United States economic program for China because he thought China would need massive outside aid to be able to industrialize fast enough to overcome its population explosion. I dissented only on the ground that Peking would place ideology ahead of material development, while the United States Congress would never have approved such massive aid to the Chinese communists on the eve of a Korean war I knew was coming from my 1947 experiences in the South Korean United States military government as advisor to the Korean Army OTS.

8 See the writer's *Politics of Formosan Nationalism*, University of California Press, Berkeley and Los Angeles, 1970; Jerome Alan Cohen *et al., Taiwan and American Policy: The Dilemma in US-China Relations*, Praeger, New York, 1971; and William M. Bueler, *U.S. China Policy and the Problem of Taiwan*, Colorado Associated Universities Press, Boulder, Colo., 1971. Bueler's book is by far the best on the subject (see his interview as ex-CIA agent in Taiwan in *The New York Times*, 12 March 1972, in which he points to a revolutionary potential in Taiwan).

9 Kennan's criticism of the Cairo Declaration was in his book, *Russia and the West under Lenin and Stalin*, Princeton University Press, Princeton, 1961, pp. 376–77, which I purchased in a pirated edition in Taiwan early in 1962 and quoted to local classes. Kennan elaborated his views in an interview with me in January 1964, when he doubted that Russia would ever help China to capture Taiwan.

10 Comments by Professor Reischauer at an American-Japanese symposium on the future of Taiwan, held at the Biltmore Hotel, New York, 25 March 1972, sponsored by President K. Toyama of Radio Kanto, Tokyo.

Agriculture in the People's Republic of China:
An Economic Overview

JOHN WONG

Agriculture is the mainstay of China's economy. Speaking in a country such as New Zealand where farming is an important income-producing and foreign-exchange-earning industry, I do not expect to have difficulty in getting this statement across. However, I must hasten to add that, though agriculture is a dominant sector of the economy in both China and New Zealand, there are many structural differences between the two countries' systems of agriculture: one is essentially collectivized peasant farming and the other primarily commercialized grassland farming of an advanced type. Politically, economically, and socially there must be a world of difference between a Chinese peasant and a New Zealand farmer, although both are making a living on resources directly connected with land. It is not that the Chinese peasant is not as efficient as the New Zealand farmer – most agricultural economists agree that peasant farming can be efficient in its own way and Chinese peasants are in fact among the most efficient and experienced in the world. The differences lie rather in the economic and social orientation of the two, and the kinds of problems they face. The Chinese peasant is not yet fortunate enough to have at his disposal an abundant supply of capital equipment and adequate modern inputs of industrial origin. He simply does not know the kind of rural affluence his New Zealand counterpart enjoys. On the other hand the New Zealand farmer would be amazed to find that farming in China is such an intensive operation which involves much meticulous attention and back-breaking labour. He is likely to be impressed also by the high level of skill and ingenuity with which the Chinese peasant organizes production, as commonly demonstrated in the economical use of scarce resources and the preservation of the natural fertility of the soil. Peasant farming in China, as elsewhere, is a very challenging occupation with a complex production process and many uncertain factors.

Since the communist government came to power in 1949 Chinese agriculture has undergone drastic transformation. Though some elements of peasant farming still remain, many aspects of rural life have changed beyond recognition. Working within a free-enterprise family farm system, the New Zealand farmer would be unfamiliar with such phenomena as collective labour, work-points, private plots, mass mobilization of labour for unpaid capital construction projects, and the like.

In this paper I shall attempt to outline the salient economic features of Chinese agriculture and discuss the institutional changes introduced by the communist government. Then I shall examine the economic implications of the institutional transformation in the light of agricultural development during the past two decades.

THE SALIENT FEATURES OF TRADITIONAL CHINESE AGRICULTURE

Ever since the foundation of the People's Republic the Chinese government has been making gigantic efforts to industrialize the country. This industrialization effort has made impressive strides on many fronts. In some ways China is now an industrialized nation, as can be seen by her annual output of 21 million tonnes of steel and her capacity to produce a wide range of industrial hardware, including nuclear weapons and space equipment. In an overall sense, however, China is still a poor country and a predominantly agricultural one, as her top leaders have repeatedly stressed. Today agriculture in China still produces a large fraction of the national income (at least one-third), provides a livelihood for 80 per cent of the population, and yields 40 per cent of export earnings. Chairman Mao said in 1960: 'Agriculture is the foundation of our economy', and this statement still holds true.

In 1949 the communist government inherited a war-torn economy with a depressed and stagnant agricultural sector. Compared with the pre-war peak, grain production was down by 22 per cent and cotton by 48 per cent. The agricultural structure was of the pre-industrial peasant type and faced the problem of low productivity which is universal in developing countries. In its physical aspects Chinese agriculture reflected the heavy population pressure on land. Studies show that, at the then existing level of technology, China's population had reached what might be called the optimum point by the end of the eighteenth century, and subsequent population growth had led to a decline in per capita output and the lowering of rural living standards.[1] In fact the unfavourable man-land ratio still exists. China supports between one-fourth and one-fifth of the world's population but has only 8 per cent of the world's cultivated land. China is the third largest country in the world with a total area of 9·6 million square kilometres, but with only 11 to 12 per cent of the land under cultivation. The per capita arable land works out at roughly 0·2 of a hectare, but the per capita sown area is 50 per cent larger, as a large part of China produces more than one crop a year.

Because of the shortage of cultivated land, Chinese peasants had for centuries operated one of the most intensive types of farming within the traditional production framework, as reflected in the relatively high yield per hectare but low yield per man. Most peasants lived at bare subsistence level and were trapped in the vicious circle of poverty. The farm economy as a whole failed to produce the large surplus needed for industrial development. Further, the worsening of the man-land ratio, especially after the turn of the century, produced tension and pressure on the traditional institutional structure of agriculture; and many defects were either aggravated or brought to the fore. The cracks in the traditional agrarian framework widened, giving rise to such abuses as landlordism, rent extortion, burdensome land taxes and surcharges, rural usury, and market imperfections. Before the Sino-Japanese war many Chinese rural reformers had passionately advocated institutional reform as a prelude to agricultural development.[2]

On the other hand some reformers favoured a 'technical approach' rather than an 'institutional approach' to agricultural development. Many of these reformers, including the eminent American agricultural economist J.L. Buck, saw the problems of Chinese agriculture as lying primarily in the lack of capital, the shortage of credit, and the insufficient support of modern extension services. Buck thought that increase in production was mainly dependent on farm size and technical progress.[3] Consolidation of the fragmented uneconomic holdings in China would significantly increase productivity. Schultz thought that as peasant agriculture was already efficient and its resources were being intensively utilized, a reallocation of resources along the traditional production pattern as in the case of a land tenant reform would not increase productivity.[4] In particular, it was noted that the extent of tenancy in China was not serious: 46 per cent of the rural population being owners, 24 per cent part-owners, and only 30 per cent tenants.

The above technical arguments might well have been true. But the problem of Chinese agriculture had got beyond the simplistic realm of pure economic argument. As the socio-economic conditions of rural life in China continued to deteriorate, a potentially explosive situation in the countryside developed. From the outset the Chinese communist party (CCP) had recognized the revolutionary potential of the Chinese peasants. In the late twenties Chairman Mao formulated his theory of Chinese revolution with the countryside as the base.[5] Ever since then the CCP had experimented with land reforms in its base areas. Its long involvement with the peasant movement had earned it the hallmark of 'agrarian reformer' and, above all, provided it with a unique opportunity of acquiring organizational experience and practical knowledge of working with the peasantry which formed 80 per cent of the population.

INSTITUTIONAL TRANSFORMATION IN AGRICULTURE

The CCP chose to base its long-term strategy for agricultural development on its own ideological inclination. It held that the institutional framework of traditional agriculture was a 'feudalist' one, in which, in Marxist terms, 'production relations' impeded the development of 'production forces'. To increase production this contradiction must first be resolved, which would mean the replacement of the 'old' production relations by 'new' ones based on socialist organization of production. In other words the institutional transformation of traditional agriculture was to take precedence over technological transformation. Two major developments resulted from the adoption of this strategy. First, agricultural development was given low priority in China's First Five Year Plan (1953–7). Secondly, a series of institutional reorganizations was touched off, starting with land reform and culminating in the formation of the people's communes.

FIRST FIVE YEAR PLAN

The First Five Year Plan, launched with substantial Soviet technical and economic aid, was in many ways a replica of the so-called 'Stalin Model' of development, which laid overwhelming emphasis on rapid industrial growth, especially in large-scale and capital-intensive heavy industries, while at the same time requiring agriculture to fulfil its basic developmental function by carrying the main burden of overall industrialization. The Plan earmarked only 7·3 per cent of the total state investment for capital construction in agriculture, forestry, water conservancy, and meteorology taken together, as against 64·8 per cent for industry alone. Thus the CCP relied on traditional methods rather than on new investment to generate the agricultural surplus needed for industrial development. Largely as a result of inadequate capital investment, agricultural performance during the period of the Plan was rather moderate when compared with the spectacular achievements in industry – 4·5 per cent growth rate for agriculture and 18 per cent for industry.[6] In fact agricultural production had for a time created a bottleneck for further industrial growth during this period. Nevertheless, the government had effectively extracted between 30 and 40 per cent of the marketed surplus from agriculture for economic development in other sectors (as compared with 5 per cent in India for the same period).[7] The Chinese peasants had indeed made heavy sacrifices for the nation's record economic growth which was officially 9 per cent. Western estimates range from 5·6 per cent to 8·8 per cent.[8] In the same way the Meiji peasants had carried the heavy burden for Japan's economic take-off.

Given the initial commitment to the Soviet model of economic development, with heavy industry as the leading sector, the scarce investible resources were inevitably diverted from agriculture. On the other hand some irrational elements clearly influenced the allocation of so low a priority to agriculture in the context of China's economic structure and resource endowment. No wonder that some Chinese leaders, many of whom understood the rural problem better than their Russian counterparts did, had harboured some misgivings about the Soviet strategy from the outset. The Chinese reaction against the priorities of the First Five Year Plan was fully embodied in the Great Leap Forward Movement (1958–60), which called for simultaneous development of agriculture and industry ('Walking on Two Legs'), with emphasis put on labour-intensive projects and total mobilization of labour. The Great Leap Forward eventually ended in economic crisis, partly due to planning and organizational errors and partly to bad weather. But this setback led the CCP to consolidate its development strategy and to base it on what Chairman Mao called 'agriculture as the foundation and industry as the leading sector'. This strategy resembled some form of 'balanced growth' because it appeared to recognize the structural interdependence of industrial and agricultural development as well as the need for balance between consumption and investment in both sectors. Further, this balanced growth was to be operated in the framework of 'self-reliance' which was a new policy resulting from China's worsening economic relationship with the Soviet Union. This approach to development predominated throughout the 1960s and remains basically unchanged today, not having been affected by the Cultural Revolution. At last the Chinese leaders had developed their own strategy of development which they considered to be more appropriate to conditions in China.

INSTITUTIONAL REORGANIZATION

The institutional reorganization of agriculture had been carried out smoothly throughout the 1950s. The first step was land reform (1950–2), which was designed to break up 'feudalist' production relations and to lay down the preconditions for continued institutional transformation. On the political front, land reform appeared to be a radical movement because of its association with revolutionary violence, but in terms of economic revolution Chinese land reforms were actually rather moderate. It sought only to expropriate the landlords as a class; and only 50 per cent of the land was involved in the process of expropriation and redistribution; for draught animals and farm implements the percentage was much lower.[9]

After land reform many newly-created owners were still in economic hardship. The CCP organized them into Mutual Aid Teams (MATs) on a basis of traditional patterns of rural cooperation. A few households formed a MAT by pooling their resources, mainly labour and draught animals, for cooperative use during peak seasons. In a MAT, resources remained individually owned and members were free to dispose of their own produce. In traditional China there was no lack of such cooperative arrangements, and the CCP had little difficulty in getting the poor peasants to join MATs. Usually about 40 per cent of the households formed themselves into MATs as soon as land reform was completed. Some MATs were of a permanent type in the sense that they were not dissolved during slack seasons.

Meanwhile the CCP was making separate efforts to encourage the peasants to form agricultural producers' cooperatives (APCs) on the basis of successful MATs. The APCs were considered to be semi-socialist in nature because, though land and major implements were pooled for collective use, other resources were still technically owned by individual members and were put in as shares for which their owners were paid dividends. By 1955 51 per cent of the peasants were in MATs and 14 per cent in APCs.

As in the Soviet Union, the aim was to achieve agricultural collectivization. Thus further effort was made to convert the cooperatives into full socialist collectives (called Advanced APCs in China) in which all major means of production were collectively owned and payments to members were based on a work-point system. The collectivization movement which met with so much difficulty in the Soviet Union under Stalin was achieved in China in less than four years after the completion of land reform. By 1956 over 90 per cent of China's 122 million peasant households had been collectivized.

Two years later the country was seized by the Great Leap Forward movement (1958–60) in which 750 000 collectives were merged and reorganized into 26 000 people's communes, a still higher form of socialist organization (Table 4). The first models for communes were huge organizations of 5 000 households, which existed as self-sufficient units combining the administrative, economic, and cultural functions of local government. Many communes introduced new methods of organizing production and distribution and also experimented with communal living (3·4 million communal dining halls were hastily set up in 1958). Some even declared that they had achieved 'communism' by providing for 'each according to his needs'. These early communes were widely publicized and misrepresented abroad, especially their social aspects such as communal living.

But radical tendencies were quickly checked and the momentum of the commune movement actually slackened within one year. In 1960, as an agricultural crisis was mounting, further rationalization of commune organization took place, resulting in the evolution of a three-level organization: the commune, the production brigade, the production teams. After 1962 more pragmatic measures were introduced in order to stimulate agricultural recovery, so that patterns of production and distribution actually reverted to those of the collectives, with the commune providing only an overall administrative framework. The post-1962 commune organization was stabilized and has continued to the present day, basically unaffected by the Cultural Revolution. The commune today is still an organization rather than an institution.

With the formation of the communes, the institutional reorganization sparked off by land reform had spent itself. Since 1962 the

TABLE 4

The Progress of Institutional Transformation in Chinese Agriculture
(expressed as % of total rural households involved in each process)

	Land Reform	Mutual Aid Teams			APCs (Cooperatives)	Advanced APCs (Collectives)	People's Communes
		Simple MATs	Permanent MATs	Total			
1950	32	—	—	10·7	—	—	—
1951	58	—	—	19·2	—	—	—
1952	88	29·8	10·1	39·9	0·1	—	—
1953	—	27·8	11·5	39·3	0·2	—	—
1954	—	32·2	26·2	58·4	1·9	—	—
1955	—	23·1	27·6	50·7	14·2	—	—
1956	—	—	—	—	8·5	87·8	—
1957	—	—	—	—	—	—	—
1958 July	—	—	—	—	—	—	—
August							30·4
Early September							48·1
Mid-September							65·3
Late September							98·0
December							99·1

Sources: For land reform, John Wong, *Communist Land Reform in China: The Road to Agricultural Collectivization* (to be published).
For the rest, State Statistical Bureau, *Ten Great Years*, pp. 35 and 43.

focus of agricultural development has shifted to technical transformation.

ECONOMIC IMPLICATIONS OF INSTITUTIONAL TRANSFORMATION

Evolution of the Optimal Production Organization

Though the institutional changes in Chinese agriculture in the 1950s were strongly motivated by ideological considerations, they can also be viewed as a search for an organizational form which would maximize output within the constraints of the traditional production structure. In traditional agriculture, resources were normally owned and utilized on the basis of family farms; but the actual organization units for production could be considerably larger than the family farm. This is because the 'ownership size' (determined by man-land ratio and the institutional set-up) is often different from the 'operational size' (determined by economic and technological factors), due to small landholdings and the existence of slack labour resources. To optimize production, peasants can increase the 'operational size' of the farm through some form of cooperative work teams. This pattern of resource utilization has been the economic rationale for traditional cooperative activities in China's peasant agriculture as well as for the formation of MATs.[10]

Suffice it to say that the MATs were close to the optimal level of organizing production, and they could eliminate many structural shortcomings inherent in small peasant farming. In the cooperatives, which were formed by merging a few MATs, the limit of exploitation of the production scale was reached – economic benefits from agricultural cooperation being the net difference between the advantages of large-scale farming and the diseconomies of mismanagement of factors arising from over-expanding the size of operation. In the context of the production structure of China at the time there was little economic rationale for the CCP to go into larger organizational units like the collectives, much less the communes. In particular the early communes, each comprising 5 000 households, were really too large to be organized effectively for agricultural production. These big communes were efficient for mobilizing a huge labour force for extra-agricultural activities such as building a dam, but were certainly the wrong size for agricultural production, which requires effective decision-making and efficient use of resources at a low level. Hence the later decentralization of the communes by scaling down production units to the small brigade. Today the organizational units for production have been stabilized at the team level, which will remain the most practicable unit in which to organize resources for maximum output until Chinese agriculture has completed its technological transformation.[11]

The Peasant Response

Despite its success in achieving rapid institutional revolution and its skill in the mass mobilization of peasants, the CCP could not always take the peasants for granted. Although the CCP gained effective centralized control over the rural sector after collectivization, it lost some leverage of peasant initiative and some positive peasant response to certain economic challenges. The problem became all the more important for three reasons: first, the process of economic development currently taking place in China still requires the peasants to make sacrifices or to deliver their agricultural surplus to the government; secondly, rapid and often radical institutional transformation in the past has also created some tension within institutions; and, thirdly, the peasants themselves are also in the process of adaptation and adjustment. Hence China shares the problem of peasant economic incentive with other socialist countries with collectivized agriculture.

From time to time the CCP has had to adjust its degree of centralized control over the processes of production and distribution and make some allowance for individual incentive, usually through decentralization or even the normal marketing channels. In the 1950s, for example, the government's procurement policy was a combination of market control with some room for private incentive. With the formation of communes, the question of peasant economic incentives became even more crucial as the proportion of collective life in all spheres increased. This problem is best reflected in the ownership of private plots and in the wage structure. To party zealots private plots were ideologically repugnant because they fostered the 'spontaneous growth of capitalism'; but the CCP could not afford to discount the economic significance of private plots, especially in the area of subsidiary production. While many party zealots thought that an egalitarian system of rewards was of fundamental importance, the CCP had to recognize the incentive scheme in the wage structure with its work-point system which incorporated differential rewards.[12]

There is nothing unusual about the Chinese peasants in their self-seeking economic behaviour, and it should not be interpreted as a kind of opposition to the government. The whole problem of peasant response highlights the interplay of two conflicting forces at work in agricultural policy: ideological commitment and economic reality. The Cultural Revolution with its colossal political and social effort to educate the peasants to sacrifice self-interest for the collective good, and to play down the influence of material incentives, represents the latest or last institutional change designed to reconcile this conflict.

Agricultural Performance since 1949

The immediate task of the CCP upon assuming power was the rehabilitation of agricultural production. This was successfully completed by 1952. The restoration of production was undertaken at the same time as land reform, which indicates that the land reform campaign had genuine peasant support. During the First Five Year Plan (1953–7) the agricultural sector performed quite well, with a growth rate of 4·5 per cent despite the inadequate attention it received. For food production, if 1952 is taken as the base year, the index for 1957 is 119·8, giving an average rate of growth of 3·7 per cent, which is well above the population growth rate of 2·2 per cent. During this period China was a net food exporter, mainly to the Soviet Union.

During the Great Leap Forward (1958–60) the index for food output shot up to the all-time high of 175. But production could not be stabilized at that level. In 1960–1 China experienced its worst agricultural crisis since the formation of the People's Republic, and food production was thrown back to the level of the early 1950s. China had to import wheat from Australia and Canada. Ever since then wheat purchase from abroad has been maintained at the level of 4 to 5 million tonnes a year.

Agricultural production recovered in 1963, and since then has maintained a steady, albeit moderate, rate of increase. The Cultural Revolution (1966–9) largely spared the agricultural sector. Most observers agree that agricultural production, especially of food and cotton, is now proceeding on a sound basis. However, China has continued to buy wheat abroad at great cost to her foreign exchange reserve. In 1970 she spent about US $300 million on wheat imports, mainly from Canada. But this is no indication of lack of agricultural self-sufficiency, for during the same year China's food exports to Hong Kong alone netted her US $248 million. The most reasonable argument for her continuing purchase of wheat is that it pays her to

TABLE 5

Agricultural Production, 1949–71

	Food Grain[a]			Cotton[a]	
	(million tonnes)	Indexes		(million tonnes)	Index
1949	108	70·1	43·2	0·4	30·8
1950	125	81·1	50·0	0·7	53·8
1951	135	87·6	54·0	1·3	100·0
1952	154	*100*	61·6	1·3	*100*
1953	157	101·9	62·8	1·2	92·3
1954	160	103·8	64·0	1·1	94·6
1955	175	113·6	70·0	1·5	115·4
1956	183	118·8	73·2	1·4	107·7
1957	185	119·8	74·0	1·6	123·0
1958	250	161·9	*100*	2·1	161·1
1959	270[b]	175·2	108·0	1·8	138·4
1960	150	97·4	60·0	1·0	76·9
1961	162	105·1	64·8	0·88	67·7
1962	174	112·9	69·6	1·03	79·2
1963	183	118·8	73·2	1·24	95·4
1964	200	129·8	80·0	1·70	130·7
1965	200	129·8	80·0	2·10	161·5
1966	—	—	—	—	—
1967	230	149·3	92·0	—	—
1968	—	—	—	—	—
1969	—	—	—	—	—
1970	240	155·8	96·0	—	—
1971	246	159·7	98·4	—	—

[a] Food grain comprises rice, wheat, coarse grains, and potatoes, but excludes soya-beans and groundnuts. Potatoes are converted into grain-equivalent at the ratio of 4 to 1. Cotton means ginned cotton.
[b] The grain output for 1959 is obviously statistically upward-biased.

Sources: 1 For grain and cotton, 1949–58, the direct official source as contained in the State Statistical Bureau, *Ten Great Years*, Foreign Languages Press, Peking, 1960, p. 119.
2 For grain 1959, Li Fu-ch'un's report, *Peking Review*, 5 April 1960, p. 6.
3 For cotton 1959–65, see Kang Chao, *Agricultural Production in Communist China, 1949–1965*, University of Wisconsin Press, 1970, p. 270.
4 For grain 1960–7, indirect official sources or references to unofficial statements from the mainland. For detailed documentation of the sources see Audrey Donnithorne, *China's Grain: Output, Procurement, Transfers and Trade*, Economic Research Centre, the Chinese University of Hong Kong, 1970, pp. 26–7.
5 For grain 1970–1, official source; see *Far Eastern Economic Review*, 8 January 1972, p. 27.

import wheat to supply metropolitan cities such as Shanghai and Peking rather than to transport it from the grain-surplus provinces of the interior.[13]

On 1 January 1972 Peking announced that grain production for 1971 was 246 million tonnes, representing a 60 per cent increase over 1952 (154 m.t.; Table 5). This is not quite an impressive record. The two developing regions, the Near East and the Far East (excluding China), show approximately the same level of performance for the same period: 61 per cent for the Near East and 56 per cent for the Far East.[14] Thus in food production China did neither better nor worse than the average of the other countries in the developing world, despite her sharply different institutional set-up. Ideological factors do not appear to speed up agricultural production faster than other factors. Compared with advanced countries, China's productivity level is still a long way down: her unit yield is about 150 per cent lower than Japan's and 50 per cent lower than France's or the United States', although 50 per cent higher than India's.[15]

Technical Transformation of the Production Structure

The agricultural crisis in 1960–1 sharply focused nation-wide attention on the vulnerability of traditional patterns of production to unfavourable weather influences and the weaknesses of relying on institutional changes as a source of agricultural growth. From 1962 the technical transformation of agriculture and the new overall development strategy of giving priority to agriculture were stepped up. Thus an increasing supply of new modern inputs was made available to agricultural production, especially commercial chemical fertilizers and electric pumps. At first the modernization effort was concentrated on the stable high-yield farms in the river plains and delta areas in Central, East, and South China. In recent years technical transformation has spread to other regions. By 1971 agricultural production had returned to the 1958 peak, with the new dynamic inputs obviously providing the main impetus for growth: for example, the increased application of chemical fertilizers. Before 1949 Chinese farms used hardly any chemical fertilizer. Even up to 1957 only 2 million tonnes were used, which was clearly too little to be effective. By 1971, however, 23 million tonnes were reported to have been used, of which 17 million tonnes were produced at home and about 6 million tonnes imported.[16] Similarly with mechanization. From the outset Chairman Mao held that collectivization should precede mechanization. Thus very little effort had gone into mechanization until the late 1950s and the early 1960s. In 1971 Peking reported that 90 per cent of the counties had set up plants to manufacture and repair farm machines.[17]

Although a substantial start has been made in the last ten years, the technical transformation of Chinese agriculture is still in full swing. In 1971 about 150 kilograms per hectare of chemical fertilizers were used in China; though this is a higher rate than India's 16 kilograms, it is still only about one-third as high as Japan's and half as high as the United States' rate of use. In fact these figures, more than any other, explain the variation of productivity between these countries.[18] No doubt the input mix in Chinese agriculture will continue to change and will become increasingly the mainspring of agricultural growth, and the traditional character of the production structure will be gradually phased out.

Conclusion

In conclusion I should like to recapture two strategic considerations relevant to the continuing development of agriculture in China. They are the relationship between agriculture and other sectors of the economy, particularly industry; and the balance between food and population. The first concerns the basic development strategy of the economy. Will China return to the Stalinist model of development, with top priority given to heavy industry at the expense of agriculture, as in the First Five Year Plan? Or will she launch another Great Leap Forward and make an all-out effort to push ahead on all fronts? Judging by the existing political climate and economic reality, neither alternative appears possible. Further, the present leaders, all with their 'peasant mentality', are unlikely to adopt a strategy with any distinctive urban bias. This means that the existing cautious development policy will be maintained, with agriculture continuing to make an important contribution to urban industrial development, but with a considerable resource feedback for development in the agricultural sector itself. Such a strategy also serves China's fundamental policy of 'self-reliance' well. Because agriculture is a low-productivity sector as compared with industry, the present strategy, however 'balanced', will not yield any record performance for the economy as a whole.

The second issue concerns the growth potential of the agricultural sector itself. With such a large population base, agricultural production (almost 80 per cent for food) in China has always competed with population growth. The present government of China should be given credit for its success in the past two decades in staving off famine and eliminating malnutrition, both of which still threaten many developing countries today. However, food production is increasing at the rate of less than 3 per cent while the rate of population growth is close to 2 per cent. For long-range political and economic stability, food production should secure a larger edge over population growth. This could be achieved through a substantial increase in unit yield and would mean that the technological transformation of Chinese agriculture needs to be stepped up.

Notes

1 See Ping-ti Ho, *Studies on the Population of China, 1368–1953*, Harvard University Press, Cambridge, Mass., 1959, and Dwight H. Perkins, *Agricultural Development in China, 1368–1968*, Aldine Publishing Co., Chicago, 1969.
2 See, for example, *Agrarian China: Selected Materials from Chinese Authors*, London, 1939.
3 J.L. Buck, *Land Utilization in China*, Nanking, 1937.
4 See Theodore W. Schultz, *Transforming Traditional Agriculture*, Yale University Press, New Haven, 1964.
5 Mao expounded his theory powerfully in his 'Analysis of the Classes in Chinese Society' (March 1926) and 'Report on an Investigation of the Peasant Movement in Hunan' (March 1927). See *Selected Works of Mao Tse-tung*, vol. i, Foreign Languages Press, Peking.
6 State Statistical Bureau, *Ten Great Years*, Foreign Languages Press, Peking, 1960.
7 See John T. Macrae, 'Mobilization of the Agricultural Surplus in China for Rapid Economic Development, 1952–1957', *The Developing Economies*, vol. viii, no. 1, March 1970, pp. 79–92, and Shigeru Ishikawa, 'Resource Flow between Agriculture and Industry: the Chinese Experience', *The Developing Economies*, vol. v, no. 1, March 1967, pp. 3–49.
8 Ta-chung Liu, 'Quantitative Trends in the Economy', in Alexander Eckstein *et al.* (eds), *Economic Trends in Communist China*, Aldine Publishing Co., Chicago, 1968.
9 See John Wong, *Communist Land Reform in China: The Road to Agricultural Collectivization* (to be published).
10 John Wong, 'Peasant Economic Behaviour: The Case of Traditional Agricultural Cooperation in China', *The Developing Economics*, vol. ix, no. 3, September 1971, pp. 332–49.
11 See John Wong, 'Small Production Teams in Chinese Agriculture: A Structural Analysis of the People's Communes', Paper of Centre of Asian Studies, University of Hong Kong, 1970.

190

12 John Wong, 'Socialization of Agriculture and Peasant Response to Economic Incentives in China', Paper of the Centre of Asian Studies, University of Hong Kong, 1971.

13 Audrey Donnithorne, *China's Grain: Output, Procurement, Transfers and Trade*, Economic Research Centre, the Chinese University of Hong Kong, 1970.

14 Compiled from the *FAO Yearbook*, 1970.

15 *Ibid.*

16 *Far Eastern Economic Review*, 8 January 1972, p. 27.

17 *Far Eastern Economic Review*, Yearbook, 1972, p. 151.

18 Compiled from the *FAO Yearbook*, 1970.

Modern Science in China

HO PENG YOKE

By modern science I mean the form of science that grew up in post-Renaissance Europe and that is now regarded as universally valid. I do not refer to this as 'Western' or 'European' science for two reasons. First, the civilizations of other peoples, such as the Arabs, the Indians, and the Chinese, have made important contributions in the past towards the development of modern science in Europe, although no one can deny Europe the credit of having played the main role. Secondly, although some scientific theories in post-Renaissance Europe – for example, the phlogiston theory in chemistry – must be regarded as European, they do not contribute to the development of modern science.

In this paper the word 'China' is used in a geographical sense, without any political or racial connotations, although, as we all know, politics exerts a profound influence on the development of science and technology. I include under 'China' the work done by American and European scientists in China during the last hundred years, but not the work done by Chinese scientists in other parts of the world: for example, the Parity law of Yang and Lee in modern physics.

During the sixteenth century European scholars like Francis Bacon (1561–1626) in England, Jean Fernel (1497–1558) in France, and Jerome Cardano (1501–76) in Italy, were talking about the three great inventions in science and technology: the compass, printing, and gunpowder.[1] In the science of magnetism, which led to the first of these inventions, the Chinese with their knowledge of the magnetic compass, the directive property of the lodestone, the phenomenon of induced magnetism, magnetic declination, and the polarity of the magnet, had been far ahead of European scientists. Europe took the lead only in the year 1600 with the work of William Gilbert (1540–1603).[2]

In Europe movable types were first used in printing in the year 1447 by Johannes Gutenberg (*c.* 1397–*c.* 1468). It is said that the first movable types used in China were devised about the year 1045 by Pi Sheng (畢昇, fl. 1045), but recent archaeological discoveries have indicated that movable types were used as early as the sixth century B.C. for the casting of inscriptions on bronze sacrificial vessels.[3] The earliest extant printed book in the world is a Chinese version of the *Diamond Sutra,* dated 11 May 868, now in the British Museum. This book was obviously the result of long experience in block-printing: hence the art of block-printing must have been known in China much earlier.[4] Printing has always been closely connected with paper-making. This art also originated in China not later than the first century A.D. Remains of paper made during that period have been found recently. The technique of paper-making was improved by Ts'ai Lun (蔡倫) in the year 105 A.D. and after that paper came into general use in China. It reached Europe by the old Silk Route across central Asia some time during the thirteenth century. The spread of printing in Europe has always been recognized as a necessary precursor of the Renaissance[5] and hence of post-Renaissance science.

Gunpowder also originated in China. The earliest reference to the gunpowder formula in Europe can be traced back only to the year 1327 or at earliest 1285. In China the earliest references to the use of gunpowder in war occur in the book *Wu-ching tsung-yao* (武經總要), edited by Tsêng Kung-liang (曾公亮) in the year 1044. This book contains a formula for making gunpowder. The Taoist alchemists had also hit upon a formula a few centuries earlier when they mixed saltpetre, sulphur, and carbon in some of their experiments. Some of their laboratories may have caught fire or else some of the Taoists may have got their beards singed when this explosive substance went out of control, as a Taoist alchemical text gives warning that it must be approached with extreme caution. It has been suggested that the Mongol invasions of Europe in 1235 and 1261 brought gunpowder to the western world.[6]

In the thirteenth century, the century of St Thomas Aquinas (1227–74) and the English Franciscan monk, Roger Bacon (1214–94), when European science was at its dawning, China was already in full possession of the compass, the art of printing, and gunpowder. By that time also Chinese mathematics had reached its peak of development. For example, a method used by the thirteenth-century Chinese algebraists Ch'in Chiu-shao (秦九韶, 1202–*c.* 1261),

Li Chih (李治, 1192–1279), and Yang Hui (楊輝, fl. 1261–75)[1] to solve cubic equations and numerical equations of higher orders was not rediscovered in Europe until more than five centuries later by William George Horner (1786–1837) and Paolo Ruffini (1765–1822). Alchemy and the science of observational astronomy also were highly developed in China. In biology China had monographs on certain plants, such as tea and citrus fruits, and the pharmaco-poeias. Fossils were first identified by the great neo-Confucian Chu Hsi (朱熹, c. 1130–1200) in the middle of the eleventh century; Europe had to wait for Leonardo da Vinci (1690–1730) for their recognition.

Despite these early advances in science and technology, modern science developed not in China but in post-Renaissance Europe. Indeed Chinese science declined rapidly from the beginning of the fourteenth century. A question of considerable interest is: why didn't modern science develop in China? This question cannot be dealt with at length in this paper. First, space would not permit and, secondly, it would be rather presumptuous for me to attempt to do something which so illustrious a scholar in Chinese science as Joseph Needham will attempt only in the last volume of his monu-mental work, *Science and Civilisation in China,* after spending at least thirty-five years pondering over this question. I shall thus be very brief in trying to account for the decline of traditional Chinese science and its failure to develop into modern science.

In China it is now fashionable to attribute the decline of traditional science and the failure to develop modern science to the conflict between materialism and idealism, to the neo-Confucian schools of Chu Hsi and Wang Yang-ming (王陽明, 1472–1529) if not to the bureaucratic social structure in the past. In one of Joseph Need-ham's recent books, *The Great Titration: Science and Society in East and West* (London, 1969), he sees modern advances mainly in terms of social and, particularly, political factors. There was no modern science in China because there was no democracy – the kind of democracy associated with the rise of the merchants to power in the West; the revolutionary democracy associated with consciousness of technological change; Christian individualistic and representative democracy with all its agitating activity which characterized many of the movements that were unknown in China until our own day.[8]

Social and political factors as inhibitors of the development of Chinese science had been discussed earlier by a very eminent

American scholar, John K. Fairbank. He attributed the non-development of Chinese science to the Chinese failure to work out a fuller system of logic whereby ideas could be tested by ideas; to the fact that the Chinese language was not alphabetic; to the educational system which laid great emphasis on memory work, and especially on the classics, thus forming a natural matrix for authoritative thinking; to the state monopoly over large-scale economic organization; and to the over-abundance of manpower.[9]

It is possible to think of other political and social reasons, and also of factors connected with inter-cultural contact with other countries. However, I shall discuss only a few inhibiting factors that are intrinsic to Chinese science. First let us consider the logic or order which formed the basic scientific ideas worked out by the ancient Chinese. These ideas include the theory of the two fundamental forces in nature, Yin (陰) and Yang (陽). Through the eternal interaction of these principles the five primary elements come into existence: water, fire, wood, metal, and earth. The proto-scientific use of a very elaborate symbolic structure derived from the *I-ching* (易經) or the *Book of Changes* and a form of numerology reminiscent of the activities of the Pythagorean school in ancient Greece. The Chinese five-element theory appears to have been even more advanced than the four-element theory which Europe inherited from the ancient Greeks, but Robert Boyle made the four-element theory obsolete with the publication of his *Sceptical Chymist* in 1661. In China, however, traditional scientific ideas lasted much longer. In fact the Chinese were unable to disentangle themselves from these ideas until they felt the full impact of modern western science in the middle of the last century. Until then they were completely contented and would not venture a step further once they could give some sort of 'explanation' to a phenomenon in terms of their proto-scientific theories, although the so-called 'explanation' might sometimes be just as much a mystery as the phenomenon which it tried to 'explain'. Let us take a simple illustration in biology from the *Ta-Tai Li-chi* (大戴禮記), a book written during the first century B.C. To explain why the gestation period of a dog is about sixty-three days, it says: 'Seven times Nine gives Sixty-Three, the number Three governs the Great Bear Constellation, which in turn governs the dog. Hence, the dog is only born during the third month [of its conception].'[10]

If the Chinese were satisfied with this kind of explanation and engrossed and diverted by their ancient proto-scientific ideas, how could they look for mathematical formulations and experimental verifications? According to Joseph Needham, these proto-scientific ideas acted like huge filing cabinets where all information was stored, without being taken out and subjected to further analysis. These proto-scientific reasonings also applied to astronomy, alchemy, medicine, politics, and even to fate-calculation, the last of which in fact has become the fate of traditional Chinese concepts in modern times.

Another factor inhibiting the development of modern science in China was the method and terminology used in traditional Chinese mathematics. Calculations were performed on counting-boards, and until the fifteenth century on the abacus. Unlike written arithmetic, all traces of intermediate workings on the counting-board and the abacus were automatically erased, leaving only the final answers. Thus there was quite often no way to follow the methods used by past masters in Chinese mathematics.

The question of terminology leads us to Chinese algebra and brings to mind the Greek mathematician Diophantus (*c.* 250 A.D.), the inventor of algebra in Europe. Diophantus used the Greek alphabet as algebraic symbols but, because at that time some letters of this alphabet were already used as numbers, this caused confusion. Chinese algebra suffered from an even greater handicap than early Greek algebra because its terminology and notation lacked the flexibility of the Greek alphabet. Chinese characters or words were used as 'dummies' to represent algebraic quantities. For example, the length, breadth, and area of a rectangle were used as 'dummies' by the thirteenth-century mathematician Yang Hui (fl. 1261–75) when applied to solve such problems as those involving weight and money. However, because the characters also had other meanings of their own, the learner was often confused. Another example is that of the fourteenth-century mathematician Chu Shih-chieh (朱世傑, fl. 1280–1303), who represented equations involving four unknowns by the four elements: heavens (*t'ien* 天), earth (*ti* 地), men (*jen* 人), and things (*wu* 物). But his method was so involved that no Chinese mathematician seemed to understand it until more than four centuries later. I was delighted to learn that a New Zealand university mathematician is writing a doctoral thesis on the work of Chu Shih-chieh, the last of the great traditional Chinese mathematicians.[12]

The above reasons are only a few of the many one could give to account for the failure of traditional Chinese science to develop into modern science. As mentioned earlier, Chinese science even began to decline from the beginning of the fourteenth century. This was exactly the state of affairs that Matteo Ricci (1552–1610) found when he arrived in Peking in 1601. Everyone knows that the Jesuits brought European scientific knowledge with them. Let us now discuss how much of this can be considered as modern science.

Chemistry can be ruled out at once because modern chemistry had not been born in Europe at that time, although there is evidence to show that the Jesuits brought with them the knowledge of strong acids. In mathematics they introduced China to Euclidean geometry, algebra of the time of Vieta, trigonometry, logarithms, and written arithmetic. Today of course all of these studies are regarded as elementary mathematics, and some students may think of non-Euclidean geometry or coordinate geometry as more modern. However, we may think of these Jesuit-introduced studies as modern because they are still in use today.

Let us now turn to astronomy. Here we can say that, except for the Galilean telescope, what the Jesuits brought to China was not modern science. Their world picture was still that of Aristotle and Ptolemy, in spite of the revolutionary changes in astronomy introduced to Europe by Copernicus (1473–1543), Galileo (1564–1642), and Kepler (1571–1630). It was not until 1640 that Johann Adam Schall von Bell (1591–1666) introduced China to the names of Galileo and Copernicus, but he also asserted that there was no difference in principle between Ptolemy and Copernicus. James Rho (1590–1662) had even stated that Copernicus believed in the sun's rotation about the earth. Schall von Bell also introduced China to the system of Tycho Brahe (1546–1601) and to a diagram of the Tychonic system. This diagram, which asserted that the planets rotated round the sun, which in turn rotated round the earth carrying the planets with it, was reproduced in the *Tu-shu chi-ch'êng* (圖書集成), the Imperial Encyclopaedia of 1726. When in 1760 another Jesuit gave a correct description of the heliocentric system it was not accepted by Chinese scholars because it contradicted earlier statement made by the Jesuits. In fact, as a result of the uncertainty of the views expressed by the Jesuits, the heliocentric theory was not generally accepted in China until the nineteenth century.[13]

All in all, except for some mathematics and the telescope, and perhaps also the art of cartographic survey, very little of what the Jesuits brought to China can be regarded as modern science. Then in 1773 the Society of Jesus was suppressed by Pope Clement XIV.

At the same time the emperor of China issued an edict which forbade foreign missionaries to enter China and expelled those already there, except for a few Jesuits who were giving useful service in the Astronomical Bureau. For more than a hundred years China shut its door to contact with the West. But the Jesuits' influence had made the Chinese ready to accept the inflow of modern science, which came in the middle of the nineteenth century soon after the Opium War of 1839–42.

Modern science came to China with the Protestant missionary movement, the merchants, and professional people such as doctors. It is interesting to note that the first book on modern science written in China was by an English doctor, Benjamin Hobson (1816–73), who was then working in Shanghai. It was the *Po-wu hsin-p'ien* (博物新編), a book on general science. It was published in 1855 and soon afterwards reprinted in Japan. It is worth mentioning that the first book on chemistry had appeared in Japan some fifteen years earlier than Hobson's book. This was Udagawa Yōan's (宇田川榕菴) *Seimi Kaiso* (舍密開宗) or *Treatise on Chemistry*, which was a translation of William Henry's *Elements of Experimental Chemistry*. It was issued in parts between 1837 and 1846.

One of the first tasks facing the Chinese at that time was the translation of scientific books from western languages.[14] Two translation centres were established, first in Peking and then in Shanghai. Most scientific books were translated in Shanghai where John Fryer (1839–1928) worked. Together with a number of Chinese collaborators, Fryer worked on one hundred and twelve scientific textbooks, of which nine were on pure chemistry and fifteen on chemical engineering. One of the most interesting features of the work in the translation bureau in Shanghai was the constant necessity to invent new Chinese technical terms. Here Fryer and his colleagues did a splendid job, although the technical terms were not finally accepted until the twentieth century with the establishment in 1932 of a successor organization, the National Bureau of Compilation and Translation (*Kuo-li pien-i-kuan* 國立編譯館). It is worth mentioning that, when John Fryer retired from the translation bureau, he became the professor of Chinese at the University of California.[15]

Because chemistry was probably the subject that fascinated the Chinese most at the time of the second influx of Europeans during the nineteenth century, let us look at the problems involved in coining new technical terms for chemistry. In fact modern chemistry provides a perfect example of the age-old dilemma that has confronted translators of alphabetical languages into Chinese, although naturally the chemistry problem has its peculiar complexities also. From the second century onwards the Buddhists had faced the same problem: should one first transliterate foreign polysyllabic words into strings of meaningless monosyllabic words and then define these words; or should one borrow existing Taoist words and run the risk of distorting their original meaning? The Buddhists adopted the first alternative, with the result that Buddhism retained to the end an indelible quality of foreignness within Chinese culture.

The Chinese resolved the dilemma in a number of ways: by adopting a large number of archaic or obsolete characters and giving them precise technical significances; by coining totally new characters according to the classical radical-phonetic system; and by joining the archaic and new characters together with numbers to make polysyllabic formulae which are as clearly comprehensible as a term like carbon dioxide is to us.

For readers who are not familiar with Chinese, a few words about the Chinese script may be helpful. It is about the only non-alphabetic script that is still a living language. It consists of some 50 000 characters, of which about 10 per cent are in common use. Some of these characters are pictograms, like the words for sun (*jih* ☉ and then 日) and tree (*mu* 米 and then 木). However, most characters consist of two parts: a radical, which is some kind of a classification; and a phonetic component, which is the qualifying part. For example, the character for 'walking stick' (*chang* 杖) consists of a tree radical (*mu* 木) to indicate that the stick is made of wood, and a phonetic component (*chang* 丈) to indicate that it is something made of wood and is called *chang*. On the other hand, 'forest' (*lin* 林) is written with a qualifying component, 'tree' (*mu* 木), next to the tree radical (*mu* 木), to indicate the plural number of trees in a forest. There are altogether 214 different radicals in the Chinese writing.

Let us now see how the Chinese coined terms for modern chemistry. Of course they already had names for common elements like sulphur, iron, copper, zinc, silver, tin, mercury, lead, and gold. Through the use of radicals, these elements had also already been classified into metals, non-metals, and liquids. Thus iron, copper, zinc, silver, tin, lead, and gold all have the metal (*chin* 金) radical; sulphur has the non-metal or stone (*shih* 石) radical; and mercury, whose natural state at room temperature is liquid, has the water (*shui* 水) radical. This principle was applied in coining new technical terms. To coin a word for hydrogen, the gas (ch'i气) radical was used to denote its gaseous state and a phonetic component (ch'ing 巠) derived from the word 'light' (ch'ing 輕) was used to indicate that hydrogen is the lightest of the elements. Of course this was by no means the only way in which the Chinese coined words. Sometimes they employed transliteration, for example 'radar' is called lei-ta (雷達), and 'pulsar' is called po-sha (波霎). Sometimes they borrowed scientific terms from the Japanese; for example, wa-ssu (瓦斯) for 'gas' and hsien (腺) for 'glands'.[16]

Modern institutions of higher learning began to appear in various parts of China as early as the year 1865, when an educational institution, called the wên-hui-kuan (滙文館), was established in the province of Shantung by American missionaries. In the year 1905 this institution combined with a similar institution set up by British missionaries to form the university of Chilu (Ch'i-lu ta-hsüeh 齊魯大學). In 1885 American missionaries also established a number of colleges in Canton and Macao; thirty years later these were grouped together to form the Lingnan University in Canton. In 1888 American Methodists established a college called the Hui-wên shu-yuan (滙文書院) in Peking; this college later became the Yenching University. Other universities were also established, some by the government and others by the missionaries. Modern science found an important place in most of them.

Chinese students were also sent abroad. In 1866 a magistrate by the name of Pin Ch'un (斌椿) was sent on an overseas tour to study the educational systems of other countries. In 1872 the first batch of students, thirty in all, set out to study in the United States under the leadership of two officers, Ch'en Lan-pin (陳蘭彬) and Yung Hung (容閎). Further batches of thirty students at a time were sent to the United States in 1873, 1874, and 1875. After 1875 some students also went to France and Britain. In 1890 a ruling was made that every ambassador appointed to Britain, Russia, Germany, France, and the United States must take two students with him. In 1896 students were sent to Japan for the first time. Many of these students returned with a knowledge of modern science. It may be of interest to mention that in the year 1907 Chinese women students were sent to study abroad for the first time in history – three women went to the United States in that year.[17]

With the establishment of the Republic in 1911 the Chinese became still more keenly aware of the importance of modern science and technology to the building of a nation. In 1915 the Chinese

Society of Science (*Chung-kuo k'o-hsüeh-shê* 中國科學社) was established. Its inaugural meeting was held on the campus of Cornell University, Ithaca, New York, and membership was open to scientists in every field in China. By 1935 its membership was about 1 500 and it represented the vast majority of scientists working in China. It published a journal called *K'o-hsüeh* (科學 – *Scientia*).

The most important organization devoted to scientific research was the Academia Sinica, established by the Chinese government on 20 November 1927, with Ts'ai Yuan-p'ei (蔡元培) as its first president. It started with only four research institutes but by the 1930s there were ten institutes devoted entirely to research in science and technology, namely:

1 Research Institute of Mathematics
2 Research Institute of Astronomy
3 Research Institute of Physics
4 Research Institute of Chemistry
5 Research Institute of Earth Science
6 Research Institute of Animal Science
7 Research Institute of Plant Science
8 Research Institute of Meteorology
9 Research Institute of Medicine
10 Research Institute of Engineering

There were only two research institutes devoted to the study of the humanities and social sciences, thus indicating the Academia Sinica's sharp bias towards science and technology.[18]

In 1929 the National Academy was founded in Peking. In October 1949 it merged with the Academia Sinica of Nanking to form the Academia Sinica of Peking. One of the research institutes of the Academia Sinica of Nanking had been moved to Taiwan at the time, but we are not concerned with it here as it is engaged in the study of linguistics and history and has little to do with the natural sciences. By 1960 there were forty-six institutes and laboratories in the Academy of Science of Peking, grouped into five departments: mathematics, physics and chemistry; biology; geology and geography; technology; philosophy and the social sciences. Affiliated to these departments were many scientific institutes, such as the Institute of Mathematics, the Institute of Chemistry, the Institute of Applied Physics, and the Institute of Atomic Physics. The president of the Academy of Science of Peking is Dr Kuo Mo-jo (郭沫若), a famous writer and a vice-president of the People's Republic of China.[19]

By 1937 the number of universities and research centres totalled

124. Of this number 73 were concerned with science and technology, 34 of them being connected with the natural sciences. Ten universities had facilities for research in science.[20] After 1949 the universities were re-organized: for example, the universities of Peking, Ts'ingHua, and Yenching merged to form the National Peking University, though the old names are still often heard; missionary universities ceased to function. A glance at the list of Chinese universities and technical institutes, such as that published in *The World of Learning*, 1960–1 (London, 1961), will quickly show the strong emphasis on scientific education in China.

A very brief survey now of the progress made in some branches of modern science in China during the past fifty years or so,[21] beginning with astronomy, which has indeed had a very long history in China.[22] Before the Second World War there were about half a dozen observatories in different parts of China. Their work included positional astronomy, the study of the minor planets, sunspots, variable stars, and time-keeping. Among them was the Purple Mountain observatory outside Nanking. Completed in 1934, it became the first modern astronomical research centre in China. It made solar and variable-star observations with its 60 cm equatorial-reflector and 20 cm equatorial-refractor telescopes. Meteorological and seismological observations were carried out at the Zokawei observatory. There are now observatories in the cities of Peking, Nanking, Shanghai, Hangchow, and Kunming. The Zokawei observatory in Shanghai gives time-signal broadcasts at various intervals. Since 1938 a team of astronomers at the Zo-Se observatory has made observations of minor planets and studied their general perturbations and aberrations. The results of their studies are published in the annals of their observatory, the *T'ien-wên nien-k'an* (天文年刊), *Academia Sinica Annals of the Shéshān (Zô-Sè) Section of Shanghai Observatory*. The Purple Mountain observatory continues to be the major research centre. It not only builds its own astronomical instruments but it studies the planets, the stars, the sun, artificial satellites, radio astronomy, and applied astronomy. The *Chung-kuo t'ien-wên nien-li* (中國天文年曆), *Chinese Astronomical Ephemeris,* of 1969 and 1970 are based entirely on calculations made by electronic computer at the Purple Mountain observatory.[23]

To return now to chemistry, which was by far the most popular science subject in China during the first few decades of this century. At first what little research there was in chemistry was confined to problems in industrial chemistry. An impetus to research was given by the Union Medical College in Peking which came under the Rockefeller Foundation in 1915. It was there that American and European scientists conducted full-scale research in the fields of biochemistry, food chemistry, and pharmacology. Other research centres were established soon after, for example, in Peking University, Ts'ingHua University, and Yenching University in Peking, and Central University in Nanking. Two other research centres were founded by Europeans: the Lester Institute of Medical Research in Shanghai and the North China Chemical Laboratory in Tientsin. The Japanese also established a research centre, called the Research Institute of Natural Sciences, in Shanghai. Of course, as we know, almost all of these organizations have ceased to function after the establishment of the People's Republic in 1949. However, from accounts given by groups of foreign scientists who have visited China in recent years we cannot help but be impressed by the vast development of the chemical industry, of analytical work, and of university education.[24] Proof of these advances is exemplified by the great achievement of Chinese chemists and biochemists (not without severe international competition) in one of the most striking areas of our own time, the synthesis of active insulin in 1965.

Let us now come to physics. Although some Chinese students began to go abroad to study science as early as 1866, it was not until the present century that some of them turned their attention to physics. In 1918 it was first introduced as a teaching subject in an institution of higher learning at Peking University. By the mid-thirties physics was taught in more than thirty universities throughout the length and breadth of the country. The first paper by a Chinese physicist to be published in an international scientific journal was written by Wu Yu-hsuan (吳有訓), a professor at Ts'ingHua University, Peking. It was published in *Nature* in 1930. Within the next five years Chinese physicists had contributed more than fifty papers to scientific journals in the United States, France, Britain, and Germany. In 1932 the Chinese Physical Society (*Chung-kuo wu-li hsüeh-hui* 中國物理學會) was established. In 1932 this society began to publish its own journal called the *Chung-kuo wu-li hsüeh-pao* (中國物理學報), *Journal of the Chinese Physical Society*.[25] An account of research work in nuclear physics and other branches of physics is contained in a private report given to the Fellows of the Australian Academy of Science by Professor Sir Mark Oliphant in 1964 after a visit to China.[26]

Before the Second World War the Chinese had every reason to be proud of the work carried out at the Institute of Geological Survey (*Ti-chih t'iao-ch'a-so* 地質調查所): with the cooperation of the Academia Sinica it had produced a geological map of the whole of China, discovered 'Peking Man', and made numerous seismological observations. The most renowned personality in Chinese geology at that time was the Glasgow-trained geologist Ting Wên-chiang (丁文江), a biography of whom has recently been written in English.[27] The Central Agricultural Experimental Institute had carried out a considerable amount of research in agriculture, and the Academia Sinica and other research institutes were making a full-scale study of the flora and fauna of China. Beautifully illustrated books on Chinese botany were produced by Hu Hsien-su (胡先驌), the director of one of these research institutes.

One can say then that by the third decade of this century science in China was fully integrated into the mainstream of modern science. Then in the year 1937 came the Sino-Japanese War, which interrupted the progress of education and research in modern science in China. The full story of the difficult conditions under which Chinese scientists laboured is told by Joseph Needham in *Science Outpost* (London, 1948). During the period following the civil war of 1945–9, the foundation of the People's Republic of China in 1949, and the moving of the seat of the Nationalist government to Taiwan, science was almost at a standstill. In 1960 Soviet scientists and technicians left China and some laboratories and factories were almost denuded of staff.[28] Finally, in 1965 came the Cultural Revolution, as a result of which some scientific activities probably were curtailed. The achievements of Chinese scientists are the more remarkable when we take into account all these problems that have confronted them. Today science in China is already in the nuclear age and the space age, and the Chinese participate actively in the world-wide enterprise of modern science along with all other cultures.

Notes

1 See Joseph Needham, *Science and Civilisation in China*, Cambridge, 7 vols: vol. 1 (1954); vol. 2 (1956); vol. 3 (1959); vol. 4, pt 1 (1962); vol. 4, pt 2 (1965); vol. 4, pt 3 (1971); and especially vol. 1, p. 19, and vol. 4, pt 2, p. 7.

2 For the full story of the Chinese invention of the compass see Joseph Needham, *Science and Civilisation in China*, vol. 4, pt 1, pp. 229–328.

3 See Chêng Tê-k'un, *Archaeology in China*, Cambridge, vol. 3 (1963), pp. 222–3.

4 This will be discussed in Joseph Needham, *Science and Civilisation in China*, vol. 5 (in press). For the present see, for example, Raymond Dawson, *The Legacy of China*, Oxford, 1964, or H.J.J. Winter, *Eastern Science*, London, 1952. I saw in the Peking National Library in November 1973 another Buddhist sutra, printed in the year A.D. 448.

5 This will be discussed in Joseph Needham, *Science and Civilisation in China*, vol. 5 (in press). For the present see, for example, Chang Tzu-kao· *et al.*, *Chung-kuo hua-hsüeh shih-kao* (Draft History on Chemistry in Chinese), Peking, 1964, pp. 161–3.

6 This will be discussed in Joseph Needham, *Science and Civilisation in China*, vol. 5 (in press). See also J.R. Partington, *A History of Greek Fire and Gunpowder*, Cambridge, 1961.

7 Ulrich Libbrecht did a Ph.D thesis on Ch'in Chiu-shao in 1970. A full study of the major work of Yang Hui, the *Yang Hui suan-fa*, has been made by Lam Lay Yong of Singapore and is being published by the University of Singapore Press.

8 See Joseph Needham, *The Great Titration: Science and Society in East and West*, London, 1969.

9 See John King Fairbank, *The United States and China*, Cambridge, Mass., 1962, pp. 64–7.

10 See Joseph Needham, *Science and Civilisation in China, op. cit.*, vol. 2.

11 See Ho Peng Yoke, *The Birth of Modern Science in China*, Kuala Lumpur, 1967.

12 He is Mr J. Hoe of the Department of Mathematics, University of Wellington.

13 See Ho Peng Yoke, '*Ting Wen-chiang, Science and China's New Culture* by Charlotte Furth' (book review), *Journal of Oriental Studies*, 1971, vol. 9, pp. 369–70.

14 This issue will be fully discussed in Joseph Needham, *Science and Civilisation in China*, vol. 5 (in press).

15 See Adrian Arthur Bennett, *John Fryer: the Introduction of Western Science and Technology into Nineteenth-century China*, Cambridge, Mass., 1967.

16 See Ho Peng Yoke, 'Traditional Chinese Scientific Terminology and Modern Scientific Terminology', *The Modernization of Languages in Asia*, Kuala Lumpur, 1970, pp. 83–90. See also Alleton, Vivians, and Jean-Claude, *Terminologie de la chimie en Chinois modern*, Mouton, Paris and The Hague, 1966.

17 See Ting Chih-p'ing, *Chung-kuo chin-ch'i-shih-nien-lai chiao-yu chi-shih* (Records on Education during the Past Seventy Years in China), Shanghai, 1935.

18 See Ministry of Education, Republic of China, *Ti-êrh-ch'i Chung-kuo chiao-yü nien-chien* (The Second Chinese Educational Year Book), Shanghai, 1948.

19 See *The World of Learning, 1960–61*, London, 1961.

20 The ten institutions of higher learning which offered facilities for research were the Ts'ing Hua, the Peking, the Central, the Sun Yat-sen, the Wuhan, the Peiyang, the Nankai, the Yenching, and the Chinling universities together with the Union Medical College. See Liu Han, *Chung-kuo k'o hsüeh êrh-shih-nien* (Twenty Years of Science in China), Shanghai, 1937.

21 For an earlier survey see C.H. Peak, 'Some Aspects of the Introduction of Modern Science into China', *Isis*, vol. 22, 1932, pp. 173–219.

22 For the history of Chinese astronomy see, for example, Joseph Needham, *Science and Civilisation in China*, vol. 3, and Ho Peng Yoke, *The Astronomical Chapters of the CHIN SHU*, Paris, 1966.

23 See further Ho Peng Yoke, 'Astronomie', *China-Handbuch*, Hamburg (in press).

24 There are many such reports. To name a few, one of the most recent reports is by H.P. Tam Dalyell in 'Chemical Industry in China Today', *Chemistry and Industry*, 1 January 1972. C.H.G. Oldham, in an article 'Science for the Masses' in *Far Eastern Economic Review*, vol. 60, 1968, pp. 353–8, tells about the effort made in China to bring science to the people. Great emphasis also appears to be given to applied science. A survey of 51 scientific publications in China and Taiwan shows that 19 of them are concerned with agriculture, 3 with irrigation, and 2 with soil

science. They also confirm Oldham's observation, because many of the publications have a popular appeal rather than being meant for the specialists. The author is indebted to Mr Y.S. Chan of the Australian National Library for providing him with the list of scientific publications in China. Oldham has also published an earlier article on science in China, 'Science and Superstitions', *Far Eastern Review*, vol. 48, 1965, pp. 14–18.

25 See Liu Han (ed.), *Chung-kuo ko-hsüeh êrh-shih-nien* (Twenty Years of Science in China), Shanghai, 1937.

26 In Report on a Visit to China, 22 September–18 October, 1964, by Delegates of the Australian Academy of Science (unpublished report circulated among Fellows for discussion).

27 See Charlotte Furth, *Ting Wên-chiang – Science and China's New Culture*, Cambridge, Mass., 1970.

28 Mikhail A. Klochko (*Soviet Scientists in China*, London, 1964) tells about the activities of Soviet scientists in China in the early days of the Chinese People's Republic and the deterioration of relations between China and the Soviet Union in 1960.

Medicine in China

DOUGLAS ROBB

The long history of the Chinese people, partly recorded and partly traditional, is an impressive story. The many ups and downs – infiltrations, invasions, the warring states, and periods of stability and enormous achievements – make it a human document of intense interest. Its eclipse by the West in the last three hundred years, followed by its recent emergence in a new form on the world stage, is a phenomenon of the greatest importance for mankind. Its sheer dimensions assure it of that, as do its unusual approaches to present-day problems.

From prehistoric times the Chinese system of medicine has been closely interwoven with the attitudes of the Chinese towards life and the world around them. Whatever cataclysms may have shaken China in the twentieth century, no one can ignore these ancient influences.

The age-old outlook of the Chinese people was a conservative one. They saw themselves as a part of the total order of things, physical and spiritual, and thus as inextricably linked with what we now call the biosphere of all living things – plants, animals, and the physical forces of nature, which they often had good reason to fear and struggle with. They had great regard for the continuity of the generations and had strong family and ancestral ties. Their own puny lives thus shared in the whole, and this belief gave them patience, determination, and hope. It was a humanist, perhaps materialistic attitude, not a God-centred one; unlike our modern western attitude, with its emphasis on individualism and business drive, it was a very social, ecological, and biological attitude. Western salesmanship, planned obsolescence, the share market, the disregard of natural resources, and the rat-race generally must have seemed completely unintelligible to the Chinese.

The cosmic forces surrounding the Chinese were sometimes in

harmony, in equilibrium and order, and sometimes in disharmony and disorder. They sensed two great forces or principles underlying philosophy, the arts, crafts, astronomy, magic and religion, science and medicine: Yin: negative, passive, female, cold, darkness, disease and weakness; and Yang: positive, active, male, warmth, light, health, and strength. These forces may get out of balance in the community or in the individual, and need adjustment and restoration. The Yin-oriented forces called for stimulation, and the Yang-oriented for sedation, and each had again radical, moderate, and conservative elements.

The story of Pien Ts'io (c. 430–350 B.C.) is extraordinary. He founded the study of the pulse (mo-fa) as a basis for diagnosis and prognosis and used drugged wine (perhaps hashish) for anaesthesia. His proposal for heart transposition – one patient had a strong will but a weak spirit; the other patient had a weak will but a strong spirit – was most interesting. Whether the operation was carried out, and what type of bypass machine was used, are not recorded. The fact that these ideas could be conceived and measures for carrying them out mooted, is astonishing.

The basic ideas of Chinese medicine have much in common with Greek and Arabic medicine. The Greek pairs water and fire, cold and heat, moist and dry and, in medicine, innate heat and radical moisture provide better counterparts to the Yin and Yang than to other elementary pairings. These basic ideas were based on the five elements: wood, fire, earth, metal, and water; on the five organs: the spleen, the liver, the heart, the lungs, and the kidneys; and on the three souls, which resided in the head, the abdomen, and the feet respectively.

The methods of examining the patient were as follows: observation; listening to the voice and breathing; taking the history; and feeling the pulse. The latter was best done at sunrise, without looking at the patient. This was the dominant clinical procedure for over two thousand years.

Anatomical dissection and surgery were practised early but were proscibed by Confucius (551–479 B.C.) as impious. There were some notable exceptions, Hua T'o (A.D. 141?–208) for example, who was the great surgeon of this period. He used drugged wine as an anaesthetic and carried out splenectomy and the celebrated operation on the humerus of General Kuan Kung. But in general anatomy was not resuscitated and regularized until 1913 under western influence.

Until the twentieth century therefore the Chinese relied on fictitious anatomy and physiology. However, it must not be forgotten that imaginary anatomy is to be found in all early medical systems, which lacked the ability to carry out extensive autopsies. In Europe this situation had existed from Galen (A.D. 130–*c.* 201) until well into the seventeenth century. China did not benefit as did the West from the three hundred years of experimentation after Galileo (1564–1642) and Harvey (1578–1657).

We do not know very much about prehistoric Chinese medicine. There were three legendary emperors in this period, Fu Hsi, Shen Nung, and Huang Ti (the Yellow Emperor). Later medical practices were attributed to them, although no written information survives from those times. The earliest medical texts can be found in the *Tso-chuan* (*c.* 540 B.C.).

Among the giants of early Chinese medicine are Pien Ts'io, Chang Chung-ching, and Hua T'o. Pien Ts'io (*c.* 430–350 B.C.) lived a century after Charaka and Susruta in India and has already been referred to. Chang Chung-ching (A.D. 200), 'the Hippocrates of China', wrote on typhoid and other fevers. The Sung version of his work filled fourteen volumes. He established the enema, using pig bile. He veered away from acupuncture, favouring clinical observation and single-drug prescriptions in contrast to the customary shot-gun variety. He inveighed against commercialism in the profession and against ignorance on the part of the public. Hua T'o (A.D. 200) graduated as a Master of Arts but refused literary posts in favour of practising surgery and physical treatments. He used few drugs and needles, and perfected the traditional technique for castration. His offer to trephine the head of a general led to his execution.

Traditional Practice and Treatment

Chinese medical treatments fall broadly into three fields: drug and herbal treatments; physical medicine, including hydrotherapy and manipulation; and acupuncture and moxibustion.

Drug Treatment and Herbals There is an age-old tradition of drug and herbal treatments in China which is still strong in hospitals and apothecaries' shops. The current pharmacopoeia stems from Li Shih-chen (1518–93). Traditional herbs are smilax (China root), sarsparilla, camphor, eumenol, hyoscyamus, gelsemium, aconite, belladonna, and ginger. Powdered thyroid, seaweeds, and seahorse are used for goitre, and liver for a variety of blood disorders. Today

a growing range of antibiotics and hormones is appearing. Minerals of various kinds and odd animal products are still used. I did not hear much of modern research or rationalization in this field.

Physical Medicine, Hydrotherapy, and Manipulation These forms of treatment are still prevalent and are well done.

Acupuncture and Moxibustion The traditional treatments of acupuncture and moxibustion have had their ups and downs, having been forbidden in the early nineteenth century and again in the twentieth century by the Kuomintang. They were reinstated after 1949 and are now officially recognized, rewarded, and taught on a basis equal to western techniques. The old crude splinters of bone and bamboo and coarse needles used in acupuncture have given place to very fine needles which are manipulated and sometimes connected to electric-current sources. A great wealth of lore has grown up, and many millions have faith in acupuncture for many conditions. So far as I know, no real explanation or understanding of it is available, and some of its success at least may be attributable to faith – and stoicism. A new development since my visit is the use of acupuncture in anaesthesia. Many medical and lay persons' accounts of this development have received great publicity in lay media, but again adequate scientific observations, to my knowledge, are not yet available through professional channels. The subject at present must be left *sub judice*.

Moxibustion is a form of counter-irritation. One or more small cones, made from the downy covering of the leaves of *Artemina moxa* or from the pith of various plants are placed on the skin over the affected part. Combustion gradually proceeds through the cone and causes a superficial scar to form on the skin. Moxibustion may have a local or long-distance effect. The pain and scarring have restricted its use in the West. Moxibustion and acupuncture may be combined, either by passing the needle through a moxa already applied or by applying the moxa on withdrawal of the needle.

Public Health

Public health has always been of great concern in China and perhaps the greatest current achievement in this field is the extension to each home and individual of basic requirements in nutrition, shelter, and child care. Successful attacks on such pests as flies (by the use of pyrethrum), bed bugs, and lice are noteworthy. Whether the claim to have eradicated venereal disease by stopping prostitution and providing employment for women can be accepted is debatable.

Other hazards like schistosomiasis, and perhaps tuberculosis, are far from conquered. Smoking and spitting are still very common. A variation of vaccination against smallpox was in vogue before Jenner in the form of the dried vesicles from a patient which were applied to the nose.

Population Control

Population control is difficult to record and to document in China but we were told that there is no great problem. Oral and other contraceptives are readily available, but the emphasis on directing one's personal behaviour towards social ends is also important. Men are discouraged from marrying before the age of twenty-seven or thirty and women before about twenty-five, and two children are regarded as the ideal number. This behaviour, and reasonable behaviour in general – for example, during the long travels of the Red Guards in 1966–70 – seem to be effectively enforced through social pressures. Social pressures are also effective in China in discouraging corruption and dishonesty.

Medical Training

Parallel with the state civil service examinations for the mandarin class (a career open to the talented but one which later became ossified in ivory-tower remoteness) there were state examinations in medicine for two thousand years down to the Sung period, seven hundred years ago. A candidate's success was judged by the number of his patients who lived. Those with the highest grades were told to take official appointments, to teach and to write; those with middle grades were directed into practice; those with poor grades were told to undertake more studies; and the rest were advised to change their career.

The Imperial University had 3000 students in 10 B.C. The university moved to Loyang in A.D. 224 and in the Tang period there was a full professorship system. The first imperial medical college was established in A.D. 618 and was soon followed by others. Hospitals, which were free to the poor, were provided out of taxation from A.D. 1000.

Traditional Medicine Today

With the advance of western medicine through government, missionary, and private doctors in the nineteenth century and the establishment of western medical schools from about 1900 onwards, the traditional practitioner fell into relative disrepute. Under Sun Yat Sen, and later the Kuomintang, western medicine was favoured. The communists promised in 1944 to rehabilitate traditional medicine but were ambivalent for six or seven years. Then came full rehabilitation, traditional practitioners being granted equal status with western-trained doctors, and the two groups were instructed to cooperate, both within a given institution and in general, and to study each other's methods in order to evolve the best united form of medicine for present-day use.

The traditional doctor has his own schools, trains for the same number of years, and is paid the same as the western doctor, whom he outnumbers by two to one. For example, in the hospital and health centre of the Tang Wang agriculture commune near Shanghai, which we visited, there were nine traditional doctors, four western doctors, and one dentist.

A traditional school which we visited in Peking in 1966 was, as far as we could see, anything but a hotbed of research and development. The doctors seemed quiet and rather relieved at their reinstatement. We saw them busily at work prescribing and treating patients by manipulation, acupuncture, and moxibustion. Neither Chinese nor westerners can explain how acupuncture works in anaesthesia, nor do we know how effective it would be in other countries. For centuries there have been fads in western countries for Chinese and other strange methods; perhaps the current one for acupuncture is just another, which is likely to be as effective as many others in the treatment of superficial and functional complaints.

There is no doubt that traditional practices, dating back thousands of years, mean a lot to the Chinese peasant and citizen generally. It would have been cruel to have withdrawn suddenly the comfort they give, particularly when there was no possibility of replacing them on a country-wide scale with something more rational and effective. Like many western practices, traditional Chinese treatments aim to comfort, and who are we to call for the withdrawal of this 'opium for the people' when we cling to our own opia.

Public Health: 'Half-doctors' and 'Barefoot Doctors'

Before going on to western medicine in China, a little more should be said about the great traditional and continuing concern of the Chinese for basic health measures such as nutrition, sanitation, and mother and child care. These things are now mediated by the party machinery and reach down to each village, street, and dwelling. The children of factory workers are bright, alert, and well cared for.

The 'half-doctor', who is said to receive three years' training in post-primary school and three years in college, is ubiquitous and most useful. He corresponds to the Russian 'feldsher' and without him the spread of health and medical measures to anything like their present extent would be impossible. We did not to our knowledge meet any of these half-doctors, nor did we hear of their educational establishments.

The 'barefoot doctor' has been receiving favourable comment recently. As far as I can gather he is similar to our ambulance men in scope and training. Often he is the first one a peasant will approach for medical advice, although the local midwife fulfils this function in many streets. It is interesting to note that the use of the feldsher or half-doctor is being discussed in Britain, America, and other western and affluent countries. It is becoming increasingly expensive to train and equip doctors, and it is being realized that these half-doctors can do as well, or even better, many of the tasks that are now done by fully-trained doctors. One of the reasons for this is that they and only they are paid to do these tasks. It is likely that we shall see great development in this field in the next few years, with training of the various kinds of assistants being carried out alongside that of medical students. The medical school thus expands to become a 'health sciences' school as at McMaster University in Ontario.

A 'Chinese puzzle' in relation to this is the Chinese practice of sending city specialists, even national figures, round rural areas for three months of each year. This is allegedly to spread their knowledge and skill among the 'broad masses', who are loud in their gratitude to Chairman Mao for giving them such privileges for the first time. It is said also to be in the interest of the specialist himself, because it keeps him in touch with the needs of the people and discourages academic, scientific, and professional pride. I cannot see that it is in the people's interest to dilute the services of the all-too-rare highly-skilled specialist in this way. All professional people seem to be obliged to spend periods away from their regular work partici-pating with artisans and peasants in their basic tasks.

The practice of sending the specialist on rural circuit caused us to miss my chief Chinese surgical acquaintance in Peking, Dr Wu Ying-k'ai, chief of the cardio-vascular services at Fu Wai hospital.

I had met him twice at the International Surgical Association meetings, where he was a delegate from the People's Republic of China.

WESTERN SCIENCE AND MEDICINE IN CHINA

Professor Ho Peng Yoke refers in his paper to the lack of interest in China in the scientific and technological revolution from 1600–1900, initiated by Galileo and Harvey, which gave the commercial and military advantage to the European powers. This lack of interest was encouraged by the traditionally in-turned view of the Chinese in their walled-off 'Middle Kingdom'. The celebrated reply of the emperor to George III in 1793 epitomizes this attitude: 'As your Ambassador can see for himself we lack for nothing. I set no store by strange and ingenious objects and I have no use for the products in your country.' But the Europeans did not hesitate to use gunboats to force trade concessions from the Chinese. They humiliated the Chinese in their own land. One might sense the same disinterestedness or dislike as that shown in 1793 in some of the attitudes of China to the West today.

From the Jesuit doctors of the eighteenth century through the growing variety of private, diplomatic, and missionary doctors from all European countries of the nineteenth century, we come to the early years of the twentieth century. The first medical schools were established in Peking, Tientsin, and Canton. They were helped by the official recognition of anatomy in 1913. A number of hospitals were built and medical journals launched about this time. In 1916 there were twenty-six schools of medicine; in 1935 there were thirty-three, with a total of 3 528 students. By 1949 there were some 30 000 western-trained doctors in China, many with European experience, and by 1957 this number had risen to 73 537. By 1968 western-trained doctors numbered 120 000, compared with 500 000 traditional doctors.

The relationship between traditional and western-trained doctors has already been touched on. Chairman Mao has aimed at and largely achieved a symbiosis between the two. The training of each group overlaps, and they are supposed to be learning from each other. I personally learnt almost nothing of the daily *modus vivendi* as they work alongside each other in the same hospital, and I note the same experience in the writings of other visitors.

In 1966 the Cultural Revolution had reached its early heights and we could not gain access to any university. The universities were presumably housing the roving Red Guards. We visited medical schools in Harbin, Shenyang, Sian, and Shanghai, all of which were associated with hospitals, not with universities. The curriculum in medical and other schools was the subject of heated debate, and abbreviated courses, with periods of agricultural work and rural service for the doctors, were being forecast. This new curriculum is said to have been realized now. The state of research and journal production can only be guessed at; perhaps they are at a complete standstill. All observers record difficulty in eliciting information on these subjects.

We witnessed positive achievements in the practice of western medicine in 1966 and achievements in fields such as cardiology have been recorded by more recent observers. I saw an intracardiac operation successfully carried out in Shanghai, and we were told that several other centres were doing this work in Shanghai, Sian, and Peking. Advanced operations on blood vessels for aneurism, liver disease, etc. were also being carried out, as well as run-of-the-mill thoracic and orthopaedic operations. Much was made of several cases of restoration of a severed limb or hand, and of the successful treatment of particularly extensive burns. In Shanghai some of the older surgeons we met had had overseas training before the revolution, but none of the younger ones had. On the whole equipment was simple and at times Spartan, but effective. Some two hundred heart-lung bypass machines had been built in Shanghai on recognized American and British lines. How many were in use then, and are in use now, I do not know. I do not think that this service was in any sense generally available (and free) as it is in New Zealand; it seemed rather to be a showpiece or development plant here and there. We visited a factory for the production of surgical instruments, such as operating tables, dental chairs, and diathermy machines. Much was done by hand, and the products were of good quality.

The future of western medicine and surgery did not look very bright in 1966. Western methods existed almost under sufferance and were handicapped by the prominence given to traditional methods. But neither side would say much about the other, or how they delineated fields of work and individual cases. Full-scale western medicine is of course costly to mount and to run, in terms of both equipment and personnel, and it may be some years before widespread development is seen in China. It could well be a sound decision on the part of the Chinese government to leave things as they are for the next ten years or so.

There are accounts of considerable developments in the pharmaceutical industry in producing penicillin and other antibiotics, hormones, etc. These developments too may be held in abeyance for the time being, judging by the obvious activity of the herbal pharmacists. But drugs for infectious diseases are certainly widely used.

In 1957 an Academy of Medical Sciences was reorganized with sections for physiology, pathology, biochemistry, pharmacy, etc. distributed throughout the country, and research institutions for nutrition, industrial medicine, epidemiology, etc. A large series of sanatoria for tuberculosis and chronic illness has been set up by the unions and extensive measures for protecting workers' health against such things as silicosis in mines are in force.

The Chinese Medical Association, which was our host, is a semi-government organization, in which many laymen hold prominent positions. Several centres had women doctors as secretaries. Both traditional and western doctors belong to the Association, which organizes area meetings for discussions. The local officers met us, arranged our visits, and entertained us in our hotels. We were taken to the home of only one Chinese doctor; my wife, who sat in at all the official functions, was often the only woman present, and at other times met only the women doctors present.

In view of China's history and experiences I think we can abandon any idea of expecting close parallels between her system of medicine and that of the West. Something is being evolved there, born of her past and moulded by her current needs, that will be very different from what we know. We may hope that the best of ours will find a place in it, just as there are signs that some of her concepts may well be incorporated into our practice. The attitude should be one of mutual interest and sympathy, and readiness to emulate and cooperate wherever this is desirable and possible.

To sum up, the good features of Chinese medical and health practice as I saw them are the following:

1 First and foremost, attention is given to basic needs: public health, sanitation, nutrition, mother and child care, and population control, and these services are extended to every village and family. (It should be borne in mind that 80 per cent of the Chinese people live by agriculture.)

2 Every grade of assistance needed is employed, without regard to purely professional considerations and interests. Barefoot doctors, half-doctors, nurses, fully-trained doctors, and all sections play their part, with, I would guess, considerable economy and a much wider spread than is the case with our system.

3 The customary social reactions and traditional allegiances of the people have been supported.

4 Some aspects of modern scientific medicine are available to some sections, and there is reason to believe that this will increase with the increase in living standards and availability of equipment and the like.

The less favourable features of medicine in China today, as seen by western eyes, centre on the relative neglect (or even suppression) of the intellectual and the scientist.

1 The comforts of, for example, traditional herbal treatments or acupuncture are admittedly great to those who have always relied on them. But their persistent use may cause some serious trouble to be neglected at an early and curable stage. They may also involve a waste of effort and resources; for example, hunting for seahorses and dispensing them to cure a goitre when a few drops of tincture of iodine would be quicker, cheaper, and more reliable.

2 There seems to be an almost complete lack of serious scientific research, which to us is the only sound way of carrying out Chairman Mao's edict that the best elements of both systems of medicine should emerge for general use. By now we should be hearing of results, such as drugs, herbs, and procedures that have been found wanting and are to be abandoned, and vice versa. No real information has yet been forthcoming on acupuncture, for example.

3 The *Chinese Medical Journal*, which for some years was 95 per cent political propaganda, finally ceased publication in 1968, and no professional medical publications now reach us. This surely represents a serious internal lapse, and one may well wonder how long the situation can continue.

4 Personnel is ruthlessly directed into functions and places by the central control. This is possible only because the Chinese are so socially conscious and adhesive and therefore amenable to social pressure rather than the punitive pressures of police and prisons.

5 The constant bombardment by repetitious propaganda in the interest of social conformation is intolerable to free-thinking westerners, however admirable the social reactions and behaviour of the Chinese may be. The Cultural Revolution of 1966–70, with its virtual cessation of ordinary education and training, was a colossal example of this. How often and for how long must this be repeated? How long can it be expected to succeed in the face of growing affluence, contacts with the rest of the world, and the growing self-consciousness of Chinese youth?

One always hopes, in great cataclysms such as the French, the Russian, and the Chinese revolutions, that the good results will outweigh the obvious sufferings. 'Religion is the opium of the people: abolish it, let the people's minds become clear and un-clouded' is the cry. But why not the medical opia too? They have not yet been abolished, nor does it seem that any real encouragement is given to better things. Some of the reasons, or at least explanations, for this in the medical and other fields in China are:

1 The change required is so colossal that it cannot be achieved overnight.
2 An effective substitute is by no means generally available.
3 Present-day China requires people to conform and to be docile; independent spirits (in science and elsewhere) are difficult or impossible to cope with.
4 Medicine is not of first importance in China; therefore it can do without first-class brains. When it comes to developing nuclear energy and steel works, it may be different.

One cannot but have great hopes of the great Chinese people. They are tough, hardworking, good to each other, patient, and have a long-range view and long-range hope. China is much more than a communist or cultural revolution, and she will come through and give us greater Han, Tang, Sung, and Ming epochs. She may yet show us how to handle affluence, power, and sex with greater human dignity than we have shown so far. A friend of mine, Sir Theodore Fox, who visited China in 1957 while he was editor of the *Lancet* ended his comments thus:

To any of us who merit Job's sardonic rebuke 'No doubt but ye are the people, and wisdom shall die with you' a visit to China is a chastening experience. Any such distemper in my own mind has now, I hope, been finally dispelled. Indeed I came to feel that if humour, ingenuity, kindness, and fortitude are the human qualities that need preservation, there is no reason to be much disturbed by the thought that the Earth might be ultimately inherited by the Chinese rather than ourselves.

Suggestions for Further Reading

General Works

A Concise History of China, Foreign Languages Press, Peking, 1964.

Fitzgerald, C.P., *China: A Short Cultural History*, Praeger, New York, 1961; Cresset Press, London, 1962.

Greene, Felix, *The Wall Has Two Sides*, Jonathan Cape, London, 1966.

Grousset, Rene, *The Use and Splendour of the Chinese Empire*, University of California Press, Berkeley, 1965.

Huard, P. and Wong Ming, *Chinese Medicine*, Weidenfeld & Nicholson (World University Library), London, 1968.

Hume, C., *The Chinese Way in Medicine*, John Hopkins Press, Baltimore, 1940.

Latourette, K.S., *The Chinese: Their History and Culture*, 4th edn, Macmillan, New York, 1964.

Mackerras, C. and Hunter N., *China Observed*, Nelson, London, 1967.

Roper, Myra, *China in Revolution 1911–1949*, C. Arnold, 1971.

Schurmann, F. and Schell, O. (eds), *China Readings*, 3 vols, Penguin, Harmondsworth, 1969.

Shabad, T., *China's Changing Map: A Political and Economic Geography of the Chinese People's Republic*, Praeger, New York, 1956.

Snow, Edgar, *Red Star over China*, Gollancz, London, 1968.

Suyin, Han, *The Crippled Tree, Birdless Summer, A Mortal Flower* (trilogy), Jonathan Cape, London, 1965–8.

Terrill, Ross, *800,000,000 The Real China*, Heinemann, London, 1972.

Wallnoefer, H. and Von Rottauscher, A., *Chinese Folk Medicine*, New American Library, New York, 1972.

China's Traditional Civilization

Fairbank, J. King, *The Chinese World Order, Traditional China's Foreign Relations*, Harvard University Press, Cambridge, Mass., 1968.

Fung Yu-lan, *A History of Chinese Philosophy*, Princeton University Press, Princeton, 1952.

Hucker, C.O., *The Traditional Chinese State in Ming Times, 1368–1644*, University of Arizona Press, Tucson, 1961.

Lattimore, O., *Inner Asian Frontiers of China*, 2nd edn, American Geographical Society, New York, 1951.

Legge, James, *The Chinese Classics*, 3rd edn, 5 vols, Hong Kong University Press, Hong Kong, 1961.

Moule, A.C. and Pelliott, P., *Marco Polo: The Description of the World*, Routledge & Kegan Paul, London, 1938.

Watson, B., *Early Chinese Literature*, Columbia University Press, New York, 1962.

Zurcher, E., *The Buddhist Conquest of China*, 2 vols, Brill, Leiden, 1959.

Chinese Literature

Buck, Pearl, *All Men Are Brothers*, translation of *Shiu-hu chuan*, Grove Press, New York, 1957.

Liu, J.J.Y., *The Art of Chinese Poetry*, University of Chicago Press, Chicago, 1962.

Suggestions for Further Reading

Prusek, J., *Chinese History and Literature*, Academia, Prague, 1970.

Waley, A., *Monkey*, translation of *Hsi-yu chi*, Grove Press, New York.

Wang Chi-chen, *The Dream of the Red Chamber*, translation of *Hung-lou meng*, Twayne, New York, 1958.

Yang Hsien-yi and Yang, Gladys, *The Courtesan's Jewel Box. Chinese Stories of the X–XVII Centuries*, Foreign Languages Press, Peking, 1957.

Yoshikawa, K., *An Introduction to Sung Poetry*, Harvard University Press, Cambridge, Mass., 1967.

Chinese Society

Balacs, E., *Chinese Civilization and Bureaucracy*, Yale University Press, New Haven, 1964.

Ho Ping-ti, *Studies in the Population of China 1368–1953*, Harvard University Press, Cambridge, Mass., 1959.

Hucker, C.O., *The Censorial System of Ming China*, Stanford University Press, Stanford, 1968.

Wittfogel, K.A., *Oriental Despotism: A Comparative Study of Total Power*, Yale University Press, New Haven, 1957.

China and the West

Banno, M., *China and the West, 1858–1867: The Origin of the Tsungli Yamen*, Harvard University Press, Cambridge, Mass., 1964.

Cohen, P.A., *China and Christianity*, Harvard University Press, Cambridge, Mass., 1963.

Franke, Wolfgang, *China and the West, the Cultural Encounter, 13th to 20th Centuries*, Harper Torchbooks, New York, 1967.

Hu Sheng, *Imperialism and Chinese Politics*, Foreign Languages Press, Peking, 1955.

Levenson, J.R. (ed.), *European Expansion and the Counter-example of Asia, 1300–1600*, Prentice-Hall, New Jersey, 1967.

Purcell, W., *The Boxer Uprising, a Background Study*, Cambridge University Press, Cambridge, 1963.

Reichwein, A., *China and Europe*, Knopf, New York, 1925.

Schwartz, B.I., *In Search of Wealth and Power: Yen Fu and the West*, Harvard University Press, Cambridge, Mass., 1967.

Teng Ssu-yü and Fairbank, J. King, *China's Response to the West: A Documentary Survey, 1839–1923*, Harvard University Press, Cambridge, Mass., 1954.

Waley, A., *The Opium War through Chinese Eyes*, Allen and Unwin, London, 1958.

Wang, Y.C., *Chinese Intellectuals and the West, 1872–1949*, University of North Carolina Press, Chapel Hill, 1966.

Wright, M.C., *The Last Stand of Chinese Conservatism*, Stanford University Press, Stanford, 1957.

Revolution in China

Adshead, S.A.M., *The Modernization of the Chinese Salt Administration, 1900–1920*, Harvard University Press, Cambridge, Mass., 1970.

Alley, R., *Sandan, an Adventure in Creative Education*, Caxton Press, Christchurch, 1969.

Alley, R., *Yo Banfa!*, China Monthly Review, Shanghai, 1952.

Chesneaux, G., *The Chinese Labor Movement, 1919–1927*, Stanford University Press, Stanford, 1968.

Chow Tse-tsung, *The May Fourth Movement: Intellectual Revolution in Modern China*, Harvard University Press, Cambridge, Mass., 1960.

Ho Kan-chih, *A History of the Modern Chinese Revolution*, Foreign Languages Press, Peking, 1959.

Isaacs, H., *The Tragedy of the Chinese Revolution*, Stanford University Press, Stanford, 1951.

Meisner, M., *Li Ta-chao and the Origins of Chinese Marxism*, Harvard University Press, Cambridge, Mass., 1967.

Schiffrin, H.Z., *Sun Yat-sen and the Origin of the Chinese Revolution*, University of California Press, Berkeley, 1968.

Schram, S., *Mao Tse-tung*, Pelican, Harmondsworth, 1967.

Snow, Edgar, *Journey to the Beginning*, Random House, New York, 1958.

Snow, Edgar, *Random Notes on Red China; 1936-1945*, Harvard University Press, Cambridge, Mass., 1968.

People's Republic of China

Acupuncture Anaesthesia, Foreign Languages Press, Peking, 1972.

Asia Research Centre, *The Great Cultural Revolution in China*, Rutland, Vermont and Tokyo, 1969.

Chiang Ch'ing, *On the Revolution of Peking Opera*, Foreign Languages Press, Peking, 1960.

Cohen, J.A. (ed.), *Contemporary Chinese Law: Research Problems and Perspectives*, Harvard University Press, Cambridge, Mass., 1970.

Donnithorne, A., *China's Economic System*, Praeger, New York, 1967.

Friedman, C. and Selden, J. (eds), *America's Asia: Dissenting Essays on Asian-American Relations*, Pantheon Books, New York, 1971.

Gittings, J., *The Role of the Chinese Army*, Oxford University Press, London, 1967.

Griffith, W.E. (ed.), *Communism in Europe: Continuity, Change and the Sino-Soviet Dispute*, MIT Press, Cambridge, Mass., 1966.

Griffith, W.E., *Sino-Soviet Relations, 1964-1965*, MIT Press, Cambridge, Mass., 1966.

Hinton, W., *Fanshen: A Documentary of Revolution in a Chinese Village*, Monthly Review Press, New York, 1966.

Hinton, W., *Hundred Day War: The Cultural Revolution at Tsinghua University*, Monthly Review Press, New York, 1972.

Horn, J., *Away with All Pests: An English Surgeon in People's Republic of China, 1954-1969*, Monthly Review Press, New York, 1971.

Hu Chiao-mu, *Thirty Years of the Chinese Communist Party*, Foreign Languages Press, Peking, 1954.

Hunter, N., *Shanghai Journal, an Eyewitness Account of the Cultural Revolution*, Praeger, New York, 1969.

London, K. (ed.), *Eastern Europe in Transition*, John Hopkins Press, Baltimore, 1966.

MacFarquar, R., *The Hundred Flower Campaign and the Chinese Intellectuals*, Praeger, New York, 1960.

Mao Tse-tung, *Selected Works*, Foreign Languages Press, Peking, 1961-5.

Myrdal, J., *Report from a Chinese Village*, Pantheon Books, New York, 1965.

Myrdal, J. and Kessle, Gun, *China: The Revolution Continued*, Pantheon Books, New York, 1970.

Selden, M., *Yenan Way in Revolutionary China*, Harvard University Press, Cambridge, Mass., 1971.

Schurmann, F., *Ideology and Organization in Communist China*, University of California Press, Berkeley, 1966.

Vogel, Ezra, *Canton under Communism, Programmes and Politics in a Provincial Capital, 1949-1968*, Harvard University Press, Cambridge, Mass., 1969.

Zagoria, D.S., *The Sino Soviet Conflict, 1956-1961*, Princeton University Press, Princeton, 1962.

Translation Series

Current Background, US Consulate General, Hong Kong.

Extracts from China Mainland Publications, US Consulate General, Hong Kong.

Hung-ch'i (Red Flag), US Joint Publication Service.
Jen-min jih-pao (People's Daily), US Joint Publication Service.
Kuang-ming jih-pao (Kuang-ming Daily), US Joint Publication Service.
Kung Jen jih-pao (Workers Daily), US Joint Publication Service.
Selections from China Mainland Magazines, US Consulate General, Hong Kong.
Survey of the China Mainland Press, US Consulate General, Hong Kong.
Ta-kung pao (Ta-kung Daily), US Joint Publication Service.

Chinese Periodicals in English
China Literature (monthly).
China Pictorial (monthly).
China Reconstructs (monthly).
Chinese Medical Journal (monthly).
Peking Review (weekly).
Scientia Sinica (quarterly).

A complete list of works published in English by the Foreign Languages Press may be obtained from Guozi Shudian, PO Box 399, Peking, People's Republic of China.

English Periodicals
Asian Survey, Berkeley.
China Now, London.
China Policy Study Group Broadsheet, London.
China Quarterly, London.
Eastern Horizon, Hong Kong.
Far Eastern Economic Review, Hong Kong.
Ta Kung-pao Weekly Supplement, Hong Kong.

Radio Peking English Language Transmissions
Australia and New Zealand

Peking time:	11.30 – 17.30	
	17.30 – 18.30	
Local time:	18.30 – 19.30	(Aust. ST)
	20.30 – 21.30	(NZ ST)
	19.30 – 20.30	(Aust. ST)
	21.30 – 22.30	(NZ ST)

Metre bands	25, 19, 16
Kc/S	11600, 11720, 15060, 15435, 17835, 11600, 11720, 15060, 15435, 17835

APPENDIX

PROGRAMME AND TIMETABLE OF THE FIRST NEW ZEALAND INTERNATIONAL CONFERENCE ON CHINESE STUDIES

A   Public Lecture Series   C   Scholarly Papers
B   Public Seminar Series   D   Workshops

A   PUBLIC LECTURE SERIES

WEDNESDAY, 17 MAY 1972

7.30 p.m.   CHINA'S FOREIGN RELATIONS: TRICK AND TREAT DIPLOMACY

Mr W.A.C. Adie, Senior Research Fellow
Department of International Relations
Australian National University

Chairman: Professor W.T. Roy
University of Waikato

THURSDAY, 18 MAY 1972

7.30 p.m.   TAI-HSU'S CONTRIBUTION TO MODERN CHINESE BUDDHISM

Professor D. Lancashire, Head, Department of Asian Languages and Literatures
University of Auckland

Chairman: Dr S.A.M. Adshead
University of Canterbury

FRIDAY, 19 MAY 1972

7.30 p.m.   JAPANESE POLICY TOWARDS THE TWO CHINAS

Professor D.H. Mendel, Department of Political Science, University of Wisconsin

Chairman: Professor J.H. Jensen
University of Waikato

SATURDAY, 20 MAY 1972

7.30 p.m.   MODERN SCIENCE IN CHINA

Professor Ho Peng Yoke, Head, Department of Chinese Studies, University of Malaya

Chairman: Professor A.T. Wilson
University of Waikato

Organization of the Conference on Chinese Studies

As far as China is concerned it seems that the Sinologists have a special responsibility to show the public something of the heavy burden of misunderstandings – some going back several centuries – between China and the West. China is still a misunderstood phenomenon for the West, a country about which every generation must form its own impressions. In the past these impressions were often based on contemporary Western ideology and attitudes; it is to be hoped that our generation will be able to observe both worlds for themselves and to come to a better understanding. The Conference may contribute to this.

The Conference, which is entirely non-political, is open to all scholars studying any aspect of life in China, past or present. It may also be noted that there has been a divergence from the traditional academic conference, and that the community has been invited to participate.

The Conference combines three major sections which will run concurrently throughout the four days.

Further, there is a comprehensive film programme and a number of special workshops dealing with the following topics: China's economy, Impressions of the New China, Education in the People's Republic of China, Japanese Studies. Registration allows attendance at any of the conference sessions.

PATRON: SIR DOUGLAS ROBB, formerly Chairman of the New Zealand Medical Council and Chancellor of the University of Auckland

HOST: Dr D.R. LLEWELLYN, Vice-Chancellor, University of Waikato

PRESIDENT: Professor D. LANCASHIRE, Head, Department of Asian Languages and Literatures, University of Auckland

CHAIRMEN: Professor W.T. Roy, Head, Subject of Politics, University of Waikato

Professor J.H. JENSEN, Head, Subject of History, University of Waikato

SECRETARY: Mr D. BING, Subject of Politics, University of Waikato

STEERING COMMITTEE: Miss MARGARET E. AVERY, Subject of History, University of Waikato

Mr P.M. GRAYSON, University Extension, University of Waikato

Dr P.R. HART, Subject of History, University of Waikato

Dr MARGARET T.S. SOUTH, Department of Asian Languages and Literatures, University of Auckland

SPONSORS: Subject of Politics, University of Waikato; Subject of History, University of Waikato; University Extension, University of Waikato

B   PUBLIC SEMINAR SERIES

WEDNESDAY, 17 MAY 1972

9.00 a.m.   Assembly and Registration

10.00 a.m.   Official Conference Opening

11.00 a.m.   THE SEARCH FOR PERPETUAL YOUTH IN CHINA: WITH SPECIAL REFERENCE TO CHINESE ALCHEMY

Professor Ho Peng Yoke, Head, Department of Chinese Studies, University of Malaya

Chairman: Professor A. Zulauf
University of Waikato

1.30 p.m.   THE ART OF CHINESE LANDSCAPE PAINTING

Dr Liu Wei-ping, Department of Oriental Studies
University of Sydney

Chairman: Dr Margaret T.S. South
University of Auckland

3.30 p.m.   CHINA AND THE WEST: AN HISTORICAL PERSPECT-IVE

Mr D. Bing, Subject of Politics, University of Waikato

Chairman: Professor D.H. Mendel
University of Wisconsin

THURSDAY, 18 MAY 1972

9.00 a.m.   SINO-AMERICAN RELATIONS: A NEW DEPARTURE?

Professor D.H. Mendel, Department of Political Science, University of Wisconsin

Chairman: Dr J.S. Hoadley
University of Auckland

11.00 a.m.   THE CHINESE POET AND HIS ART

Dr Margaret T.S. South, Department of Asian Languages and Literatures, University of Auckland

Chairman: Dr Liu Wei-ping
University of Sydney

1.30 p.m.   THE GREAT PROLETARIAN CULTURAL REVO-LUTION

Dr S.A.M. Adshead, Department of History
University of Canterbury

Chairman: Mr W.A.C. Adie
Australian National University

3.30 p.m.   THE ECONOMY OF THE PEOPLE'S REPUBLIC OF CHINA

Professor Audrey G. Donnithorne, Director
Contemporary China Centre, Australian National University

Chairman: Professor A.J.L. Catt
University of Waikato

FRIDAY, 19 MAY 1972

9.00 a.m.   NEW ZEALAND FOREIGN POLICY TOWARDS CHINA

Professor W.T. Roy, Head, Subject of Politics
University of Waikato

Chairman: Dr N.R. Bennett
University of Canterbury

11.00 a.m.   AGRICULTURE IN THE PEOPLE'S REPUBLIC OF
CHINA

Dr J. Wong, Department of Economics and Statistics
University of Singapore

Chairman: Mr T.G. Tay
University of Canterbury

1.30 p.m.   ASIAN STUDIES IN NEW ZEALAND

Professor P.N. Tarling, Head, Department of History, and
Dean of the Faculty of Arts
University of Auckland

Chairman: Professor J.H. Jensen
University of Waikato

3.30 p.m.   CHINA AND EASTERN EUROPE: THE RUMANIAN
EXAMPLE

Professor J.H. Jensen, Head, Subject of History
University of Waikato

Chairman: Professor P.N. Tarling
University of Auckland

SATURDAY, 20 MAY 1972

9.00 a.m.   EDUCATION IN THE PEOPLE'S REPUBLIC OF CHINA

Mr R.I.D. Taylor, Department of Politics
University of Auckland

Chairman: Professor W.T. Roy
University of Waikato

11.00 a.m.   MAO TSE-TUNG'S REVOLUTIONARY DIPLOMATIC
LINE: The Revolutionary Experience of the Chinese
Communist Party and Its Role in China's International
Relations

Mr W.A.C. Adie, Senior Research Fellow, Department of
International Relations, Australian National University

Chairman: Mr D. Bing
University of Waikato

1.30 p.m.   CHINESE CERAMICS, THEIR PLACE AND THEIR
INFLUENCE ON BOTH WESTERN AND EASTERN
CIVILIZATIONS

Mr T.J. Bayliss, Curator of Applied Arts
Auckland Institute and Museum

Chairman: Professor D. Lancashire
University of Auckland

3.30 p.m. MEDICINE IN THE PEOPLE'S REPUBLIC OF CHINA

Sir Douglas Robb, formerly Chairman of the New Zealand
Medical Council and Chancellor of the University of
Auckland

Chairman: Dr H.R. Bennett, Medical Superintendent,
Tokanui Hospital, and Pro-Chancellor of the University
of Waikato

C SCHOLARLY PAPERS

WEDNESDAY, 17 MAY 1972

11.00 a.m. SIKANG AND THE REVOLUTION OF 1911

Dr S.A.M. Adshead
University of Canterbury

Chairman: Professor Wang Chien-min

1.30 p.m. THE INFLUENCE OF THE CHINESE EXAMINATION
SYSTEM UPON BRITISH IMPERIAL ADMINIS-
TRATION

Professor W.T. Roy
University of Waikato
Chairman: Dr J.S. Hoadley

2.30 p.m. CH'EN TU-HSIU AND THE CHINESE REVOLUTION
OF 1911

Professor Wang Chien-min
Chengchi University

Chairman: Professor D. Lancashire

4.00 p.m. PROBLEMS OF MODERNIZATION IN CHINA
SINCE 1942

Miss Ti-hou Han
University of Auckland

Chairman: Mr H. Chan

THURSDAY, 18 MAY 1972

9.00 a.m. EARLY SINO-RUSSIAN CONTACTS

Mr Chen Chu-yuan
University of Auckland

Chairman: Dr N.R. Bennett

10.00 a.m. CHINA'S ATTEMPT TO RE-ESTABLISH HER
NAVY 1895-1911

Dr N.R. Bennett
University of Canterbury

Chairman: Professor W.T. Roy

11.00 a.m.   PROBLEMS OF GROUP SOLIDARITY IN THE
             FORCES OF CULTURAL-HISTORICAL RESEARCH IN
             NON-EUROPEAN SOCIETIES: THE CONTRIBUTION
             OF CHINESE STUDIES

Dr Magdalena von Dewall
University of Heidelberg

Chairman: Mr D. Bing

1.30 p.m.   SOME REMARKS UPON THE ORIGIN AND THE
             NATURE OF THE ART OF ANCIENT CHINA–A
             NECESSARY PRELUDE TO ASSESSMENTS OF
             INFLUENCES FROM THE CHINESE SPHERE INTO
             THE PACIFIC
             (illustrated with slides)

Dr N. Barnard
Australian National University

Chairman: Dr A.C. Moore

2.30 p.m.   THE MAITREYA FIGURE IN CHINA–A BRIDGE IN
             PAN-ASIAN BUDDHISM
             (illustrated with slides)

Dr A.C. Moore
University of Otago

Chairman: Professor D. Lancashire

4.00 p.m.   SOME SOURCES FOR THE STUDY OF EARLY T'ANG
             HISTORY

Mr W.G. Lewis
Macquarie University

Chairman: Dr Margaret T.S. South

ᵀRIDAY, 19 MAY 1972

9.00 a.m.   A PROBLEM IN THE SIYUAN YUFIAN:
             THE JADE MIRROR OF THE FOUR UNKNOWNS

Mr J. Hoe
Victoria University of Wellington

Chairman: Professor Ho Peng Yoke

10.00 a.m.   CHINESE PARTICIPATION IN HONG KONG

Dr J.S. Hoadley
University of Auckland

Chairman: Mr S.W. Greif

11.00 a.m.   SELECTED POLITICAL AND SOCIAL ATTITUDES OF
             THE NEW ZEALAND CHINESE

Mr S.W. Greif
University of Otago

Chairman: Mr H. Chan

1.30 p.m.   THE PLA AND THE GPCR:
             PERSPECTIVES FROM AN INDONESIAN EXAMPLE

229

Dr J.S. Hoadley
University of Auckland
Chairman: Dr S.A.M. Adshead

2.30 p.m. LATE NINETEENTH-CENTURY AND EARLY
TWENTIETH-CENTURY NEW ZEALAND IMAGES
OF THE CHINESE AND OF CHINA
Mr H. Chan
Massey University
Chairman: Professor J.H. Jensen

4.00 p.m. HAN AND TA-CH'IN: CHINA'S ANCIENT RELATIONS
WITH THE WEST
Dr Brian E. Colless
Massey University
Chairman: Dr Magdalena von Dewall

D   WORKSHOPS

i   Japanese Studies
ii   Education in the People's Republic of China
iii   Impressions of the New China
iv   China's Economy

The following scholarly papers will form part of the various workshops:

WORKSHOP: (1) CHINA'S ECONOMY

AGRICULTURAL PRODUCTION AND SOCIALIST TRANS-
FORMATION IN CHINA – TWO DECADES AFTER
Dr J. Wong
University of Singapore

INCOME vs SURPLUS MOTIVATION:
THE CONFLICTS BETWEEN THE SOCIALISED AND
THE PRIVATE SECTOR IN CHINESE AGRICULTURE
Mr K.K. Fung
Victoria University of Wellington

IMPACT OF LAND TO THE TILLER PROGRAMME ON TAIWAN'S
AGRICULTURAL DEVELOPMENT
Professor Feng-hue Tee
Academica Sinica

WORKSHOP: (2) EDUCATION IN THE PEOPLE'S REPUBLIC OF CHINA

EDUCATIONAL REFORM OF THE GREAT
PROLETARIAN CULTURAL REVOLUTION
Mr R.C. Hunt
Victoria University of Wellingtaon

UNIVERSITY ENROLMENT POLICIES IN THE
PEOPLE'S REPUBLIC OF CHINA SINCE THE
CULTURAL REVOLUTION

Mr R.I.D. Taylor
University of Auckland

WORKSHOP: (4) JAPANESE STUDIES

THE APPLICATION OF ROSTOW'S MODEL OF
ECONOMIC DEVELOPMENT TO THE CHUKYO AND
CHUBU REGION IN JAPAN

Associate Professor A.M. Gorrie
University of Auckland

TEACHING METHODS AND CURRICULUM DEVELOPMENT
AT UNIVERSITY LEVEL

Mr F. Kinoshita

SPECIAL WORKSHOPS – JAPANESE STUDIES

Host:

Dr P.F. Wells
Head, Subject of Language Studies
University of Waikato

Chairman:

Professor E.S. Crawcour
Head, Department of Japanese
Australian National University

WEDNESDAY, 17 MAY 1972

9.00 a.m. Assembly and Registration

10.00 a.m. Official Conference Opening

11.00 a.m. Welcome to Japanese Studies Workshop by Host,
Dr P.F. Wells

11.15 a.m. Workshop Session A:

Teaching Methods and Curriculum Development
at Post-Primary Level

Introduction to Informal Discussions:

Dr P.F. Wells
Head, Subject of Language Studies
University of Waikato

Participants:

University Teachers and Post-primary
Japanese Language Teachers

THURSDAY, 18 MAY 1972

11.00 a.m. Workshop Session B:

Teaching Methods and Curriculum
Development at Polytechnics

Introduction to Informal Discussions:

Mr R.A. Midwinter
School of Languages
Wellington Polytechnic

Participants:

Polytechnic Teachers, University Teachers,
Post-primary Teachers

Miss Hisako Mizukami
Subject of Language Studies
University of Waikato

Mr P. Knight (not confirmed)
Modern Languages
Massey University

Miss Yoko Wakiya (not confirmed)
Modern Languages
Massey University

Mr R.A. Midwinter
School of Languages
Wellington Polytechnic

SPECIAL WORKSHOPS – EDUCATION IN THE PEOPLE'S REPUBLIC OF CHINA

Honorary Chairman:

Professor I.A. McLaren
Subject of Education
University of Waikato

Chairman:

Mr N.J. Northover
Senior Inspector of Secondary Schools
·Department of Education, Hamilton

Most participants in this workshop have had teaching experience in the People's Republic of China.

WEDNESDAY, 17 MAY 1972

11.00 a.m.   EDUCATIONAL REFORM OF THE GREAT PRO-
LETARIAN CULTURAL REVOLUTION
Mr R.C. Hunt
Victoria University of Wellington
Chairman: Mr D. Bing

1.30 p.m.   UNIVERSITY ENROLMENT POLICIES IN THE
PEOPLE'S REPUBLIC OF CHINA SINCE THE CUL-
TURAL REVOLUTION
Mr R.I.D. Taylor
University of Auckland
Chairman: Mr R.C. Hunt

232

THURSDAY, 18 MAY 1972

10.00 a.m.   TEACHING IN PEKING DURING THE GREAT CUL-
TURAL REVOLUTION

Mrs Ruth Lake
Post-primary Schoolteacher
Wellington

FRIDAY, 19 MAY 1972

10.00 a.m.   Session C: Scholarly Papers:

Associate Professor A.M. Gorrie
University of Auckland

The Application of Rostow's Model of
Economic Development to the Chukyo
and Chuba Region in Japan

Chairman: Professor E.S. Crawcour
Head of Department of Japanese
Australian National University

The following paper on Japanese Studies will appear in the Public Lecture Series:

Professor D.H. Mendel
University of Wisconsin

Japanese Policy towards the Two Chinas

Chairman: Professor E.S. Crawcour
Australian National University

5.00 p.m.   Reception given by the Honourable Mr T. Asada, Consul
General of Japan

SATURDAY, 20 MAY 1972

11.00 a.m.   Workshop Session D:

Teaching Methods and Curriculum Development
at University Level

Introduction to Informal Discussion:

Mr T. Kinoshita
Acting Head, Department of Asian Languages
University of Canterbury

Teaching Methods and Curriculum Development

Participants:

Mr G.W. Perkins
Department of Asian Languages and Literatures
University of Auckland

Mr H. Noto
Department of Asian Languages
University of Canterbury

Dr P.F. Wells
Head, Subject of Language Studies
University of Waikato

Chairman: Mr E.R. Bloomfield
Hamilton Teachers College

11.00 a.m. EDUCATION IN THE PEOPLE'S REPUBLIC OF CHINA:
EXPERIENCE OF A NEW ZEALAND TEACHER

Mr J. Ewen
Post-primary Schoolteacher
Auckland

Chairman: Mr R.I.D. Taylor

1.30 p.m. EDUCATION IN THE PEOPLE'S REPUBLIC OF CHINA:
a As part of the social reform
b The need to look at the history of education
c Old education system pulled down, new being built

Mr J. Wong
Post-primary Schoolteacher
Auckland

Chairman: Mr A.W. Knight
Morrinsville College

FRIDAY, 19 MAY 1972

10.00 a.m. PANEL DISCUSSIONS:
EDUCATION IN NEW ZEALAND AND EDUCATION
IN THE PEOPLE'S REPUBLIC OF CHINA:
A COMPARATIVE APPROACH

Chairman: Mr R.I.D. Taylor

SPECIAL WORKSHOPS – IMPRESSIONS OF THE NEW CHINA

Honorary Chairman:

Sir Douglas Robb, formerly Chairman of the New Zealand
Medical Council and Chancellor of the University of Auckland

Chairman:

Mr R.C. Hunt
Lecturer in Chinese
Victoria University of Wellington

All participants in this workshop have visited the People's Republic and/or Taiwan
recently.

WEDNESDAY, 17 MAY 1972

11.00 a.m. TAIWAN AND POLITICAL REALISM

Mr Michael K. Moore
Auckland

11.30 a.m. A VISIT TO TAIWAN

Miss Rosemary A. Young
Wellington

THURSDAY, 18 MAY 1972

9.00 a.m. IMPRESSIONS OF THE PEOPLE'S REPUBLIC OF
CHINA:
1969 and 1971

Mr R. Evans, J.P.
Auckland

9.30 a.m. IMPRESSIONS OF THE PEOPLE'S REPUBLIC OF
CHINA AND TAIWAN

Mr David F. Caygill
Christchurch

11.00 a.m. CHINA: A NEW SOCIETY UNDER PROLETARIAN
DICTATORSHIP

Mr Ah Fo Wong
Wellington

FRIDAY, 19 MAY 1972

9.00 a.m. AGRICULTURE IN TAIWAN TODAY

Mr Eric R. Ellis
Carterton

9.30 a.m. IMPRESSION OF THE NEW CHINA: TAIWAN

Mr Roger L.D. Wiig
Auckland

SATURDAY, 20 MAY 1972

9.00 a.m. INDUSTRIAL RELATIONS: CHINA 1971

Mr Frank Hogan
Auckland

9.30 a.m. THE QUESTION OF LAND AND AGRICULTURAL
DEVELOPMENT IN CHINA

Mr R.C. Hunt
Victoria University of Wellington

SPECIAL WORKSHOPS – CHINA'S ECONOMY

Honorary Chairman:

Professor A.W.H. Philips
Emeritus Professor of Economics
Australian National University

Chairman:

Professor A.J.L. Catt
Subject of Economics
University of Waikato

235

CHINA: CULTURAL AND POLITICAL PERSPECTIVES

A   Theoretical Papers

WEDNESDAY, 17 MAY 1972

11.00 a.m.   AGRICULTURAL PRODUCTION AND SOCIALIST
TRANSFORMATION IN CHINA: TWO DECADES
AFTER

Dr J. Wong
University of Singapore

Chairman: Professor A.J.L. Catt

1.30 p.m.   IMPACT OF LAND TO THE TILLER PROGRAMME ON
TAIWAN'S AGRICULTURAL DEVELOPMENT

Professor Feng-hue Tee
Academica Sinica

Chairman: Mr K.K. Fung

2.30 p.m.   INCOME vs 'SURPLUS' MOTIVATION: THE CON-
FLICTS BETWEEN THE SOCIALIZED AND THE
PRIVATE SECTOR IN CHINESE COLLECTIVIZED
AGRICULTURE

Mr K.K. Fung
Victoria University of Wellington

Chairman: Dr J. Wong

The following scholarly papers will appear in the Public Seminar Series:

THURSDAY, 18 MAY 1972

3.30 p.m.   THE ECONOMY OF THE PEOPLE'S REPUBLIC

Professor Audrey G. Donnithorne
Australian National University

FRIDAY, 19 MAY 1972

11.00 a.m.   AGRICULTURE IN THE PEOPLE'S REPUBLIC

Dr J. Wong
University of Singapore

B   Practical Papers

THURSDAY, 18 MAY 1972

10.00 a.m.   NEW ZEALAND-CHINA TRADE RELATIONS

Mr R. Howell
Managing Director
Vadco Traders
Auckland

Chairman: Professor A.J.L. Catt

11.00 a.m.   TRADING WITH THE PEOPLE'S REPUBLIC
OF CHINA

Mr L.W. Tattersfield
Woolbroker

236

Chairman: Mr F.G. Tay
University of Canterbury

1.30 p.m. TRADING WITH THE PEOPLE'S REPUBLIC:
THE CANTON TRADE FAIR OF APRIL 1972

Mr V.F. Percival
Sales Director
Kelvin Industrries (1958) Ltd
Auckland

Chairman: Dr J. Wong

2.30 p.m. PANEL DISCUSSION:
NEW ZEALAND TRADE PROSPECTS WITH THE
PEOPLE'S REPUBLIC OF CHINA

Chairman: Professor A.J.L. Catt

4.00 p.m. PANEL DISCUSSION:
NEW ZEALAND TRADE PROSPECT WITH TAIWAN

Chairman: Mr K.K. Fung